LIMESTONE

100 best limestone climbs in Britain

LIMESTONE

100 best limestone climbs in Britain

Chris Craggs

CICERONE PRESS

MILNTHORPE CUMBRIA

Frontispiece: Mike Owen powering up the fiercely leaning crux of Malham Cove Main Overhang, pitch one (E6 6c) in Yorkshire.

ACKNOWLEDGEMENTS

I would like to thank several people who have made this book possible. First and foremost to Sherri Davy who has given me continuous moral support throughout the project, as well as posing on routes, taking photographs and looking after the team as chief cook and bottle washer over a very hectic year.

To Colin Binks, who has given up his precious holidays to be dragged around the country to do the routes I wanted pictures of rather than the ones on his hit list.

To John Addy, Nigel Baker, Derek Carter, Christine Kell, Pete O'Donovan, Mike and Elaine Owen, Graham Parkes, Mike Riddings, Brian Rossiter, Jim Rubery, Dave Spencer, Steve Warwick and Richard Watkinson, who were happy to come out and be directed on a variety of routes or offered advice on the contents and direction of the book.

To all the total strangers I have 'dropped in on' in the last year - never a one has complained.

To Kodak for supplying the film and Pentax for helping with the photographic equipment.

Finally to Walt Unsworth who had the faith in me to give the project the thumbs up; I hope it is up to scratch.

Now it is time to get back to the gritstone.

CONTENTS

INTRODUCTION

A number of Selected Climbs volumes has been produced in recent years, concerned with picking out the best of the country's rock climbs (or ice climbs) within a range of grades, or within a particular geographic region. The majority of the climbs covered in these books are to be found in the mountainous areas of our islands where the longest and arguably the most significant routes are located.

Inevitably many of these major routes are not climbed as regularly as they might be, because of problems associated with inaccessibility and inclement weather. In reality the majority of climbers spend the majority of their leisure time and physical energy engaged in 'outcrop climbing'. 'Outcrop' has always been used as a loose and perhaps slightly derogatory term for any piece of rock not intimately associated with our higher hills. The fact that some of the so-called 'outcrops' are larger, more impressive and more serious than many a mountain crag clearly indicates that this definition is at best a rather blurred one.

Once upon a time most climbers used their easily accessible local cliffs purely as training for bigger things, getting out whenever the weather allowed and pushing their ability in well known and relatively friendly settings. Since the earliest days of our sport many of the country's most difficult and boldest climbs have been created on these 'backyard crags' and they remain to this day a forcing and proving ground for technique, stamina and ethics. Nowadays there exists a generation of young climbers, many of whom have never climbed on a mountain cliff, and have no desire to do so. The 'outcrops', with their elevated standards of difficulty have become the ultimate horizon for many such climbers.

These 'outcrops' provide a vast selection of routes of all grades and in widely varied settings. From dingy holes in the ground to unbroken miles of magnificent sea cliffs; from high draughty edges to secluded wooded dales, this variety adding to the appeal of the sport. All these many and varied outcrops have their devotees and their own particular charm. The routes available run the whole gamut from one-move wonders, through the lengthy and amiable ambles, today's hardest route in the world (and perhaps tomorrow's 'path'), all the climbs have their own value and as such are worth seeking out and doing.

The two commonest types of rock for outcrop climbing are limestone and gritstone, and this suggested the format for this book - a selection of climbs bound together by their shared geology. The pick of the country's limestone climbs of whatever grade, brought together in one volume. This approach has allowed me to include climbs across a broad spectrum of difficulty and from a fascinatingly diverse selection of settings.

The Selection

What makes a classic? A few years ago an up and coming (shooting?) star told me that the best route he had ever done on limestone was UNE CRIME PASSIONNEL in Chee Dale. Acting on this recommendation I did the route and enjoyed it. It gave steep climbing on rather dusty rock, with dubious peg protections, the odd loose hold and a finish on near vertical grass where a knotted rope hung down to assist the exit. I concluded that either he had not done many routes on limestone, (and certainly none of the ones included in this book!) or he was using different criteria in defining the quality of his routes. There is more than a grain of truth in the old adage; "One man's meat is another man's poison".

In terms of what makes a classic I must confess to being very much a traditionalist. For inclusion in this book a climb needs to follow a clearly definable physical feature up the rock face, be inescapable at the grade and finish on the cliff top. These definitions are descriptive rather than prescriptive and I have bent the rules to include routes that simply could not be left out - such is an author's prerogative! A good example of this rule bending is in the case of PINK WALL TRAVERSE at Avon. From the top of MIKE'S MISTAKE, the easiest way to the cliff top is via the Diff route GREY WALL, whereas the selected route is a devious connection away to the left. A party which has just enjoyed MIKE'S MISTAKE will hopefully want more of the same and so the logic of seeking out difficulties in this selection.

Another example of this 'flexibility' is AXLE ATTACK at Craig Pen Trwn - a leader who has just succeeded on the E5 rock climb could certainly cope with the easy rock and vegetation that leads to the cliff top some distance higher and then spend time grubbing around on the grass bank above in search of belays. This would fulfil the stated criteria but it would not add a lot to the climbing experience. Hence the reason behind the lowering bolts on the route, and why I feel able to include it here. Despite this occasional bending of the rules I hope that most climbers, irrespective of what grade they personally climb at, would agree with the inclusion of the vast majority of routes in this book. With every climber having their own idea of what makes a great route, there can never be a truly definitive 'best of' list. So here is a personal selection of the cream of many thousands of climbs on the 'white stuff' - whether you do just one of them or all of them, I don't think you will be disappointed.

The routes described cover the spectrum of difficulty from V.Diff to E8, with the majority of climbs being in the H.V.S. to E3 range. This is the grade that most climbers operate at or aspire to operate at, and many of the country's great limestone classics are encompassed within this range of difficulty.

I have tried to give a broad geographical spread to the routes included, and especially to avoid too much of a northern bias in the selection. Doubtless someone living, for example, in Bristol or Exeter would have produced a 'definitive' list that would differ in detail but I trust would still hold the basic core of classics. Apologies to anyone whose latest 'Best Limestone Route in Britain' has been missed out!

The Format

The climbs in the book are described in ascending order of difficulty, in effect forming a graded list. As always this is a rather touchy subject, filled with problems of personal preference and 'the bullshit factor'. As with any graded list, individual placings should be taken with a pinch of salt. The overall ordering is as accurate as I have been able to make it, so at least there should be an element of consistency in the gradings, and in any event it should provide meat for that old pub game 'slag off the author'. Every chapter has enough information to enable a stranger to an area to locate the cliff (perhaps also using a road atlas) and the appropriate climb. There are notes on any special equipment that is needed, any access restrictions that may be in force at different times of the year as well as any other relevant details, e.g. tides, descents etc. This information is followed by an essay that provides a bit more general background to the climbs in a form that I hope is both readable and informative.

I have done all the climbs included in the book (though not quite all of them in their freest form, I hasten to add) and I believe all the details to be accurate at the time of going to press.

Photography

The question "What makes a good photograph?" is liable to cause even more disagreement than "What makes a classic rock climb?" Despite this I have tried to produce a single photograph of each route that sums it up - this has proved to be no mean task. Trying to get a team on the required route at the right time, in the right clothes and with decent light has given hours of endless 'fun'. In the event of being unable to get the required photographic coverage the route has had to be left out. A good example of this was SILVER SHADOW on Stackpole Head. We visited the route on three occasions, on the first two it was wet and on the third the light was so poor that no decent shot was possible, so sadly it has had to be omitted.

Except where stated otherwise all the photographs in this book are from my own collection. I have used 35mm slide film throughout. Whenever the light has allowed I have used Kodakchrome 25 and 64 film very kindly supplied by Kodak. The fine grained quality and accurate colour reproduction of these films has long been a bench mark in the photographic industry and I have been very pleased with the results.

I use a Pentax SLR autofocus camera with a 35-70mm zoom lens as a standard and a 70-210mm telephoto lens for getting in close to the action. These zoom lenses have proved to be a great asset in helping with the composition of photographs when you are in a position where you can not easily move i.e. on an abseil rope. This camera is rather too bulky to carry on difficult climbs so I use a compact Pentax which also has a zoom facility.

Many of the more distant shots have been taken by my long-suffering girlfriend who has been dangled off various cliffs and had instructions shouted at her from great distances. She has endured my heavy-handed criticism of her artistic work with great stoicism and without her help this book would largely have contained a collection of bum shots (in more ways than one).

Gear

It is not uncommon today to see a climber embarking on a 15 metre pitch carrying a fortune, and a fair poundage, in modern protection equipment. Most of this will not be needed on the majority of climbs and is carried 'just in case'. It only serves to act as ballast and an encumbrance to upward progress. To try and ease the delibera-

tion as to whether to carry every piece of equipment that you possess I have included notes based on the idea of a 'standard rack' in the equipment section for each route. Climbers who feel the need of a runner to protect every upward move may need to supplement this rack, but it should be adequate for most undertakings in this book. Where a pitch is especially long, or needs a large number of runners of the same size, this has been pointed out in the EQUIPMENT section before each essay.

This STANDARD RACK includes a double set of wired nuts (Rocks, Stoppers, Gems, etc.) sizes 1 to 9, with the larger sizes on rope if preferred, ten quick draws/extenders, and half a dozen single karabiners for clipping in with and reducing rope drag. Added to this for protecting wider cracks should be either a couple of middle-sized Friends (size 2 and 2½) or a couple of Hexes (size 6 & 8). Two or three tape slings are always useful for spikes, trees and threads as well as for extending runners that are under overhangs or well off the line of the route.

Any more specialised gear that is required e.g. R.P. type nuts, large Friends and Hexes, or large numbers of similar sized wires, are specifically mentioned in the notes for the relevant route. Double ropes are taken as standard equipment except on very easy or very hard (bolt protected) routes. The advantages of double ropes on long and devious pitches are well explained in climbing textbooks. I assume that climbers who prefer to use a single rope are able to cope with problems associated with rope drag and unexpected retreat.

Grading

The British grading system is a complex and much maligned beast. It has been evolving since the dawn of guidebooks and continues to do so. The present system has been used and abused in a variety of ways over the years and there are still experienced climbers around who fail to grasp the subtleties that are available within it.

The grade of any climb above Severe in standard normally includes two sections, firstly an adjectival description that gives an overall impression of the difficulties of the climb, including size, seriousness, strenuousness, sustained difficulty and 'feel'.

These adjectival grades are: Very Difficult, Severe, Hard Severe, Very Severe, Hard Very Severe and Extremely Severe, which is subdivided into E1, E2, E3, E4, E5, E6, E7, E8 etc.

Added to this is a pitch by pitch technical grade that attempts to assess the difficulty of the hardest move on the pitch as it would feel approached, on sight, on a top rope. (Some schools of thought maintain that the technical grade is purely for the hardest move taken in isolation, but as it can never be done in isolation this does not seem to make a lot of sense and I have stuck to the more traditional definition.) The technical grade therefore takes account of strenuousness and sustained difficulty but has no regard of protection or lack of it, or the state of the rock.

The two grades taken together and used sensibly give a general impression of the difficulties likely to be met on any particular route.

A few examples of 5c pitches included in the book might help to illustrate how the system is supposed to work.

E1   (5c)   LIGHT   Pitch 1   A short, safe crux near the ground. The rest of the route is much easier.

E2	(5c)	HEAVEN'S DOOR	Pitch 2	A safe strenuous crux as part of a long intimidating pitch.
E3	(5c)	DREADNOUGHT	Pitch 3	A short strenuous pitch in a serious setting, as part of an 'expedition'.
E4	(5c)	STAR WARS		A serious start followed by safer but bold and sustained climbing above.

On the hardest routes with largely fixed gear the 'E' grade has little to do with seriousness and more to do with the likelihood of getting up the pitch first time, and in a single push, i.e. an E for effort grade. There is a growing feeling amongst many climbers that the French system should be used on routes that are wholly bolt protected. This would appear to make a lot of sense, but only where the climbs are fully fixed with solid regular protection. It is perhaps more than a little illogical to grade, for example, the short and safe (though utterly desperate) free version of Whore of Babylon (HUBBLE) on Raven Tor E10, whilst the terminal (and still utterly desperate) INDIAN FACE on Cloggy is graded E9. Perhaps the former should be graded 8c+ French leaving the "E" system to fulfil its original route.

If the system is still causing you problems, try starting with the easiest route in the book and working through it. By the time you have done all of them you should have at least a minimal grasp of how U.K. grades are supposed to work!

For foreign visitors (and Brits who have not yet climbed abroad), I include a comparison of British grades with the French and American equivalents. These may not tally exactly with other published lists, especially the ones in continental guides, but are at least based on personal experience coupled with a broad consensus from a number of widely travelled climbers. Rather than comparing routes, it attempts to compare climbers, i.e. if you climb E4 6a at your limit in Britain, you should find French 6c and American 5.11d require a roughly similar expenditure of physical and nervous energy, though the actual style of climbing will also affect the grade you climb at.

A couple of points are worth highlighting:

Firstly, and most importantly, any grading system attempts to compare things (moves on infinitely variable rock done by infinitely variable people) which in reality are not comparable with each other. Attempting to compare one grading system with another is even more of an impossible task - but here goes anyway!

Secondly, the French system presupposes that the routes, of whatever grade, are fully equipped with bolt runners. The time and energy saved by not having to place nut protection and the certainty in the solidness of the bolts means that it is normally possible to climb closer to your physical limit than is usual back home. The climbing tends to suit strong fingered climbers and is rarely bold. The inherent safety of this style of climbing perhaps explains its increasing popularity in Britain.

It always takes a little while to get used to a new style of climbing and this should be borne in mind when choosing an objective in a new area and before dismissing the local grading system as totally unworkable.

GRADES: A comparison of U.K., French and U.S. systems

BRITISH	FRENCH	AMERICAN
V.Diff	3	5.5
Severe	4	5.7
V.S. (4c)	4+	5.8
H.V.S. (5a)	5	5.9
E1 (5b)	5+	5.10a
E2 (5c)	6a	5.10c
E3 (6a)	6b	5.11a
E4 (6a)	6c	5.11d
E5 (6b)	7a	5.12a
E6 (6b)	7b	5.12d
E7 (6c)	8a	5.13b
E8 (7a)	8b	5.14a
E9 (7a)	8c	5.14c

The 'missing' French and American grades can be worked out by extrapolation, e.g. French 7a+ is roughly equivalent to hard E5 or 5.12b/c.

All grades included in the book are taken to be for on-sight leads, with no previous knowledge of the route apart from that available in the appropriate guidebook. The very hardest routes in the book have yet to receive on-sight flashed ascents but their time will come! (Note: See the comment at the end of the essay about the SUPER DIRECTISSIMA (TOTALLY FREE) at Malham.)

Additional information, especially top-roped ascents, tends to dramatically reduce the adjectival grade of the route concerned, because it removes 'the uncertainty factor'. Sitting on runners, for any reason whatsoever (and there are always plenty) reduces the climb to a mixed aid/free route and perhaps suggests that an easier route should be sought out, unless of course this is your 'n'th day of working the pitch, in which case you can frig away to your heart's content. There is no disgrace in failing but plenty of stigma attached to cheating (and there is always somebody watching) even in these days of 'the modern approach'.

The Rock

Under the broad umbrella of limestone there is a tremendous variation of rock type and quality available in Britain. Unfortunately we have nothing to compare with the fantastic sheets of grey limestone that are found in southern France, but all is not lost. Variety is the spice of life, and we certainly have plenty of that. Strictly speaking, chalk is a form of limestone, but only in a fairly loose use of the definition! I have had no difficulty in leaving chalk climbs out of this book; perhaps someone someday will produce a Soft Rock Selected Climbs volume.

A few years ago I was chatting to a very depressed American visitor on the first day of his U.K. climbing tour. He had failed on a series of Stoney Middleton test pieces, starting with toughies and gradually working his way down the graded list. I asked if they had similar rock back in Montana, to which he replied, "Oh yeah, but we sure don't climb on it." Perhaps if he had started his tour in Pembroke his initial impressions would have been more favourable, and he would have grown to appreciate the subtleties of our limestone in all its various guises.

The majority of the routes described in this volume are on rock that is between 350 and 400 million years old. The exceptions are the routes at Swanage, Ogmore and on the North Yorks Moors where the rock is much younger (and can't you tell).

All the limestones were laid down in warm shallow seas not unlike those around the Bahamas today. The rock was formed from layer upon layer of the remains of various sea creatures often preserved in a lime-rich mud, hence the large numbers of fossils that are often visible. Occasionally this deposition was broken by influxes of clay or volcanic ash. These thin layers are usually easily eroded and nowadays form conspicuous horizontal breaks cutting across many of our cliffs, with CHEE TOR GIRDLE being perhaps the premier example. In some areas huge domed coral reefs existed. Here the horizontal layering is much less evident - High Tor and Beeston Tor in the Peak District are good examples of these 'reef knolls'.

Varying pressure on the rock throughout its history has caused the formation of major vertical cracks (joints). These have controlled the erosion of the rock and account for the great steepness of the majority of limestone climbs. Only where the whole rock pile has been tilted by earth movements are there relatively easy-angled limestone routes, e.g. in parts of Pembroke.

The rock is usually peppered with solution pockets and small flakes where part of the solid rock has been dissolved away by ground or rain water. The form of the holds coupled with the angle of the rock means that strong fingers are a great asset, as is a high resistance to pain on many of the hardest routes. In some areas precipitated limestone from percolating ground waters has re-cemented the rock so that unstable looking features are relatively solid. This can create unusual 'stuck on' holds which can be used (carefully) to aid upward progress, such as on THE ARROW at St Govan's in Pembroke.

Loose holds are not uncommon, either as minor flakes or major blocks. A circumspect attitude is a good idea and a heavy-handed approach could have nasty consequences. The fine grained texture of the rock leads to it polishing all too easily. Sloppy footwork is liable to aggravate this problem and make upward progress erratic at best. Repeated top roping also leads to the premature ageing of routes. Although this is a great way of getting fit, it is a pity that it cannot be avoided on classic routes as it will inevitably lead to their eventual destruction.

The nature of the rock tends to lend itself well to traditional British nut protection techniques. Pegs were often used for aid and runners on early ascents of many of the classic climbs in this book. Most of these pieces of iron have rusted away and have not been replaced, as a higher degree of safety is now offered by wired nuts. These can be extremely fiddly to place, so perseverance and a touch of cunning are great assets. In recent years climbers have moved onto the open and often leaning faces between existing routes in search of new sport. Bolt protection is the norm on many of these climbs, though they are often 'sportingly' placed, and a long fall is a very real possibility.

The Areas
Below is a brief 'pen portrait' of the various limestone regions from which the routes have been selected. These should give visitors a general idea of what to expect when going to a new area for the first time. The number of routes in each area is intended as a rough guide to the amount of climbing available there and should not be taken as a definitive total.

DORSET: Over eight kilometres of south-facing cliffs up to 40 metres high, running west from Swanage. There are several less important outlying areas. Recent developments have centred around the Isle of Portland where many short bolt-protected routes have been put up. Access to the main cliffs is often by abseil and there are seasonal restrictions on several areas due to nesting sea birds, as well as the usual tidal problems. The south-facing aspect and a mild climate means that climbing is possible all year round. The routes tend to be steep, strenuous and quite serious. The area used to have a reputation for looseness on a large scale that was not totally unfounded and many of the finishes are distinctly unstable. (*c.*800 routes)

SOUTH DEVON: One pleasant and quite extensive inland cliff (Chudleigh) and a series of sea cliffs and 'almost sea cliffs' at either end of Tor Bay. Access is usually straightforward, with only the Old Redoubt having major tidal problems, and a seasonal bird ban (as the best cliff in the area this is perhaps inevitable). Several areas have been quarried and might best be described as esoteric. Sea level traversing is a popular diversion in some areas, (rubber rings and waterproof chalk bags are taboo). Recent developments have produced a series of hard bolt-protected routes at Anstey's Cove and adventure climbs on the Sanctuary Wall as well as impressive solos at Berry Head. (*c.*500 routes)

AVON and SOMERSET: Two major centres (Avon and Cheddar gorges) and a series of small cliffs and rather unsavoury quarries.

The Avon Gorge provides a series of long and easily accessible routes on good rock. The style of climbing on the Main Wall takes a bit of getting used to and protection is often rather poor. The Suspension Bridge Buttress offers rather more 'normal' limestone climbing, whereas the Unknown area has some strenuous test pieces and some longer climbs on 'interesting' rock. The cliffs face west and dry quickly, so climbing is possible throughout the year. At the moment major civil works are being carried out at Avon. The Main Wall and Central Buttress areas are closed to climbers probably until 1993.

The Cheddar Gorge has a lot of rock and there has been much development of late. The cliffs are up to 100 metres high and the rock is generally good. Unfortunately many of the faces have a northerly aspect and are rather vegetated. The cliff is closed to climbers throughout the summer and in the winter the whole place is rather gloomy and grim. (*c.*700 routes)

THE WYE VALLEY: One major cliff (Wintour's Leap) and several other crags that are well worth a visit. The settings are very pleasant and most of the cliffs face west, catching the afternoon sun. The Wyndcliffe is the main exception and this faces east. Large areas on Wintour's have been quarried in the relatively recent past and so the climbing tends to be on flat holds and protection is often rather spaced. Many of the most important pegs are cemented in places, especially on the more popular and easier climbs. There are routes up to 100 metres in length. The other cliffs

Dorset: The view eastwards from the foot of Marmolata Buttress at Boulder Ruckle is typical of much of Swanage; a steep and imposing line of cliffs fronted with huge fallen blocks.

Avon: An abseil down the upper section of the Unknown Wall. Hidden just around the corner are the Sea Walls, in the middle distance is the Main Wall, and out of sight in the far distance is Suspension Bridge Buttress.

Pembroke: Looking east from near St Govan's Chapel. The white walls of Trevallen Cliff are in the middle distance and beyond stretches the ever popular St Govan's itself.

Clwyd: Craig Arthur dominates the upper section of the Eglwyseg Valley. Its lofty position means that there is almost always a wind blowing on the cliff, but as some compensation the outward views are superb.

North Wales: The very popular cliffs at the Great Orme are seen here from Marine Drive, the Mayfair Wall on the left extends round to Craig Pen Trwyn, and below this is the tidal Lower Pen Trwyn.

The Peak District: High Tor at Matlock seen from the valley below. The main face is crisscrossed by many fine climbs and catches the sun for much of the day.

in the Wye valley offer more typical limestone climbing, with good protection and routes up to 30 metres high. (*c*.600 routes)

SOUTH EAST WALES: Two distinct areas are available within this region. The Gower peninsula contains generally short and unserious routes on excellent rock and in beautiful settings, as well as some fine beaches. The Yellow Wall has a selection of longer, harder climbs, and is covered by a seasonal bird ban.

The rest of south east Wales offers climbing on high windy escarpments, in deep secluded valleys and in a series of fairly unprepossessing quarries. There are also the steep and unusual sea cliffs at Ogmore. Some of the rock is rather poor. (*c*.500 routes)

PEMBROKE: Many kilometres of south-facing sea cliffs, up to 50 metres high, offering the finest concentration of quality limestone climbs in Britain. The rock is almost invariably superb, although it can be rather rough and some of the exits require care. Nut protection is usually perfect. Access problems are common due to various combinations of the birds, the army and the sea getting between you and your chosen objective. Climbing is possible all the year round. (*c*.1,500 routes)

CLWYD: A neglected area of fine limestone escarpments and a few fairly grotty quarries. Many of the routes are quite short but the rock is usually excellent and the climbing fingery. Most of the better cliffs face west and are rather exposed to the vagaries of the weather. World's End offers a selection of routes at a lower grade than is usual on limestone. (*c*.500 routes)

NORTH WALES: One excellent but banned inland crag (Craig y Forwen), and a series of cliffs on Great and Little Orme at Llandudno. There are many short, hard routes as well as some much longer and more serious undertakings on cliffs that face every direction except south. There have been access problems on the most popular cliffs above the Marine Drive on the Great Orme. The availability of much steep rock suggests that this area will be a forcing ground for many years to come. (*c*.900 route)

THE PEAK DISTRICT: A compact area containing an almost bewildering selection of routes, every available piece of rock has been scrutinised and criss-crossed with routes. The area is the most popular climbing centre in the country and the classics of all grades see a lot of traffic, hence they are becoming polished. There are routes of every grade, and they vary in quality from the best to the very worst. Many of the cliffs are sheltered in deep wooded dales and the south-facing ones that are unaffected by major seepage are climbable throughout the year. (*c*.3,000 routes)

THE NORTH YORK MOORS: Two interesting cliffs of rather loose and blocky rock. Peak Scar is a gloomy ravine whilst Whitestone is a high exposed escarpment. Worth a visit for something a little out of the ordinary. (*c*.150 routes)

THE YORKSHIRE DALES: Three main cliffs, Malham Cove, Gordale Scar, and Kilnsey Crag, and a host of lesser (at least in stature) ones. The rock is usually excellent and the settings are often sublime. Many of the really good climbs are hard to very hard. The whole area is understandably very popular with tourists. Several of the cliffs are reached across farmland, so a responsible attitude is required to preserve the present liberal access situations. (*c*.1,500 routes)

NORTH LANCASHIRE and THE SOUTHERN LAKE DISTRICT: A set of fairly unpleasant quarries and a few fine but generally small natural outcrops. The most important of these is Chapel Head Scar which contains a number of hard bolt-protected climbs and a selection of more traditional fare. The area is a nature reserve and access is denied in the spring and early summer. (*c*.500 routes)

The Yorkshire Dales: Malham Cove is the show case of Yorkshire limestone climbing, a magnificent arena set above the timeless charm of the Dales.

THE ROUTES

1: WOGS

Situation:	Chudleigh Rocks, South Devon
Aspect:	South facing
Grade:	Very Difficult
Length:	40m (130ft)
Equipment:	A standard rack.
First Ascent:	I.B.Prowse, 1923
Guidebook:	*South Devon and Dartmoor* by Pat Littlejohn and Pete O'Sullivan. Published by Cordee, 1985.

Approaches: Chudleigh Rocks are approached from the village of Chudleigh, a short distance off the A38. When travelling into the village from the south a right turn (the second one) is made by the police station. The lane narrows then widens again close to a quarry entrance. There is room to park on the right by a small iron gate. Pass through the gate and follow the path for a couple of hundred metres to a flat area in the wood. An easy though polished descent leads down to the left to the start of the cliff. WOGS is almost at the other end of the crag and takes an obvious wall, crack line and groove to the left of a couple of steep walls and to the right of a long streamer of ivy. The start is further identified by the polished state of the rock.

The Route: Although rather polished WOGS provides an excellent way up a steep cliff. All difficulties are well protected.

Description: The climb can be done in one runout but is better split into three pitches so as to savour the experience. An initial steep and well-polished wall leads rapidly to a good ledge and a variety of excellent belays. Pitch two goes up and then left to gain the crack line that is the main feature of the route, this has some awkward moves but great protection, and leads to a spacious stance on top of the buttress. There are a variety of finishes but the best one is to climb into a recess and then follow a delicate slab until it is possible to get out right onto an exposed ledge from where a finish up the 'garden wall' is made. At the end of the route is a sheltered little bay ideal for a picnic, watching the setting sun or spending a lazy half-hour 'far from the madding crowd'.

WOGS

Chudleigh is a crag that is very much out of vogue these days but despite that it is an idyllic place to spend a few hours cragging. The rock is excellent solid limestone, the cliff gets all the sun that is going and the outlook from the crag could have been painted by Constable. The sheen on some of the routes correctly suggests that the crag was much more popular in the past, but today attention has been diverted away to the big and butch sea cliffs around Torbay.

Many of the routes on the cliff are worth doing but the most remarkable thing about WOGS is its great antiquity. It was put up in 1923 and it was almost 40 years before another route was added to the crag. I wonder what were the circumstances of that first ascent? Was the rock loose? Was the route soloed? - if a rope was used was there any kind of protection? What kind of footwear did they use - surely not nailed boots? After that why was the cliff left for so long when there were other easy, though perhaps inferior lines to be done? Doubtless the answers to these questions are lost in the mists of time. One thing can be sure - there must have been a great sense of adventure and a feeling of considerable danger, setting out on a long route on a steep and unexplored cliff. Today that sense of adventure has been muted by the knowledge of the grade and exact line of the route, and the danger has been reduced with modern rope techniques. Even so, the route is still there to be enjoyed by anyone who sets aside an hour of their time; the setting is as beautiful as it ever was and the feeling of satisfaction at having conquered your own little Everest still takes some beating.

WOGS: Approaching the top of the crack line that forms the substance of the second pitch. It "has some awkward moves but great protection, and leads to a spacious stance on top of the buttress".
Climbers: Chris Craggs and Sherri Davy

2: CENTRAL RIB ROUTE III

Situation:	The South Bay, Wintour's Leap, The Wye Valley
Aspect:	West facing
Grade:	Very Difficult
Length:	70m (230ft)
Equipment:	Only a limited amount of gear is needed as the pitches are generally short and they are not over-endowed with protection possibilities.
First Ascent:	Unknown but sometime pre-1960
Guidebook:	*The Wye Valley* by J.Wilson, D.Hope, T.Penning and M.Ward published in 1987 by Cordee.

Approaches: The most satisfying way of reaching this route is by the Easy Way Down. This is quite straightforward, though a complete novice may require a little coaching, as there is a touch of exposure in one or two places. The village of Woodcroft is on the B4228 a couple kilometres north of Chepstow. Five hundred metres north of the Rising Sun public house is a small pull off on the left of the road with room for about four cars. Climb up to the left onto a promontory and drop off the right corner of this. The route down from here is well scratched and easy to follow. Towards the bottom a long ledge is reached, cross to its far end and finish the descent. At the bottom turn left (looking out) and follow paths for about 100 metres. An odd, square-cut, buttress about three metres wide, in the back of a concave bay is the route and the base of it (a large ledge with trees) is reached by a short scramble.

The Route: A long climb up a large cliff. The stances are excellent, but protection is only fair. A great route for beginners (on the right end of the rope).

Description: Climb out to the right and follow the crest of the ridge on large flat

holds to a small ledge on the left (peg belay or runner). Climb the steep groove above (peg runner) until it is possible to step left to reach ledges leading to a twin tree belay. Step out right onto the crest of the buttress and climb up its front (peg runner secreted on the left) steeply to reach two ledges both of which contain a pipe belay, though the lower one also has a cemented peg as a back up. From here climb straight up the buttress front, all rather steep, to reach

CENTRAL RIB ROUTE III
The steep groove that forms the upper section of the first pitch has rather slippery rock and is not too well protected.
Climbers: Jim Rubery & Sherri Davy (belayed on the first peg runner).

more good ledges and belay trees. The final pitch trends right up grassy ledges to finish up a short buttress in a fine position. Belay to the fence.

CENTRAL RIB ROUTE III

It has to be admitted that from below the whole of the South Bay, as this area is known, looks a bit scrappy. It is dotted with trees and there is a scattering of grassy ledges that give the whole area a rather unkempt air. The only feature that looks worth climbing is a fine clean corner that our route manages to avoid. Fortunately when you rub your nose against the rock there is a nice surprise, for the route gives three (or four) interesting pitches on excellent rock with good stances and a glorious outlook.

The first pitch sets the scene, large flat holds are awkwardly spaced, but have good sharp edges, so progress is safe and rapid to a small ledge above which are the first real difficulties. A groove of rather slippery rock is ascended crabwise, as all the footholds are in the groove but the handholds are out on the right edge. A peg runner (on a V.Diff?) backed up by nuts protects a couple of awkward moves up and out left to a big tree and fine stance. The next pitch gets out onto the rib that gives the route its name, by a rather exposed shuffle around a corner, from where steep moves on excellent handholds and indifferent footholds, protected by a peg around to the left (on a V.Diff.?) should see you arriving on more good ledges.

The third (or fourth) pitch is probably the crux though the main difficulties can be avoided rather unsportingly on the left. A distinctly steep and reachy wall (good wires in a horizontal crack on the left) is climbed to more ledges this time complete with tree belays. The final pitch is away to the right up a fine little wall, to a very sudden ending right by the Offa's Dyke footpath, with solid belays around the wooden fence. The present guide describes the route thus "A classic: a perfect introduction to rock climbing on a fine day". This is perhaps just a bit of an understatement.

3: CORMORANT BUTTRESS WEST

Situation:	Cormorant Ledge, Swanage, Dorset
Aspect:	South facing
Grade:	Very Difficult
Length:	30m (100ft)
Equipment:	A standard rack supplemented by some larger protection for the flake crack on pitch two.
First Ascent:	J.Yaldren, R.J.Crewe, 11th October 1969
Guidebook:	*Swanage* by Gordon Jenkin, published by the Climbers' Club in 1986.

Approaches: From Swanage follow the A351 out of town, then turn left along the B3069 to Langton Maltravers. Take the first left turn after the King's Arms and follow the road through a gate where it degenerates into a rough track. (The sign saying 'no

mini-buses' can be ignored unless of course you are driving a minibus.) Park at the farm of Spyway Barn (honesty box) and walk through the buildings and down towards the sea. Bear left after two fields then follow the wall down to the coastal path. Cross the stile and descend a gully to quarried ledges where a cemented pipe enables you to make a fifty foot abseil to the boulders below the cliff. The rope can then be pulled down. Scramble eastwards (to the right facing the cliff) for 150 metres to a prominent jutting buttress with a great block below it.

The Route: A low grade sea cliff classic. The abseil approach and unstable exit means that the route is not really suitable for complete novices.

Description: From the tip of the block gain the wall with difficulty then trend left on big holds to reach a ledge with thread belays. Move right then climb the wall to reach the large flake crack. Up this to its top then scramble up the ridge with care. The stake belay was missing at the time of writing so get well back and take a seat!

CORMORANT BUTTRESS WEST

Swanage is not over-endowed with quality low grade routes but then again few limestone cliffs are. Here the usual problem of the steepness of the rock are compounded by difficult access and unstable exits.

CORMORANT BUTTRESS WEST used to be approached by a long and rather 'hairy' abseil from directly above. A few years ago winter storms brought down a large area of rock just to the west of the route. This unfortunately destroyed a couple of (fairly mediocre) routes but meant that access could now be gained via the much more friendly approach from Guillemot Ledge.

A scramble down leads to quarried ledges with a substantial cemented piece of pipe at the back of it. Beginners can abseil from this protected with a back rope,

CORMORANT BUTTRESS WEST
"The second pitch climbs up and right heading for the conspicuous flake stuck on the wall above".
*Climber: Colin Bink*s

and with no fear of pulling rocks onto their head, and the really timid can even be lowered down (with their eyes closed?).

Clambering over the boulders past the site of the already almost healed rock fall, a prominent pillar stands out in the upper part of the cliff. Getting started on the wall below the pillar is difficult due to the undercut nature of the rock, though fortunately a great boulder lies close enough to the face to leave only a high step to pass the overhang. Any higher off the ground the first couple of moves would command a grade a couple of notches higher than V.Diff, but here you can take your time, work out the best strategy and 'climb when you are ready'.

Once established on the wall, huge holds on fantastically convoluted flint nodules lead up and left into a shallow groove. Here steeper moves, still on great holds, lead to a commodious ledge with a variety of belays including some substantial threads.

The second pitch climbs up and right heading for the conspicuous flake stuck on the wall above. The crack down the back of the flake is wide and either a large Friend or an equally large Hex is needed to protect it. The flake itself is quite imposing but the edge is sharp and the whole affair is short-lived. A butch and bold layback is possible or for the technically proficient a more circumspect approach using small face holds is available. From the top of the flake a couple of moves to the right leads to an easy angled but distinctly unstable ridge running up to the grassy top of the cliff. With just a little care this should present no problems (but ice-axe and crampons would not go amiss) though it gives an interesting insight into the problems of exiting from some of the steeper parts of the cliff. The stake that used to act as a belay has vanished, stolen or rotted away, so it is best to get well back from the edge before taking in.

CORMORANT BUTTRESS WEST is a fine route, a perfect introduction to sea cliff climbing with just a little touch of all the ingredients that make this such a compulsive pastime.

4: THE EAST RIDGE

Situation:	Great Tor, Penmaen, The Gower, South Wales
Aspect:	East facing
Grade:	Severe (4b, -, -, 3b)
Length:	80m (250ft)
Equipment:	A standard rack.
First Ascent:	A.Osborn, S.Osborn, 1952
Guidebook:	*Gower and South East Wales* by Mike Danford and Tony Penning, published by the South Wales Mountaineering Club in 1983. A new guide is due out in 1991.

Approaches: In the centre of the small village of Penmaen on the A4118 (12 km west of Swansea) is a parking area in front of the village store/post office. Park here and walk down a sunken lane towards the sea. At the end of the lane trend right along a sandy path onto the open heath. Now fol-low narrow paths out towards the headland. At a grassy col (leave sacks here) follow an indistinct track down to the left towards sea level until ledges lead out to the tip of the headland. Non-tidal.

The Route: A long climb in a charming setting. The start is hard but short-lived, eminently protectable and if all else fails, avoidable. The rest of the route is much easier apart from a short wall towards the top.

Description: Either climb the starting polished crack at the back of the ledge with difficulty or take the easier arête on the left. Both routes lead to a good stance on the ridge crest. Move around onto the left face to avoid a steepening then continue up the ridge to a stance below a wall. The wall is steep but short-lived and easier rock leads to the summit. A short, slippery descent leads down to the col between the tower and the 'mainland'.

THE EAST RIDGE

The Gower is a delightful area of sandy beaches and rocky headlands backed by rolling farmland and tiny villages. The climbing here tends to be much easier of access than in nearby Pembroke, and is often in the middle and lower grades. The whole place has a relaxed air about it, and the odd route can easily be fitted into a family holiday.

Great Tor is the prominent lump of rock that sticks out into the sea between the two glorious beaches of Three Cliffs Bay and Oxwich Bay. The EAST RIDGE offers a fine route finishing on an isolated summit, quite a novelty.

From the rocky platform at the base of the route, a diagonal crack rises steeply to the right. It is undercut and the footholds are small and sloping. The moves to enter the crack would not disgrace a V.S. if they were further from the ground but here they can be attempted in relative safety. A runner can be placed above the tricky step or a catching team can field a falling leader. If

THE EAST RIDGE
The alternative start to the first pitch of the route avoids the traditional polished crack and offers an easier approach to the upper part of the ridge.
Climber: Sherri Davy

you think this is all a bit much on a Severe all these antics can be avoided by the pleasant left arête of the wall. Either way you arrive at a comfortable notch on the ridge. The wall above is steep (real V.S.) but a step round onto the face on the left reveals plenty of good holds heading up a shallow groove in the wall and onto the crest. As height is gained the angle of the ridge gradually eases and finely positioned scrambling leads on towards the summit. There is a possible stance part way up the ridge or you can press on to reach a good ledge below the final riser. A short steep wall blocks the whole ridge and although it looks quite tough there are good holds once the initial move has been negotiated. The last move involves a strenuous pull on a large flake, but this can be outflanked by a swing to the left. Above this final obstacle the ridge relents and scrambling leads to the summit. Here there is a comfortable sitting stance from where you can take in the view and the ropes at the same time.

Once the team is reunited and hands have been shaken in traditional fashion a slippery descent leads to the col between Great Tor and the 'mainland'. It is worth keeping the rope on if there are beginners in the party as a couple of steps are quite tricky. Then it is back to the sacks and time for a choice, perhaps a brew, or another route in Three Cliffs Bay, or even a leisurely dip in the briny.

NIGHTMARE: At the top of the groove on pitch two before traversing right to reach easier ledges.
Climber: Sherri Davy

5: NIGHTMARE

Situation: The Sea Walls, Avon Gorge, Bristol
Aspect: South-west facing
Grade: Severe (3c, 4a, 3c)
Length: 55m (180ft)
Equipment: A normal rack with a couple of long slings should be enough.
First Ascent: M.Thompson, 1960
Guidebook: *The Avon Gorge* by Steve Monks, published by Dark Peak in 1981. A new guide is due out in 1991/2

Approaches: NIGHTMARE is the best lower grade route on the Sea Walls (and probably in the whole of the Avon Gorge). When approaching the city centre along the Portway (A4) these are the series of slanting grey walls set back from the road. A huge barred cave mouth on the left further identifies the area. To the right of centre of the cliff is a large tree on a ledge, NIGHTMARE starts directly below this.

The Route: A long route on excellent though rather polished rock. Protection is poor in a couple of places.

Description: A shallow groove leads up to overhangs below and right of a rather stunted hawthorn bush. Climb this groove to its top then traverse to the left to reach the bush. Belay just above on a good ledge. Step up and right to get into another groove which is followed until it is possible to exit right to ledges and another possible belay. Easier climbing now leads up towards the big tree with a tricky little wall just below it. From a belay on the pine tree traverse to the right for ten metres then climb the wall to reach an easy ramp leading away left to the cliff top.

NIGHTMARE

The Sea Walls are a broad conglomerate of short, steep walls divided from each other by slabby rakes slanting up from right to left. The rock on the walls is almost without exception wonderfully compact, and has a coarse texture not usually associated with limestone. The shortness of the individual walls and the lack of any prominent features meant that this whole area was largely neglected while the more challenging areas of the gorge were explored. When the pioneers finally got round to giving the area a good looking-at they were rewarded with a fine little route at a remarkably easy standard.

Talking of standards, NIGHTMARE has always been graded Hard Very Difficult, but in reality it is well worth Severe. Some of the holds are polished to a high gloss and protection is not always perfect; in fact, there are a couple of places where a fall could have nasty consequences.

The first pitch starts up a slabby groove where the first set of slippery holds has to be used. A rather precarious series of bridging moves allows progress to be made up the gradually steepening groove. A much easier and rather dirty corner on the left can be gained after a few metres but does not compare with the 'proper' way. At the top of the groove a roof bars progress and a narrowing foot ledge running across the left wall allows a delicate escape to reach the sanctuary of the hawthorn, and just a little higher a good ledge and large nut belay.

From this comfortable stance any direct route is blocked, so it is necessary to step out right into another slanting groove. This is awkward and not too well protected, the whole thing attempting to push you out onto the bald and exposed rib on the right. It is worth persevering with the corner because good holds and then runners do arrive. There is a possible stance above and right of the groove but the belays are nothing special and the position of the stance leaves the second rather poorly protected; it is probably better to press on. Easy ledges lead up right then back left until just short of the tree where a short polished flake with a tricky exit has to be tackled before the shade offered by the tree can be enjoyed.

The final pitch starts by traversing out right and climbing a step to reach a line of glassy 'lumps' running up the wall. There are no runners so a steady approach is needed until you grasp a good flake and then a couple more moves lead into the base of the easy gully running up to the cliff top. Here there are stout trees to tie onto, great views of the river and an easy descent down the back.

Although the climb is a bit of a 'polished horror' in places, it remains a great little outing, the kind of nightmare you won't lose any sleep over.

6: BOW SHAPED SLAB

Situation: Flimston Bay, Range East, South Pembroke
Aspect: South facing
Grade: Severe (3b)
Length: 40m (130ft)
Equipment: A normal rack, though you may not find a lot of use for the larger pieces of equipment.
First Ascent: J.Perrin, C.Mortlock, 20th May 1970
Guidebook: *Pembroke* by Jon de Montjoye and Mike Harber, published by the Climbers' Club in 1985. A new guide is due out in 1991.

Approaches: The shortest walk in to the cliff is from the car park at Stack Rocks at the western edge of Range East. From here walk back into the range for about a kilometre (a little over half a mile). The cliff is quite difficult to find from above but is instantly recognisable from the west. It is worth a quick trip out towards the sea to get your bearings before you get too close to the cliff, then once organised you can head straight for the top of the slab. There are belays in the rocky area behind the top of the slab that allow an abseil rope to be set up, but this involves abseiling down the line of the route and so may detract somewhat from the ascent. It is possible to descend (Moderate) or abseil down the next slab to the west and traverse in to the foot of the main slab. This preserves the integrity of the ascent i.e. no abseil inspection is possible, but care must be taken if the sea is rough and a rope is advisable for non-swimmers or the timid. Start in the centre of the slab as low as the tide allows.

The Route: A long sustained pitch on excellent rock. As the name suggests the angle is amenable though protection is rather spaced.

Description: Climb directly up the centre of the slab until it begins to rear up. A series of thin cracks runs away rightward in the direction of the impressive corner. These are followed for a short distance until it is possible to step back left and continue directly to the top. Belay well back.

BOW SHAPED SLAB

Viewed from the west the logic behind the name of the route is obvious, a graceful curve of rock that sweeps majestically up out of the sea ,its lines mirroring the shape of a partly drawn longbow. Close scrutiny of the rocks on either side of the slab reveals a hotchpotch of walls and slabs at random angles. In some places the layers of rock are joined in tortured curves where the limestone has behaved as if it was so much plasticine and in others it has been ripped apart by forces that treated the solid rock like slabs of toffee. Long before the Alps were a wrinkle on the Earth's crust, an ocean that lay across southern Britain was being squeezed out of existence by colliding continents. The ripples that spread out from this centre of destruction can be seen here in South Wales and in North Devon; on the Culm coast for example.

In the case of BOW SHAPED SLAB the former ocean bed was tipped up so as to face directly at the midday sun and at such an angle so as to be climbable anywhere. If the forces of nature had gone on 'playing' with the slab a little longer we may have ended up with some very impressive and mighty tough face routes. As it is, we are left with one of the best low grade, and one of the few low angle limestone climbs in the country.

The climbing is remarkable in that it is so sustained, there are plenty of holds but

BOW SHAPED SLAB: Approaching the centre of the slab by sustained climbing on small holds, the rock and the situations are superb. *Climber: Sherri Davy*

they are all so small that there is a tendency to keep going in the hope that better ones will appear. In fact it is best to pace yourself and try to control your cramping calves whilst getting the protection you require, as things get harder before they get easier. As the rock bulges the easiest way is to trend right and then back left to regain the line though a direct link is possible at a slightly higher grade. Before you pull over the top take a last look down the sweeping curve of the route, now you known what a ski jumper is faced with at his moment of truth.

DIEDRE SUD: Laybacking the final section of Pitch Two. "The rock is superb, clean, grey and rough".
Climbers: Steve Warwick and Colin Binks

7:
DIEDRE SUD

Situation:	Mowing Word, South Pembroke
Aspect:	West facing, the crag is in the sun from shortly after midday until it sets.
Grade:	Hard Severe (3c, 4a)
Length:	40m (140ft)
Equipment:	A standard rack should be carried as well as several slings for the spikes and threads.
First Ascent:	C.Mortlock, S.Williams, 31st May 1967
Guidebook:	*Pembroke* by Jon de Montjoye and M. Harber published by the Climbers' Club in 1985. A new guide is due out in 1991.

Approaches: The nearest car park is the National Trust one at Broad Haven (50 pence per day in 1990). The coastal path is followed over Broad Haven beach and across the downs beyond to reach the cliff in about 20 minutes. Alternative and slightly longer approaches for those not in a rush are possible from either Bosherston via the Lily Ponds or from Stackpole Quay over the delightfully named Barafundle Beach. It is possible to abseil down the line of the route from a selection of rather wobbly iron spikes embedded in the grass above, although the low tide approach described below is infinitely more satisfying.

The Route: A classic corner climb with rock and protection as good as you could wish for. A low tide is required for the start.

Description: DIEDRE SUD follows the obvious corner in the centre of the west face of Mowing Word in one long pitch or two shorter ones. At higher tides, though not in heavy seas, it is possible to start from ledges just above sea level. Great care is needed to keep the ropes out of the water. *Note:* The cliff is the subject of an access restriction due to nesting auks, and is closed to climbers between 1st March and 31st July. Please respect this.

DIEDRE SUD
There are not many good limestone climbs of a modest grade in Britain. The easier lines on these generally steep cliffs tend to be vegetated and loose, and as if that was not bad enough they are often very polished. Diedre Sud, which takes a striking and central line up one of Pembroke's finest cliffs, is not just a good climb, it is a gem. The route in its own right is worthy of a journey from afar, but add to this the spice of a distinctly adventurous approach and you have an outing that every climber should experience at some time in their career. To enjoy this trip at its best requires a set of circumstances that might require a bit of waiting for, but be assured, the wait will be worth it. You should aim to leave the car park three or four hours before sunset, on a fine blue day and with a falling spring tide.

After crossing the flesh pots of Broad Haven beach and its variety of distractions, including superb sand and a welcoming sea, to name but two, the path heads across perfect grass kept in trim by myriads of rabbits. After a kilometre or so the path heads back inland to skirt round a mighty gash, filled with squawking and wheeling sea birds. This is Raming Hole. Just beyond this a faint path breaks right from the main track, and leads down a sloping terrace. At the bottom of the terrace are two substantial iron rings which allows an abseil onto another sloping terrace below. It is possible to solo down this section (V. Diff) but there is a mighty drop on the left, so a slip might well prove fatal. The terrace leads round below the impressive walls of Gun Cliff and out into the large bay beyond. This is a great place to explore with rock pools galore and huge tottering cliffs with even an unclimbed and unclimbable pinnacle. At this stage you will discover if you have got your timing right, because if all is well the bottom of DIEDRE SUD will be out of the water and a superb sandy beach will be exposed in the bed of the bay.

From directly below, the line of the climb soars skywards as a superb square-cut corner defended at its base by a set of barnacle-encrusted and dripping wet bulges. You won't need chalk here and there is not a lot of point in drying your hightec footwear; just grab handfuls of crunchy jugs and power over the overhangs to greater things just above. There is a possible stance to bring up the rest of the party if the sea threatens, otherwise continue up the steep but straightforward corner to a comfortable stance on the right. There is a choice of belays including an old peg and a low thread as well as a selection of excellent nuts.

The ever-steepening corner above looks intimidating but its bark is worse than its bite. The best way to tackle the corner is to bridge up it - that most delightful form of progress that allows the situations to be enjoyed to the full and adequate protection arranged, without the fear of arms fading and panic setting in. The rock is superb, clean grey and rough, blasted by winter gales that throw waves over the cliff top, so relax and savour the experience, the setting sun on your back, the solidness of the rock and the runners - just being there. No matter how you try to spin it out and extend the pleasure, it is all over too quickly, committed to memory with those other special days. A slow walk back with your shadow stretching out behind you, back across the now silent beach with time perhaps for a cool pint in the St Govan's Inn. Dreams are made of this.

8: GARROTTER

Situation:	Willersley Castle Crag, Matlock, Derbyshire
Aspect:	North facing
Grade:	V.S. (4b, 4b)
Length:	35m (120ft)
Equipment:	A standard rack.
First Ascent:	S.Read, K.Beech, 1959
Guidebook:	*Peak Limestone South,* published by the British Mountaineering Council in 1987.

Approaches: When driving south from Matlock on the A6 there is a large junction and right turn to Cromford after four kilometres. Just beyond this is a minor road branching left and signed to Crich. This is followed for a kilometre to a large open grassy area on the right, Cromford Meadows. Park here then cross the road and pass through the gate into the churchyard. The rocks are a couple of hundred metres along the path.

The Route: A two-pitch classic in a rather gloomy setting. The rock is becoming polished.

Description: To the right of the centre of the cliff is a rightward leaning corner with a large overhang at 12 metres. Above this is a small horizontal tree sticking out from the cliff. Climb the groove to the first roof and pass it on the right. A little higher is another overhang which is avoided by a traverse to the left to reach the tree and a comfortable stance. The second pitch steps to the right and follows the rest of the groove throughout with sustained climbing, excellent protection and fine situations.

GARROTTER: On the second pitch "Most of the corner can be comfortably bridged".
Climbers: Mike Riddings and Colin Binks

GARROTTER

Willersley Castle Crag is named, rather illogically, after the grand building that stands on the other side of the River Derwent. Unfortunately, the cliff faces almost due north, so while the residents of the castle are bathed in sunshine the cliff tends to be shady and cold (there's no justice in the world). This northerly aspect does have one advantage, as the prevailing south-westerlies tend to blow over the top of the cliff it can stay dry in showery weather. The luxuriant tree growth along the top of the cliff helps keep the rain off though once seepage starts to appear the cliff takes some time to dry out.

The cliff offers a selection of mid-grade routes that follow excellent lines, though some of the rock requires respectful handling. GARROTTER follows one of the strongest lines on the crag, running the full height of the cliff and with perfect rock throughout. The initial corner is quite polished but the holds are large and there is plenty of protection. A roof soon interrupts the upward flow and a traverse on undercuts leads out rightwards to the lip, it is worth remembering to extend the runners so as to reduce rope drag problems that might arise once you are round the roof. A large and rather glossy foothold on the right arête has to be gained and the fingerholds around the overhang are fairly indifferent. Fortunately the protection is morale boosting and there is only one hard move before a traverse leads back left to a cosy niche and a solid piece of woodwork to lash yourself to.

The top pitch is perhaps a touch easier technically than the lower one though it is considerably more sustained. Once again there are 'bomber' runners galore. From the stance easy climbing takes you up and right, then the corner starts to steepen and things look a little tougher. The rock has changed from the sharp edged blocky material of the bottom pitch to smooth textured, compact stuff peppered with excellent pockets. The crack in the back of the corner offers a myriad of protection possibilities as well as the odd hand jam. Most of the corner can be comfortably bridged, though a short steepening toward the top is best dealt with by a couple of brisk layback moves. The exit is solid and there is a selection of big trees to belay from, while you gaze out across the river. Sitting with the sun on your back, take the

ropes in and ponder, a route as good as GARROTTER would bring a lump to anyone's throat!

9:
MEDUSA

Situation:	Ravensdale, Derbyshire
Aspect:	West facing
Grade:	V.S. (4b, 4b, 4b)
Length:	46m (150ft)
Equipment:	A normal rack with a couple of long slings.
First Ascent:	D.Johnson, D.Mellor, 22nd May 1960
Guidebook:	*Peak Limestone, Stoney,* published by the British Mountaineering Council in 1987.

Approaches: Ravensdale is the deep-cut valley that runs south from Wardlow Mires on the A623 Stoney Middleton to Chapel-en-le-Frith road, meeting the Wye valley at Cressbrook Mill. A minor road runs from the mill to Ravensdale Cottages which are directly below the cliff. There is adequate parking here and a well-made path runs through a nature reserve up to the foot of the biggest buttress (Raven's Buttress) where our route is situated.

The Route: A three-pitch classic taking the easiest line up a big cliff.

Description: The climb starts six metres left of the tree at the foot of the cliff below a polished flake crack. The crack has an awkward start but soon eases and leads to ledges from which a step right gains a rather rattly wall which is climbed to another ledge. Belays are available on the right by a large pinnacle. The steep corner to the right of the pinnacle leads to a small stance and excellent thread belays. The final pitch climbs the narrowing ramp to a

small bulge which is passed on the left to reach the final groove. There are stake belays in the grassy slopes at the top of the cliff. The best descent lies down the gully to the right of the cliff, (when facing the rock).

MEDUSA

Ravensdale is a superb little valley hidden away in the heart of the White Peak. The place has a quiet air about it, oozing a tranquillity which is rare in these hectic times. The road up the valley leads only as far as the cottages and so there is no background noise of traffic rumbling past, and the footpath through the valley bed is not very popular so crocodiles of folk in dayglow orange are absent. Added to this, the heavy covering of trees muffles the sounds from below so the cliff is a great place for a bit of solitude. The cliff faces due west and its lofty situation means that it catches any weather as it is carried in on the prevailing winds. This elevated position means that the rock dries quickly after rain and if you time your ascent properly you can top out in the setting rays of the sun, and make it back to the car before dusk turns to dark.

The line that MEDUSA traces up the cliff is a fine piece of route-finding, linking together weakness to give a technically reasonable passage up an impressive and complex buttress. The first moves can be a bit off-putting as an awkward and shiny crack bars the way to easier climbing above. A couple of skiddy moves have to be made to reach better holds and some small ledges. The short wall above provides a bit of an enigma in that it is definitely loose but it is also polished! It is obvious that the holds must be more solid than they feel as they have stood 30 years of thumping, pulling and kicking. On the other hand they are definitely going to part company with the cliff at some time and maybe today's the day.

Once above the loose wall a good stance arrives. From here you step right into a steep groove which is climbed on large holds. The pitch contains some holes that have been inhabited by generations of birds. Their comings and goings had polished the sides of these holes to a glossy sheen long before we started buffing them up with our smooth rubber soles. Nowadays it is possible to adjust your tie and ensure your hair is neatly parted in these 'mirrors in the cliffs' before you press smartly on to the next stance. The belay is a very substantial thread so you can relax and take in the situation.

The final pitch is perhaps the best on the route. A slabby ramp runs upwards from your restricted stance, narrowing as it rises, and ending at a small bulge. The ramp gives interesting and well positioned climbing and the bulge is neatly outflanked by a step to the left. This takes you into the final groove which is well furnished with holds and leads to a sudden exit on the flat top of the buttress. Belays are provided in the form of a couple of not very substantial spikes well buried in a small grassy hollow a short distance to the right. If there is any possibility of your mate coming adrift from the pitch you had best sit down and dig your heels in!

MEDUSA: The final pitch. "A ramp runs upwards from your restricted stance, narrowing as it rises".
Climbers: Rich Watkinson and Lynne Robinson

10: NIGHTWATCH

Situation:	Whitestonecliffe, Thirsk, North York Moors
Aspect:	West facing
Grade:	V.S. (4b)
Length:	35m (110ft)
Equipment:	A standard rack, perhaps supplemented by a few extra Friends for the horizontal breaks.
First Ascent:	T.Sullivan and party, early 1960s
Guidebook:	*North York Moors* by Cleveland Mountaineering Club, published by Cordee in 1985.

Approaches: When driving east from Thirsk on the A170, Whitestonecliffe is the left-hand of the two large cliffs on the edge of the hills ahead. The road leads steeply up Sutton Bank at the top of which there are ample parking spaces. Cross the minor road and follow the Cleveland Way northwards for a kilometre. As the trees on the left of the path end there is a steep gully which leads down to the southern end of the cliff. This gully is the most convenient descent to the cliff but requires care, especially if at all wet as it is steep and slippery, particularly towards the bottom. An abseil is probably the best idea. At the bottom of the gully turn to the right, passing an impressive arête, to find an equally impressive left-facing corner crack.

The Route: A steep and intimidating crack system with good protection and 'interesting' rock.

Description: Climb the crack! Tree belay well back.

NIGHTWATCH: The fine corner chimney is set far above Gormire Lake and the farmland of the Vale of York.
Climbers: John Addy and Christine Kell

NIGHTWATCH

Whitestonecliffe appeared suddenly in the early 1700s as the result of a massive landslide. The small dark patch of water below the cliff, Gormire Lake, was formed at the same time. This lake has the double distinction of being the only true lake in the giant county of Yorkshire and being bottomless. (The fact that several streams enter the lake but none leave it 'prove' that it must be bottomless. The possibility that this phenomenon may be associated with the fracturing of the rock in the landslide has been ignored by locals with a keen eye on the tourist trade.) A walk along the cliff top reveals some very impressive slits in the ground that suggest the present cliff may also be a transient feature.

When Terry Sullivan and other members of the Cleveland Mountaineering Club first visited Whitestonecliffe in the early 60's looking for practice for the Dolomites they were not disappointed. The crag was (and still is) large and loose with a series of powerful lines. Huge rounded boulders protrude from the walls, suspended in a mishmash of soft yellow rock. In places the limestone is riddled with holes, perforated into lace-like filigrees. After a quick assessment of the crag they picked on the finest and most solid-looking wall and climbed the two best lines on it. It seems likely that they were pleasantly surprised by the impressive right-hand line which they christened NIGHTWATCH, because they gave it the remarkably reasonable grade of Hard Severe. The grade has stuck through successive guidebooks but the addition of the word 'traditional' speaks volumes.

When you stand at the foot of the crack line and gaze upwards it is apparent that this is no ordinary Hard Severe and a grade of at least V.S. would seem to be more appropriate. The chimney crack narrows as it rises and leans menacingly throughout its 30 or so metres. In reality the climbing is technically quite reasonable with the numerous horizontal breaks offering a series of knobbly holds. Protection is good, but the rock is rather unusual and the upward view is always intimidating. I think most climbers looking for an introduction to the Hard Severe grade would take one look at this and run a mile.

As it stands (as long as it stands?) the route is a great one. Its bark is far worse than its bite, but it provides an interesting insight into the psychology of intimidation. How good are you at mind games anyway?

11: GIANT'S CAVE BUTTRESS

Situation:	The Amphitheatre, The Avon Gorge, Bristol
Aspect:	West facing
Grade:	V.S. (4b, 3c, 4c)
Length:	80m (270ft)
Equipment:	A standard rack is more than adequate.
First Ascent:	Unknown, probably early 1950s
Guidebook:	*The Avon Gorge* by Steve Monks, published by Dark Peak in 1981. A new guide is due out in 1991/2

Approaches: The A4 (Portway) runs alongside the River Avon passing below all the climbing areas. The Amphitheatre is the rambling area of rock that is passed just before the road goes through the tunnel below the suspension bridge. There are two small parking places on the left here which can be reversed into, though *great care* is needed with fast-moving traffic. A much safer idea is to park above the cliff near the suspension bridge and follow a footpath to the west of the bridge that zig-zags down to the valley bottom. Walk through the tunnel and climb over the fence, then scramble up to the left to the base of the steeper rock.

The Route: A long climb in an interesting setting. Protection is rather poor except on the hardest moves.

GIANT'S CAVE BUTTRESS: The final easy section of the ridge, high above the speeding traffic on the Portway.
Climber: Jim Rubery

GIANT'S CAVE BUTTRESS

What makes a classic route? The last time I was climbing at Avon we decided to finish off a long day with a quick ascent of GIANT'S CAVE BUTTRESS to see if it was worthy of inclusion in a Classic Limestone volume. We parked at the cliff top and trotted down the steep path as the sun headed for the horizon. There was already a couple on the route when we set off, but they were well up the second pitch so we set off in hot pursuit. The start of the first pitch was quite tricky and the well-glazed holds had been 'roughened up' by some public spirited soul using a hammer (interesting ethics). Above the climbing was straightforward so I ran it out to the belay. Jim led through and shot up the second pitch and I followed. At this point I was feeling rather disappointed by the climbing, it was all too easy, and the good climbing was broken up by scrappy sections.

At the final stance we caught up the other team, two young ladies who were sorting their gear and double checking the belays. They were a little apprehensive and asked us to go first so I swung round the corner and climbed the steep and interesting wall on to easier rock, and 30 minutes after leaving the car we were back at the top. In the meantime Jim was quizzing the ladies about the route. They said they had done some pitches on the Sea Walls earlier in the day but confessed that this was the first 'big route' they had ever done. We paid out two pence and went to watch them from the suspension bridge. They took their time but climbed steadily and safely, reaching the top just as dusk was falling.

We bumped into them again the next day in the car park and asked if they had enjoyed the route. There was no doubt about their feelings, they both thought the climb had been brilliant; the best thing they had ever done.

I wonder who got the right feeling about the climb? Was it us racing up it as an easy tick at the end of the day, or them, savouring the experience and doing it at just the right time in their climbing career? There is certainly a lot of truth in the theory that you get out of a route what you put into it. I think perhaps their appraisal was the right one.

Description: From the foot of the steep rock get onto a block then step right on to the wall. Climb up keeping left of the edge of the wall to a ledge (peg runner). Step out left and climb steeply to the highest ledge and belay. Move round the corner to the left then follow short walls and easy rock to ledges below the impending upper wall. Back up the in-situ belay pegs. Move round the exposed corner (peg) and gain the ledge with difficulty. Continue up the steep wall to easier rock and a corner (possible belay). Step left then climb directly up large flat ledges to the top.

12: JAM WITH SAM

Situation:	Peak Scar, North York Moors
Aspect:	North facing
Grade:	V.S. (4b)
Length:	30m (100ft)
Equipment:	A standard rack backed up with a few large Hexes or Friends.
First Ascent:	T.Sullivan, V.Tosh, 1961
Guidebook:	*North York Moors* by the Cleveland Mountaineering Club, published by Cordee, 1985.

Approaches: Take the A170 Thirsk to Pickering road to the top of Sutton Bank where a minor road forks off to the left. This is followed for a couple of kilometres to a left turn by a large mast. Continue along a very straight road to a junction in a clump of trees. Turn right and follow the road gently downhill until a plantation is reached on the left. Half a kilometre further on is a small wooden gate on the left. Park here and descend into a muddy ravine.

The cliff gradually improves in quality and height until some large roofs near the top of the crag are passed. A short distance further on is a ragged bulging crack starting from a ledge five metres from the ground.

The Route: A steep crack climb on good holds in a distinctly unusual setting.

Description: Scramble up rightwards to a belay at the foot of the crack line. Follow the crack over a series of bulges taking care with the occasional detached block, to reach a good ledge. Belay here or continue up the final corner to a tree belay in the plantation.

JAM WITH SAM: The climb follows a ragged bulging crack line, the angle of which is offset, at least in part, by the size of the holds. *Climbers: John Addy and Colin Binks*

JAM WITH SAM

Peak Scar was one of the first cliffs that I climbed on many years ago. Now I remember descending into the ravine shaded with massive trees and thinking that the place had a magical air about it. Under the right conditions the crag is a very pleasant place to be, but after rain the whole area oozes a cold, clammy dampness. I once took a friend, John Addy, climbing here on his first ever trip. It was a damp dismal autumn day and we did a pleasant but horrendously greasy route called WINGS. I was a bit worried that the gloomy atmosphere and gripping climbing might have put him off forever, but he lapped it up. I thought that if he enjoyed climbing under these inclement conditions he would really enjoy it when the sun came out and ten years later he is still hitting the rock.

On another occasion, and in total contrast, a few of us stopped-off at the cliff one spring evening on the way up to Northumberland. The sun was low in the sky slanting across the cliff, the ravine was bone dry and the birds flitted and twittered away in the treetops. The place was a peaceful and pleasant place to climb.

The cliff is actually the site of a landslip, with the rock that fell away forming the north side of the gorge. The main face consists of parallel layers of limestone usually containing good holds but often interrupted by overhangs. Many of the routes are very pleasant and worth doing though there is not a lot for the 'E by gum' brigade here. JAM WITH SAM was my first V.S. lead on limestone and so stands out above a whole series of climbs of similar worth. It consists of a steep crack line that is made technically quite reasonable because of the large holds in the breaks and the odd jam offered by the crack itself. I remember being more than a little bit harassed when I first led the route because of the steepness but in reality the technicalities are quite mild and there is protection a-plenty.

Sustained jug pulling eventually leads to a fine bivi-type ledge where a belay is possible and perhaps even advisable. The outward views into the Hambleton Hills are serene and just above, a final steep corner leads to belays that get better every year.

13: CRITHMUM

Situation:	Mother Carey's Kitchen, Lydstep, South Pembroke *Note: the route is awkward to get at when the tide is high.*
Aspect:	South facing
Grade:	V.S. (4b, 4c)
Length:	40m (130ft)
Equipment:	A standard rack with a few extra slings.
First Ascent:	C.Mortlock, C.Litton, 20th August 1969
Guidebook:	*Pembroke* by Jon de Montjoye and Mike Harber, published by the Climbers' Club in 1985. A new guide is due out in 1991.

Approaches: Mother Carey's Kitchen is reached from the car park on top of Lydstep Head. This is reached through the caravan park at Lydstep Haven, or via a minor road from the village of Lydstep. The latter route is shorter but involves going the wrong way around part of the caravan park's one-way system.

Drive as far east across the car park as possible then pass through the bushes to a footpath, follow this to the left for a short distance then take a narrow path on the right heading through brambles and gorse towards the sea. On meeting the coastal path turn left for a short distance, the top of the crag becomes visible on the right as twin rocky summits.

The whole top of the left-hand tower can be used as a substantial belay for the gripping abseil into the Kitchen. **Great care** is needed if there are teams below.

CRITHMUM: At the start of the difficulties on the first pitch. The route follows the corner system to ledges, then the flake just to the right of the upper corner.
Climber: Jim Rubery

The Route: One long or two short pitches up a shallow corner, on wonderful rock and with good protection.

Description: To the left of the entrance of the great through cave is a slab leading to the main groove system in the centre of the cliff. Follow the slab to the corner and take the right-hand groove which is followed to a small ledge at 15 metres. Belay on the left. Step back to the right and climb the shallow right-hand corner over two small bulges to a ledge. Follow the twisting crack on the left to the top.

CRITHMUM

Mother Carey's Kitchen (named after Mother Carey's Chickens - an old sailors' name for the storm petrels, which used to nest on the cliff top) is a great crag. The rock is steep, grey and rugged, pitted and scalloped with innumerable holds, and containing many solid threads. The lines are often powerful cracks and corners and of

course the main walls face the midday sun. The cliff is moderately tidal with most of the routes accessible from around mid-tide, though with care and in calm weather it is possible to abseil directly to the foot of many of the routes at all states of the tide. With a bit of forethought, and a correct deciphering of the tide tables you should be able to get virtually a full day's cragging here without being too harassed by the fluctuating water line.

A due respect for the tides in the Bristol Channel is a sensible thing. At the times of spring tides (roughly one or two days after a full or new moon) the sea rises over ten metres (about 35ft) in the six hours between low and high water. In the middle two hours of the rising tide, the water comes up half of this total height, or about five metres. If you are climbing with a leader who is a bit on the slow side, it is best to keep one eye on the rock and one on the ocean. That way you can start to suggest he moves a little faster before things get too critical.

On my very first visit to Mother Carey's some years ago now, there was a sea fog blowing onto the land, and although the tide was well down, there was a big sea running. We abseiled into the swirling mist and were dismayed to find the whole cliff dripping with water from the fog and the spray in the air. Just to make sure that the visit was not a complete waste of time we did CRITHMUM, but the experience was not a particularly pleasant one. Although the rock is generally very rough, precise technique was needed to ensure that your feet stayed where they were put, and jamming up soapy cracks required considerable finesse. I felt somewhat cheated, a great route spoilt by foul conditions.

We spent the next couple of days on the north coast until the wind changed, then it was back to Mother Carey's again. The cliff was a different place, warm dry rock and the sun hammering onto the walls. We did three great routes, then as the rest of the team was packing away I nipped back down the abseil rope and soloed CRITHMUM. The crag was deserted now and the tide was well on its way back up. I lingered on each move, revelling in the wonderful rock and the positions, enjoying the solitude and the atmosphere as day slipped slowly into night. The feeling of being cheated was long gone, replaced by a sense of privilege; the waiting had made the final outcome all the more satisfying.

14: JEAN JEANNIE

Situation:	Trowbarrow Quarry, Carnforth, North Lancashire. Note: Access to the quarry is sometimes restricted. A discreet approach and politeness if challenged are sensible ideas.
Aspect:	South-west facing
Grade:	V.S. (4c)
Length:	30m (100ft)
Equipment:	A standard rack with a few extra mid-range Friends or Hexes.
First Ascent:	A.Evans and party, 1971
Guidebook:	*Lancashire and the North West* by Phil Kelly and Dave Cronshaw, published by Cicerone Press in 1989.

Approaches: Trowbarrow Quarry lies four kilometres north-west of Carnforth; which is itself ten kilometres north of Lancaster. A minor road runs towards Silverdale Station. Just before the station is a right turn over the railway. A kilometre along here the road runs through a wood. The quarry lies five minutes bushwhacking to the north (left). A direct approach by the old quarry road is best avoided if you are to stand a chance of doing your route undisturbed.

The Route: A long sustained crack on unusual rock. Protection is good.

Description: The main wall of the quarry is the prominent large wall on the right. It is split by many cracks. JEAN JEANNIE starts at the lowest point of the wall and takes a series of thin cracks to the right of a long straight wide crack, ALADDINSANE E1 (5a). The cracks are followed without deviation and although the climbing is sustained, protection is good and there are plenty of resting places.

JEAN JEANNIE

Quarries are not the most pleasant of spots in which to climb; they are the ravaged places where man has ripped away at the bones of the Earth and always they are left in a mess. As quarries go Trowbarrow is relatively pleasant, the outward view includes plenty of green countryside and the setting is open to the afternoon sun. Despite this there are all the trappings that go together to make quarries such depressing places to be in, let alone to spend a day's cragging; heaps of shattered boulders, rotting and rusting machinery, and an air of abandoned desolation hanging over everywhere.

Limestone is much in demand for the chemical industry, for the production of iron and steel and for good old hard core. These needs have to be met, but I wonder if our children's children will thank us for turning high-grade countryside into low-grade road stone.

If you visit Trowbarrow on a fine spring afternoon you will not be too disappointed by the setting, but on a grim and grey winter's day the place reeks of ravaged destruction. Unless you have no feelings for our dwindling countryside you might be better off visiting the nearby and unspoilt nature reserve to try and catch a view of the elusive bittern that stalks the reedbeds there.

Once at the foot of the climb, on a suitably decent day, the setting fades into the background as you are faced by a fine soaring crack line. The fissure zig-zags skywards in a fashion designed to draw you onwards, and the angle although steep is never pressingly so. There are fine sharp-edged holds and good, though rather aggressive jams, that tempt you ever upwards. Runners are excellent and can be slotted in as frequently as you want, though the odd upward glance is a good idea to make sure you are not going to run out of the right sizes before reaching the top. The climbing is very sustained and totally engrossing and before you know it, you are at the top. Behind the cliff is a forest of ghostly silver birch, a couple of which provide suitable belays from which to take in the ropes and think back to a jewel of a route in a flawed setting.

QUESTOR: Laybacking the lower section of the "smart clean-cut corner groove".
Climber: Jim Rubery

JEAN JEANNIE: A fine sustained crack climb in a rather blighted setting.
Climber: Chris Craggs

15: QUESTOR

Situation: The Wyndcliffe, the Wye Valley, S.E. Wales
Aspect: South-east facing
Grade: V.S. (4c)
Length: 30m (100ft)
Equipment: A standard rack with perhaps a couple of larger Friends for the jamming crack should be adequate.
First Ascent: F.Cannings, P.Littlejohn, C.Morton, 1970
Guidebook: *The Wye Valley* by J.Wilson, D.Hope, T.Penning, M.Ward, published by Cordee, 1987.

Approaches: The cliff lies above the A446 Chepstow to Monmouth road, seven kilometres north of Chepstow. A rough track branches off to the left underneath the cliff and leads up into a small disused quarry that provides ample parking. The cliffs lie a short distance above the quarry through the woods and QUESTOR is to be found on the right-hand side part of the cliff. The easiest approach is to follow the path out of the northern end of the quarry which is signposted '365 Steps' and 'The Eagle's Nest'. This soon turns left up into the woods and after a level area the crag appears on the right through the trees. Ten minutes from the car.

The Route: A long and sustained pitch on good rock and with great protection.

Description: Towards the left side of the right-hand cliff is a fine corner running the full height of the crag, starting behind a big yew tree. Further description is super-fluous, it would take real talent to get lost.

QUESTOR
The Wyndcliffe is an odd little crag that almost appears to have been displaced from some deep Derbyshire dale. The hillside is cloaked in luxuriant vegetation and the rock is bedecked with ivy and dusty dry cobwebs. The outward view is sylvan and reveals a little more of your whereabouts, with the lazy meander of the River Wye leading your eye out to the white walls of Wintour's Leap and on to the broad spread of the Bristol Channel beyond.

Close examination of the cliff shows that there are few really strong natural lines - just a collection of grooves that fizzle out before they get anywhere, the odd flake stuck on the wall in a haphazard fashion and a few fairly uninspiring blanker sections of rock. Amongst this mishmash there is one lonely but outstanding line, a smart clean-cut corner groove that runs right up the highest part of the cliff. Whether it is on the top of your annual hit list of routes to do, or it is a two-minute solo at the end of a day's climbing, QUESTOR just has to be done.

There are no moves of outstanding difficulty or of a memorable nature, though every upward step is a pleasure. There is as much protection as anybody of even the most timid temperament could desire, all of which can be placed from comfortable bridging positions. Route-finding skills are redundant, there is only ever one way on and the climbing is never intimidating, though the odd touch of loose rock adds just a little spice. So what is it that makes the route deserved of classic status? The subtle blend of everything that is the climb; its position, purity of line and above all, pleasure in execution, all add up to a little gem - do it and its quality will no longer be open to question.

16: THE RUSSIAN

Situation: Symonds Yat, the Wye Valley, Gloucestershire
Aspect: West facing
Grade: V.S. (4c, 4a)
Length: 30m (100ft)
Equipment: A standard rack.
First Ascent: Unknown, possibly members of the Nottingham Mountaineering Club in the late 1960s, though it may have been done much earlier.
Guidebook: *The Wye Valley* by J.Wilson, D.Hope, T.Penning and M.Ward, published by Cordee, 1987.

Approaches: Symonds Yat is an extremely popular tourist spot five kilometres east of Monmouth. Access routes to the large car park on top of the cliff are signed from miles around. From behind the toilet block, cross the fence and descend to the left until below the rocks. Follow the foot of the cliffs southwards crossing a couple of wide gullies until a rock archway is reached. Pass through this and the route is 50 metres further on, a fine corner deepening as it rises.

The Route: A grand bridging groove offering plenty of protection.

Description: Climb the wall to the foot of the corner and enter it with difficulty (crux). Delightful bridging leads to a final steepening and a large ledge with a tree belay. Climb the rather rattly ridge behind the stance, moving rightwards to finish in a fine position.

THE RUSSIAN
The heavily wooded nature of the area around Symonds Yat, and the lazy loops of the river far below give the area a feel of foreign climes. The setting could have been

plucked from the Belgian Ardennes or Southern Germany, and the often warm and heavy air add to this illusion. A closer examination reveals the truth: the white houses glimpsed between the trees are definitely English in style and the cliff, though fine enough by our standards, would probably have been ignored in areas richer in rock.

The earliest geologists came to Symonds Yat to wonder at the enigma of the River Wye incising great sinuous curves deep into the hills, instead of flowing across the flat plain just to the north. We now know the area to be a classic example of antecedent drainage; the river was there long before the hills. Its course meandered across level ground and as the hills rose the river kept to its bed, preserving these ancient wanderings.

Today the picturesque beauty of the area attracts a vast number of tourists who come to visit the café and souvenir shop and perhaps have a quick peek at the view before going away happy with another tick on the tourist trail.

With climbers it is much the same story, only their required tick is a competent ascent of THE RUSSIAN. The route is best done in the afternoon when the sun warms the rock and highlights its subtle colours. The climbing is technically quite straightforward, with the crux low down and with plenty of excellent protection. Progress is made by elegant bridging with the odd butch layback move thrown in for good measure. A large stance and solid tree belay are available at two-thirds height from where a blocky ridge leads to a narrow crest with expansive views.

There are plenty of other good routes at Symonds Yat, and a very pleasant day can be spent there, mellowing out and letting the pervasive atmosphere of the place get to you. If you don't have the time the quick tick approach will have to do, but in reality the place deserves better.

THE RUSSIAN: At the start of the crux moves where awkward bridging and laybacking are required to get established in the main section of the corner.
Climber: Chris Craggs

SKYLIGHT: The rays of the setting sun illuminate the crux jamming crack and the corner that has to be climbed to gain entry to the 'skylight'.
Climber: Jim Rubery

17: SKYLIGHT

Situation: High Tor, Matlock, Derbyshire
Aspect: West facing
Grade: V.S. (4a, 4c)
Length: 42m (140ft)
Equipment: A normal rack and a size 3 Friend or large Hex.
First Ascent: J.Brown, 1957
Guidebook: *Peak Limestone, South.* Published by the British Mountaineering Council in 1987.

Approaches: High Tor is the impressive sheet of rock that dominates the valley as you drive south down the A6 from Matlock. Beyond the crag is an iron bridge that allows access to the cable-car station, and there is limited parking either side of this bridge. Cross the river and go up steps behind the buildings to a narrow path that doubles back towards the cliff, which is reached in about ten minutes from the road. You may be asked to pay an entrance fee to High Tor grounds by the cable-car station or on top of the crag, please cough up graciously if you are approached. SKYLIGHT takes the prominent corner to the left of the main face that runs the full height of the cliff, ending up as an impressive chimney.

The Route: An easy lower pitch leads to a fine corner. Well protected.

Description: The first pitch of the climb takes the long flaky corner system to a belay on a good ledge. Back up the in-situ peg. The second pitch continues up the corner which becomes more impressive as it rises, until steep jamming on polished rock gains larger holds and a bridged rest. Easier moves up and right (thread) lead into the final chimney, the SKYLIGHT. This gives straightforward climbing to the top. The best descent is by abseil or walking over the top of the crag to pick up any one of a series of paths that eventually join and lead back under the cliff. ·

SKYLIGHT

In the 1950s Joe Brown and his cronies spent time picking off many of the more prominent lines on Peak limestone, especially in the winter months when the high hills were out of condition. Many of the routes relied heavily on aid, though this is hardly surprising given the rudimentary equipment available then, and apart from that, bashing pegs in was great fun.

It is strange to think that in 1957 there was only one route on the whole crag and that was up the centre of the main face, this being the aid climb High Tor Bastion, later to become ORIGINAL ROUTE. (That is unless you count the rat pit of HIGH TOR GULLY, put up in 1903, as a rock climb.) Joe picked the most amenable looking line on the cliff and came away with a classic.

The first pitch is pleasant enough though it is nothing to write home about. There is the expected polish, a smattering of loose rock and rather too much flora to make the pitch a good one, but keep glancing upwards and the upper pitch will draw you on like 'the Siren's sweetly singing'. The commodious belay ledge is soon reached and there is a peg and good nut belays in the crack at the foot of the upper corner.

The second pitch of the climb is great. It starts off steadily but the difficulties increase as height is gained. Fortunately the protection is always good and it is possible to rest frequently in a bridging position. Then just as things are going well the corner rears up and a steep strenuous jamming crack has to be tackled. A couple of slippy pulls and you can bridge again. From here steeper climbing but on much better holds leads up and right to get into the chimney that gives the route its name. The larger holds here are decidedly frictionless, a testimony to the multitudes that have passed this way, many of whom must have had pretty sloppy footwork. What is called for is a bit of precise technique and a couple of strenuous pulls, and suddenly you find yourself in the cool shade of the chimney, away from that nasty drop. After a few moments to calm down and cool off, the chimney affords technically reasonable and nicely enclosed climbing until you are forced to an exit which pops suddenly out on top of the cliff. If you have remembered to carry a little cash, the summit café is only a few minutes away for a celebratory cuppa, or perhaps something a little stronger.

18: BLUE SKY

Situation: West Face, Saddle Head, Range East, South Pembroke
Note: The route is only accessible at dead low tide and with a calm sea.
Aspect: South-west facing
Grade: V.S. (4b, 4b)
Length: 60m (190ft)
Equipment: A standard rack with a few long slings.
First Ascent: P.Littlejohn, J.Harwood, 8th April 1978
Guidebook: *Pembroke* by Jon de Montjoye and Mike Harber, published by the Climbers' Club in 1985. A new guide is due out in 1991.

Approaches: From the car park at St Govan's cross the stile into the range and walk westwards, passing Stennis Ford and Huntsman's Leap. Ahead and slightly to the left is a headland with a wire compound containing a small building on its top, this is Saddle Head. Pass the compound and scramble seaward along the rocky ridge until it is possible to double back along the west face. A steep scramble or short abseil gains the platform which is crossed (sea level permitting) to the foot of the route. Ten minutes from the car.

The Route: Steep climbing on perfect rock and with magnificent holds. Protection is as good as you would expect.

Description: Start to the left of the impressive right arête of the buttress. Trend up and right to gain a ledge then climb straight up until forced around the corner to the steep right wall. This is climbed on huge razor-edged jugs to a stance on the left by a cave half-filled with flowstone. Pitch two climbs the groove above the stance until it ends. Step left onto the face then follow rough rock up and right to the top.

BLUE SKY

Almost every one of the thousand plus routes on offer in Pembroke is well worth doing. Good rock and a sublime setting make a strong combination and when allied to the better than average weather it is hard to go wrong. Amongst so many good routes the three-star outings have to be something rather special. BLUE SKY is a true Pembroke classic, it climbs an impressive piece of rock on remarkable holds. It faces the afternoon sun and to make it more than just another good route it has that little something extra, a very tidal approach.

The simple fact is that the foot of BLUE SKY is only accessible for a few hours a month. The required combination is something approaching a spring tide, i.e. around the dates of a full or new moon, coupled with the rather less frequent occurrence of a calm sea. Below the cliff is a broad horizontal platform which is normally well under water and even when conditions are right it is occasionally swept by larger waves. The platform is pitted with a series of deep (bottomless?) rounded holes, so if you decide to try and wade to the route be warned!

The climbing starts on slippery be-barnacled rock, but a few crunchy steps lead up and right onto honest grey limestone. From a ledge on the arête the rock leans menacingly, but fortunately you can step round on to the side wall where the angle is marginally less. The face here is only plumb vertical, real fly on the wall territory. The upwards view may be daunting but have no fear, the cliff is cut with a fantastic set of huge sharp jugs, a veritable ladder in the sky. A ledge is reached all too soon, offering a stance which is small but with belays that are sound and numerous. The upper pitch offers more of the same fare, though it is a diet you will never tire of. As height is gained the rock gets ever rougher until a final few moves

are made on rock with more than a passing resemblance to splintered glass - little wonder that boots don't last long on these cliffs!

It may take several visits to get this climb done, but a bit of a wait should sharpen your appreciation of the route when the conditions are finally spot on. If friends ask whether it is really as good as it is cracked up to be, tell them they will have to wait and see.

BLUE SKY: At the top of the wall which is "climbed on huge razor edged jugs". The rather small stance is visible on the left and the second pitch follows the grooves directly above.
Climber: Chris Craggs

19: CHEE TOR GIRDLE

Situation:	Chee Tor, Chee Dale, Derbyshire
Aspect:	West facing
Grade:	V.S. (4b, 4b, 4a, 4c, 5a)
Length:	167m (530ft)
Equipment:	A normal rack with a few extra long slings and a couple of medium-sized Friends.
First Ascent:	C.Jackson, J.Atkinson, 1964
Guidebook:	*Peak Limestone, Chee Dale*, published by the British Mountaineering Council in 1987.

Approaches: The cliff lies hidden in the depths of darkest Chee Dale and as some of the railway tunnels are closed the most popular walk in is from Wormhill. This is a small hamlet on the hill above Miller's Dale, and there is limited parking at the side of the road just before a farm gate. A track is followed down past Chee Tor Cottage to an open grassy area. A newly beaten path drops down to the right here to cross a minor stream before reaching the River Wye. Turn right and walk upstream until opposite Chee Tor, either wade the river (have you had your jabs?) or continue up the river to a footbridge and return down the other side. The route starts at the right side of the cliff at a prominent open groove.

The Route: A classical (some say THE classical) girdle traverse. The rock is polished and the whole route is rather strenuous. Protection is perfect.

Description: The groove (DOGGONE GROOVE) is steep and quite polished but it eases rapidly with height until ledges and a tree belay are reached. From here the line is blatantly obvious; keep heading left! The first traversing pitch is a long one but it is quite straightforward and leads round several corners to a short descent to gain a tree-filled bay. From here easy but exposed climbing leads to a mighty yew tree sprouting from the break; belay on it or just beyond it. Now things get a little tougher. Head out to the arête then continue strenuously past threads to a good stance. The final pitch hand traverses into the corner to a good bridged rest before the final tricky section across a shield to reach ledges and a stout tree that doubles as a belay and an abseil anchor.

CHEE TOR GIRDLE

Girdle traversing is a rather odd game. The reason for climbing a piece of rock can be seen by most folks, (because it's there?) and even deliberately seeking out difficulties has an odd logic, though there is usually 'an easy way round the back', as I have been told countless times. But going sideways - that's a bit of a daft idea.

I must admit I have always enjoyed girdle traverses. The responsibilities are shared whether you are leading or seconding a pitch, you get a good look at the cliff rather than having your nose stuck in the back of a groove and most importantly, the climbing experience is prolonged beyond the normal one or two pitches up the crag. As girdle traverses go, the one that crosses Chee Tor has a rare purity of line, it must have been designed and built by a craftsman using a ruler and spirit-level. The bedding plain that forms the line of the route frequently closes up to form a series of the most magnificent threads that you could ever imagine. It used to be necessary to carry a great necklace of long slings about your person, 'a la Baron Brown,' to guarantee access to all the available protection. Nowadays, with the proliferation of half rope length pitches up to the Girdle break and the French habit of lowering off, most of the threads required are permanently in-situ. Although rather unsightly they certainly ease your sideways movement as it is much easier to quickly clip a thread than to try and untangle one from your neck and then grope about in the depths of the break trying to thread the sling and get the two ends clipped together.

I first did the route in 1968, and actually finding the crag was a major achievement, but once there we had the cliff to ourselves. The afternoon sun on the white rock was hot and the valley lay under a hush as we slowly explored our way sideways. We only used a single 120ft rope, a bunch of slings and a few rudimentary nuts, (though at the time we thought Moacs and Clog wedges were at the cutting edge of technology). After more than four hours we arrived at the abseil tree, untied from the rope and draped it double down the crag: to our surprise the ends did not reach the ground. I was elected to go and have a look. As it turned out the rope was only about eight feet off the deck and with the stretch and a short drop we were safe.

The second time I did the route was some five years later, by which time the crag had become much more popular. I think the fact that it was possible to drive your car from Miller's Dale station through the disused railway tunnels to within five minutes of the tor may have had something to do with this upsurge in popularity. We set off up DOGGONE GROOVE and moved rapidly along the next two pitches to the yew tree. Here we caught up a slow team and hung about for 30 minutes or so before boredom set in, so we abseiled off and went off to do some other routes. Later in the day we returned for another go, only to find a team just setting out up the groove at the start of the climb. Not to be outdone so easily a second time we scrambled round the side of the cliff and up to the Girdle break. The leader of the other team suddenly realised what we were about and raced us to belay. She was somewhat miffed that we beat her there but then softened slightly as we soloed past and promised that if they caught us up we would abseil off rather than hinder their progress.

To the yew tree was familiar ground so we soloed it, set up a hanging belay and put the rope on. In 30 minutes we had finished the route and five minutes later we were walking back along the base of the cliff. The other team were just about to start the first traverse pitch when we walked past and gave them a cheery wave. The double-take as they looked along the line of route and then back down to us was worth the minor hassles in actually getting the climb done. It is well worth going through a few tribulations for such a classic trip.

CHEE TOR GIRDLE:
At the start of the real
difficulties; approach-
ing the rounded arete
on pitch 4.
Climber:
Dave Spencer

20: AVENTURA

Situation:	Boulder Ruckle West, Swanage, Dorset
Aspect:	South facing
Grade:	V.S. (4c, 4c)
Length:	35m (110ft)
Equipment:	A standard rack with a few larger nuts or Friends.
First Ascent:	P.Crewe, P.A.Bell, 29th August 1964
Guidebook:	*Swanage* by Gordon Jenkin published by the Climbers' Club in 1986.

Approaches: From the car park at the Durlston Head Country Park to the south of Swanage follow the road down to the lighthouse, then take the coastal path to the west. After 1,000m a wall and stile are reached that form the boundary of the country park. Either abseil from two stakes in a gully below the stile (down OCEAN BOULEVARD) or from a single stake 20 metres back towards the lighthouse (down THE RAMP).

Scramble back eastwards (not in high seas) for approximately 100m to the grossly undercut BOTTOMLESS BUTTRESS. AVENTURA takes the groove to the left of this.

The Route: An intimidating climb on good rock and with good protection. High in the grade.

Description: Chimney up into the groove and follow it to a roof. Move right to a good ledge and variety of belays. Trend left to a roof which is crossed on good holds (gripping) to the final groove and a solid exit. Stake belays.

AVENTURA: The second and crux pitch climbs through an impressive roof on large holds. It is somewhat of a gripper.
Climbers: Graham Parkes and Colin Binks

AVENTURA

Swanage is a bit of a gripping spot, especially to the uninitiated. The whole crag is steep and the flat-fronted nature of the cliff makes the identification of individual routes quite difficult. The latest guidebook is exceptionally accurate with superbly detailed diagrams, and so has at least partly alleviated this problem. Still there are others; access is normally by a fairly committing abseil, and the steepness of the cliff means that most of the routes are strenuous rather than overly technical. Some of the rock is a little loose, though this ap-

pears to matter a lot less than it once did and many of the finishes are best described, sometimes generously as slightly unstable.

The most serious of all the cliffs is Boulder Ruckle which presents a continuous wall of rock a kilometre wide and 40 metres high. Amazingly there are several V.S. routes through this uncompromising country and even the odd Severe. AVENTURA is a great example of the way that a relatively mild route can sneak up a cliff like this, and in doing so become a classic of its grade.

From below the lower half of the route is obvious enough; a steep and impressive chimney crack slices upwards to lose itself in a broad band of overhangs that cut across the crag at half-height. Actual entry to the chimney is problematical as it is far too wide to bridge in the lower section. You are obliged to choose one or the other wall and climb it steeply until a gripping step can be made to bridge across the gap. If you try this manoeuvre too early on you are liable to miss the opposite wall altogether, or do yourself a permanent mischief.

Once established in the groove it gives very reasonable bridging on good holds and with plenty of gear. At the level of the overhangs a line of large footholds and a juggy handrail lead out rightwards to a comfortable stance. So far so good.

The second pitch looks a bit less of a pushover. A ramp runs up to the left to another line of overhangs and is followed without incident to a crouched rest under the roofs. It is at this point you will probably begin to question the sanity and ancestry of the guidebook writer, below you is only space and above you an evil-looking overhang blocks the view of whatever might lie beyond. There are plenty of good runners to bolster your flagging morale and it is worth extending them to ensure that rope drag does not pull you up short of the top. If you fail on the roof then the problems involved with a retreat are considerable, so it is time to give the overhang your best shot.

Good undercuts or a rather sharp jam allow you to lean out and grab flat jugs over the lip. There is a thread here but it is probably best to ignore it and press on, or there is a good chance you will run out of upward impetus. More large but flat holds are available for the pull over and once bridged you can regain your composure.

The final groove is much easier and leads thankfully to a solid stake belay some way up the bank.

This superb climb might only have the modest grade of V.S. but it is undoubtedly a bit of an a(d)ventura, and most certainly is not to be underestimated.

21: FRONT LINE

Situation:	St Govan's, South Pembroke
Aspect:	South facing
Grade:	H.V.S. (5a)
Length:	30m (100ft)
Equipment:	A standard rack with a few extra large nuts or medium Friends.
First Ascent:	D.Armstrong, P.Whillance, J.Lamb, 31st December 1976
Guidebook:	*Pembroke* by Jon de Montjoye and Mike Harber, published by the Climbers' Club in 1985. A new guide is due out in 1991.

Approaches: St Govan's is one of the most accessible cliffs on the Pembrokeshire coastline. It is approached from the town of Pembroke by following the B4319 southwards for six miles through Bosherston to the car park above St Govan's Chapel. The descent route is reached by walking east for about ten minutes towards the conspicuous coastguard lookout at the far end of the cliff. The top of the narrow descent chimney is marked by several iron spikes

hammered into the turf and often a scattering of rucksacks. The descent is down a slippery chimney formed by a large pinnacle standing a metre away from the cliff face. The first section of the chimney is vertical and requires care (and perhaps a rope?) - bones have been broken here. From a ledge in the chimney descend to the right (facing the sea) down a short, steep drop and pop out into the daylight. The route is on the front of the tower.

The Route: An easily accessible pitch that gives steep bridging. Holds are good and there is protection to match.

Description: FRONT LINE climbs the obvious square groove that cleaves the outside edge of the pinnacle that forms one wall of the descent chimney. It is not high in the grade and protection is excellent. An initial bulge is climbed by moving leftwards on big flat holds and provides the hardest move on the route. People who find this section a bit energetic can avoid it on the left but still enjoy the best part of the route. From the ledges thus reached, climb steeply up and right on superb holds to gain the first groove. This is followed until it steepens and a move is made right into the larger groove. This gives superbly positioned climbing to the top; a true summit.

FRONT LINE

St Govan's has never been my favourite cliff in Pembroke, its closeness to the car and non-tidal nature coupled with the fact that access is not restricted by the army and the bird lobby, means that the place is always popular. The top of the cliff is looser than most in the area and some of the exits are decidedly dangerous. Large crowds and limestone cliffs are not a healthy mixture and this crag has had more than its fair share of accidents. Falling rocks, pulled runners and broken holds are the usual causes, though over-enthusiasm often plays more than a small part in these tragedies. A modicum of respect for the force of gravity and the hardness of the ground would not go amiss, especially early in the season when the pent-up energy of a winter in the gym is being released.

Despite these reservations the cliff does have some excellent routes and a few real gems.

FRONT LINE initially feels a bit trivial, it is very close to the descent and distinctly

removed from the sea. There is a lack of seriousness that is unexpected on a large limestone sea cliff. Despite this the climbing is action-packed, bomb-proof protection is available, the line is obvious and inescapable, what more do you want? Perhaps the sun on your back - you usually get that as well.

The initial move is a bit of a pig, a shelf that is both undercut and overhung has to be gained, and whichever technique you use the moves are strenuous. Once established runners can be slotted in and easier climbing on big holds leads you up and right into a beckoning groove. This steepens as you work your way up it, but knobbly holds in the side walls and a good crack in the back of the corner more than compensate for the gradual change in angle. Eventually the groove becomes a blind alley and you have to find a way of getting out right into the continuation corner. Excellent runners are available above your head, which is fortunate as the moves you are about to embark on are steep and strenuous. With the confidence the protection provides swing right and power up into the corner, the holds are excellent but it is no place to hang about. As soon as you are ensconced in the final long groove you can really start to enjoy the situations. Bridging upwards, with good holds and plenty of sound protection, and the groove dropping away below you is sheer pleasure. No danger of getting pumped, in fact no danger at all, just dancing between the sky and the sea, a few brief moments of real living.

FRONT LINE: 'Eventually the groove becomes a blind alley and you have to find a way of getting out right into the continuation corner'.
Climber: Roland Arneson

FINALE GROOVE:
Bridging the lower groove, "there are obviously plenty of holds despite the fearful upward view".
Climber:
Colin Binks

22: FINALE GROOVE

Situation:	Boulder Ruckle Central, Swanage, Dorset
Aspect:	South facing
Grade:	H.V.S. (4c)
Length:	30m (100ft)
Equipment:	A standard rack should be adequate.
First Ascent:	G.Smith, D.Hadlum, 12th April 1966
Guidebook:	*Swanage* by Gordon Jenkin, published by the Climbers' Club in 1986.

Approaches: From the car park at Durlston Country Park to the south of Swanage follow the road down to the lighthouse then take the coastal path running away to the west. This is followed for 450m to a prominent jutting buttress (Marmolata). The top of this contains two stakes and a 35m (120ft) abseil from these down the east face of the buttress leads to boulders near sea level. Continue to the west for another 80 metres to the foot of a soaring groove line blocked by overhangs at half-height.

The Route: A steep and imposing groove that thankfully has plenty of holds and plenty of runners.

Description: Follow the groove to the overhangs. These are passed remarkably easily on the left, and the continuation groove is taken to a slightly unstable exit on the left. Stake belay.

FINALE GROOVE

Boulder Ruckle is one of the more serious cliffs at Swanage, with a gripping abseil in and no easy ways out. Despite this a crop of high quality routes ensures the area's continuing popularity. The jutting prow of Marmolata Buttress is one of the few easily identifiable features in this area, so at least you are certain that you are abseiling down in the right place; this is not always the case at Swanage.

Scramble west from the foot of the abseil, the soaring line of FINALE GROOVE is a real eye-catcher. From below it does not look like any normal H.V.S. and it certainly does not look like 4c. The groove leans throughout its whole length broken only by a massive overhang - many parties continue along the cliff convinced that the real FINALE GROOVE must lie further on.

From the foot of the climbing there are obviously plenty of holds despite the fearful upward view, so the only thing to do is to get stuck into it. The walls of the corner are covered in lumps and knobbles of something that looks a bit like coal, though it is in fact a kind of flint. These growths provide a staggering selection of foot and handholds, and so upward progress is remarkably straightforward. On top of this the crack in the back of the corner accepts nuts of almost any shape and size, and there are threads available as well.

At the level of the roof that blocks the groove there are good footledges, on which it is possible to shuffle out before grasping superb jugs and pulling quickly into the continuation corner and getting back into a bridging position. The upper groove continues to lean and taper as it rises and you begin to wonder if you are going to be forced out onto the horrifyingly exposed and leaning left arête. There are a couple of old pegs in this upper section, rusting relics of the pre-nut era and they are well worth backing up with something a little more modern. As the groove fizzles out completely good holds on the left wall allow a neat side-step and suddenly you are at the top. It is worth a quick glance down the line before you top out. The situations are quite outrageous and the remarkably low technical grade and excellent protection make this into a truly memorable outing.

23: THE LAUGHING CAVALIERS

Situation:	The Shorn Cliff, the Wye Valley, Gloucestershire
Aspect:	West facing
Grade:	H.V.S. (5a)
Length:	30m (100ft)
Equipment:	A standard rack of wires is more than adequate.
First Ascent:	G.Gibson, M.Ward, 3rd June 1984
Guidebook:	*The Wye Valley* by J.Wilson, D.Hope, T.Penning and M.Ward, published in 1987 by Cordee.

Approaches: Rather complex on first acquaintance. In the village of Tintern on the A466, almost opposite the Royal George Hotel, a minor road leads to a bridge over the River Wye (sounds like a good choice for a film title!). There is limited parking just before the bridge. Cross the river and follow the track around to the right until a steep cobbled path leads up to the left through some iron posts. At the top of the initial steepening follow the track uphill to a fork, take the right branch. A little further on the track forks again and again the right branch is followed. Shortly after this the path splits again, take the narrower right-hand fork. This is followed as it undulates through the woods until it rises more steadily and then meets a wide Forestry Commission road. Walk gently downhill for 400 metres to a thin track disappearing into the trees on the left. This is 30 metres past an orange wooden post and is easily missed. The cliff lies well hidden, a short scramble above. A rough path leads rightwards below the cliff and is followed for 100 metres or so (hint; stay low) until a large white wall with a cave formed by a huge fallen block on its left side is reached. Thirty minutes from the car park providing you don't get lost.

THE LAUGHING CAVALIERS: Just below the start of the difficult climbing, the route bears slightly leftwards to reach the flake visible just below the cliff edge.
Climber: Chris Craggs

The Route: A pleasant piece of climbing set at an unusually reasonable angle for limestone. Protection is rather spaced.

Description: Five metres right of the cave are a couple of shallow grooves, start up the right-hand one from a block. Follow the groove until you can exit leftwards onto the slab. Now trend up and right aiming for a blue thread (ignoring the tat on a peg under an overhang directly above you). From the thread move up and left to flakes and continue steeply to the top. A short scramble leads to a substantial tree belay. The best descent is by abseil.

THE LAUGHING CAVALIERS

The Shorn Cliff was developed quite late for such a large piece of rock, though not without good reason. The cliffs are visible from the main road on the other side of the River Wye but getting close to them is difficult and actually pinpointing the cliffs once you *are* close is even more difficult. Once there, the first ascentionists discovered advanced jungle bashing techniques were required both on and below the cliff. The Shorn Cliff was initially developed in the mid-1970s by climbers from Bristol and South Wales. Unfortunately the manuscript that was prepared for the 1977 Wye Valley guidebook was lost and the cliffs rapidly returned to nature. Climbers who made the trip to the place were confronted with conditions that might well have convinced them they were lost in deepest Borneo.

In 1984 Gary Gibson and Matt Ward visited the cliff and set to work with a will. Copious quantities of herbage were removed and routes were put up in rapid succession. They started with the biggest wall on the crag and on their first visit put up five excellent routes including our chosen climb. The cliff is quite popular now, the paths are well marked and the better routes are clean as a whistle, though the trees that surround the place still give it an oppressive air on warm summer days.

All the routes on the piece of rock known as Great Central Cave Area are worth doing, giving sustained balance climbing, but LAUGHING CAVALIERS gets my vote as the best of the bunch because of its central line and because the crux is high on the wall. The initial groove is easier than it looks, then the slab gives pleasant climbing with some remarkable runner slots. From the thread things steepen

45

up and turn interesting. A hanging flake is passed with difficulty (no place for a cavalier approach) to reach better holds and small wires up on the left. More steep moves lead up left or right past a shield of rock, to reach an earthy exit and some very substantial trees which double as belays and abseil anchors at the end of a great route. So who's laughing now?

24:
THE THORN

Situation: Beeston Tor, the Manifold Valley, Staffordshire
Aspect: South facing
Grade: H.V.S. (4b, 5a)
Length: 49m (160ft)
Equipment: A standard rack
First Ascent: J.Brown, 1952/4 (Some aid)
First Free Ascent: Probably done free sometime around 1970 though the aid had been reduced to two points for some years.
Guidebook: *Peak Limestone South*, published by the British Mountaineering Council in 1987.

Approaches: Beeston Tor lies on the northern side of the secluded Manifold Valley in north-east Staffordshire. A minor road runs along the valley bottom terminating at Beeston Farm, right below the cliff. This

THE THORN: Pitch Two, "the rib is steep but the rock is wonderfully knobbly". The crux bulge is directly above the climber.
Climber: Colin Binks

minor road runs between Wetton and Grindon and is best reached from the A515 Ashbourne to Buxton road. In the valley bottom turn left and follow the road to a gate just short of the farm. Park here, a fee is sometimes charged, then pass through the gate and cross the riverbed (or the well spaced stepping-stones in winter) to reach the foot of the cliff in five minutes.

The Route: A classic two-pitch route with the crux in a dramatic setting. Protection is perfect.

Description: In the centre of the cliff is a long groove starting from a small, ever-dry cave. Half-way up the cliff this groove curves over to form a massive roofed-in recess, The Ivy Gash. The first pitch of THE THORN climbs the slabby right wall of the groove to a belay on threaded chains in the depths of the Gash. Pitch two starts with an exposed traverse out to the rib on the left. This leads to a bulge with a couple of pegs in it. Steep moves over the bulge lead to easier rock and a belay on a multiple-stumped holly tree. The top of the cliff lies a little higher and is reached by a short scramble. Descent to the left.

THE THORN

THE THORN takes a central line up one of the more impressive pieces of rock in the Peak District and this alone would make it worth doing; but there is more. The rock, both in its fine texture and its grand geometry makes for a memorable outing. Add to this superb positions, the crux in just the right place and a touch of history and you end up with an evergreen classic.

The first pitch looks quite imposing from below but the right wall of the soaring corner has plenty of good holds, and the odd steep sections are skirted round or crossed on good jugs. Eventually a step left leads into the cool recess of the cleft which gives easy bridging to good ledges and some huge threads complete with equally gargantuan chains.

Pitch two is the business. A step down from the chains and an easy traverse out onto the alarmingly exposed rib leads to a sudden change in the character of the climbing. Gone is the cosy security of the big corner system and the sheltered feeling afforded by the great roof overhead. Even your second has disappeared into his own introspective world; on this one, you are on

your own. The rib above you is steep but the rock is wonderfully knobbly with an abundance of holds, so you are almost spoilt for choice. Above lurks the crux bulge, still sprouting the old aid pegs complete with mouldering tat, (do yourself a favour and clip the steel, not the string). There are also a series of good nuts and a rather fiddly thread so at least no heroics are called for. It is possible to reduce the grade to about 4c by pulling on the pegs (nobody will ever know) but the protection is so good there really is no excuse, you have got to go for it. The holds are excellent but rather spaced and the angle is well the wrong side of vertical. A neatly executed lock off and a quick skip with your feet (or a desperate grab and strenuous scrabble) lead rapidly to easier angled rock and more big holds. Relish this section, it is short but oh so sweet, easy climbing in a fine position, a big drop below you and soaring spirits. A belay on the 'thorny' holly gives you a moment to assess the route. In one word: brilliant.

25: MIKE'S MISTAKE & PINK WALL TRAVERSE

Situation:	Main Area, Avon Gorge, Bristol
Aspect:	South-west facing
Grade:	H.V.S. (4a, 5a, 3b, 3a, 4c & A1, 4c)
Length:	110m (350ft)
Equipment:	A standard rack is adequate.
First Ascent:	MIKE'S MISTAKE - M.Harvey & party 1953 PINK WALL TRAVERSE - B.Page & party 1954
Guidebook:	*The Avon Gorge* by Steve Monks, published by Dark Peak in 1981. A new guide is due out in 1991/2

Approaches: The cliffs in the Avon Gorge are arrayed in an almost continuous line rising above the north side of the A4 (Portway Road) as it runs from Avonmouth towards the city centre. Rather more than half-way along the cliffs is a large car park with a resident tea wagon and some public toilets. MIKE'S MISTAKE climbs the big dark slab right behind the toilets and PINK WALL TRAVERSE heads away leftwards to finish up a prominent slanting crack up and left of the top of the slab.

The Route: A long and varied expedition on good rock. Protection is a bit spaced on the lower section.

Description: Pass behind the toilet block, cross the fence and walk through a thin band of trees to reach the rock. The route starts directly below an orange pillar which can be seen ten metres up at the level of a band of overhangs.

Climb directly up the wall to the orange pillar then step left to a ledge and high peg belays, or press on up the next pitch. Step right into a slanting groove which is followed awkwardly past a bolt(!) to the

MIKE'S MISTAKE & PINK WALL TRAVERSE:
The crucial hand traverse; "the pitch is a bit of a gripper, but probably less so than a retreat".
Climbers: Chez de Mengel and Sue Bird.
Photo: D.Spencer

roof that caps the groove, which is passed on the left to reach open slabs. Climb straight up the slabs, easy but without much protection, to a foothold stance with tree and bolt belays. From here climb up and right via a short crack to reach ledges. Traverse left passing trees and passing below an overhang. Climb a rather grotty corner and continue leftwards to reach a small stance and peg belays. The next objective is the lowest one of three iron spikes down to your left. Traverse towards the spikes and descend a tricky groove until you can lean out and reach the bottom one. Swarm up these to a comfortable sitting stance with good belays. Follow the strenuous hand traverse crack running left above a big drop to the cliff top.

MIKE'S MISTAKE & PINK WALL TRAVERSE

On my first visit to the Avon Gorge, MIKE'S MISTAKE seemed like the ideal route to start on, offering classical V.S. slab climbing. Just the job for the warm-up, or at least that was the idea! In reality the style of climbing on most of the cliffs hereabouts takes a little getting used to, and I found this out about 15 metres up. Protection consisted of a bendy peg runner some distance below me, the holds were shelving and rather polished and there was nothing positive to aim for. Added to this was the fact that the insecure form of progress thus far meant that controlled retreat was not an option. In the event I made it to better holds and even the odd runner materialised but the lesson had been learnt - I think I found out what Mike's mistake had been!

A lot of folks climb at Avon once and never return, having been unnerved by the precarious form of progress that so much of the climbing involves. This is a pity because with a few pitches under your belt (or should it be under your boots?) a new-found confidence will emerge. Steep walls can be climbed using a subtle mixture of side pulls, layaways and pinch grips, and with a little practice your feet will stick in the most unlikely places.

MIKE'S MISTAKE remains a great introduction to the Gorge. The old pegs have been replaced and the crux has sprouted a bolt. Sticky rubber has rather offset the polish on the bigger holds and a dab of chalk makes things feel a bit more secure. From the big ledge system (Lunchtime Ledge) above the route there are a variety of pitches leading straight to the top but the best option is to traverse left to the edge of all things and do PINK WALL TRAVERSE. A tricky groove is descended, (remember your second and leave one rope free) then a bit of a lunge out left leads to the first of three massive quarryman's spikes. These are quite far apart and it is necessary to throw your leg onto this first spike and make a grab at the second one. A couple more pulls and a mantelshelf and you arrive on a superb small stance (The Aerodrome) stuck in the middle of some wild territory. The final pitch is a great climax to this mini-expedition; an uphill hand traverse on a flat-edged crack. Fortunately protection is plentiful and the distance you have to cover is not very great. Despite this the pitch is a bit of a 'gripper' - though probably less so than the prospect of retreat from here! When you are suitably fired-up take a deep breath and go for it. In a matter of seconds you should be safely established on the cliff top. Now you can wander off into the briars with a grin like a Cheshire cat spreading across your face. You may have a growing feeling that climbs like the one you have just finished can be habit-forming.

BEESTON ELIMINATE:
The first traversing pitch where the route leaves the break to cross a 'smooth' wall on a set of surprising finger pockets.

26:
BEESTON
ELIMINATE

Situation:	Beeston Tor, Manifold Valley, Staffordshire
Aspect:	South facing
Grade:	H.V.S. (4c, 5a, 5a)
Length:	80m (260ft)
Equipment:	A normal rack supplemented with several long slings for the large number of threads on the route.
First Ascent:	The first two pitches were climbed in 1963 by D.Burgess and J.R.Allen. Pitch three was added in 1965 by G.Smith and T.Burnell, using two threads to cross the initial wall. The record of the first completely free ascent has been lost.
Guidebook:	*Peak Limestone South*, published by the British Mountaineering Council in 1987.

Approaches: Beeston Tor lies above the farm of the same name at the end of a minor road running through the valley bottom, which follows in part the old mineral railway. The valley is best approached from the A515 passing through or to the south of the small village of Wetton. A minor road signposted to Grindon drops down into the valley where a left turn leads to a parking field just short of the farm. A small fee is usually charged. Pass through the new gate and cross the normally dry riverbed to a small path that leads to the cliff. The best descent is down the open gully to the left of the cliff.

The Route: A long rising traverse that is very exposed towards the end. Protection is excellent.

Description: The left side of the cliff is a rather scruffy vegetated wall sprouting several trees. The route ascends this then follows the obvious rising break that crosses the upper part of the cliff. Start below the large tree with a beaten path leading to it. Scramble up to the tree and follow the cleaned line on to another tree and possible stance. Continue up and right on gradually improving rock to a recess which is exited on the right. A pockety bulge leads to a comfy stance at the break. From here step out right but rather than following the bedding plane (5b) take a slightly descending line across the pockety wall until it is possible to climb steeply into a groove which leads back to the break at a bunch of bramble bushes where a rather restricted stance is available.

The next few moves are the crux (they may be 5b) and the object of the exercise is to regain the break. Step down and cross the short wall on finger pockets to a resting place. The rest of the pitch gives reasonable climbing in an outrageous position and with ample protection. At the end of the traverse step down and go round the corner to a giant peg belay in the grassy groove above.

BEESTON ELIMINATE

This route gives a great little expedition across a superb cliff. The line is obvious and the situations, especially on the last pitch, are exciting to say the least. Although the climb is a girdle traverse, its gradually rising line gives it more of the feel of a traditional 'up and down' route and a cautious second can get a lot of help from a leader who knows what he is doing with the ropes.

The first pitch is pretty grotty, and although the rock is good you definitely get the feeling that given the chance it would soon return to nature. Don't worry though, things soon improve. From the cave stance you swing out onto the wall and suddenly you are a long way off the ground. The rock looks steep and smooth but is in fact peppered with pockets that provide finger and toeholds a-plenty and the odd thread runner to boot. Eventually the wall drops away below you and a couple of strenuous pulls on good holds leads into a groove. At the top of this is an uncomfortable and prickly stance. The final pitch is superb, but a little test has to be undergone before you get to the rewards beyond. A piggish little wall is crossed on sharp finger pockets to regain the bedding plane. The situations are great with a big roof above you and a massive one below you. There are plenty of good solid threads in the break (providing you remembered the slings) so the crabwise motion can be relished. All too soon a short wall is crossed and it is all over, another memory and another tick in the book, but a rather special one.

27:
MOONRAKER

Situation:	Berry Head, Torbay, South Devon
	Note: A local by-law protecting nesting auks prohibits climbing on Berry Head from mid-March to July 15th. There is a standard fine of £1,000 for breaking this by-law. The route is good, but not that good!
Aspect:	East facing
Grade:	H.V.S. (5a, 4b, 4c)
Length:	75m (250ft)
Equipment:	A normal rack with a few extra mid-range Friends or Hexes.
First Ascent:	P.Biven, P.Littlejohn, 6th August 1967
Guidebook:	*South Devon and Dartmoor* by P.Littlejohn and P.O'Sullivan. Published by Cordee, 1985.

Approaches: Berry Head is a country park situated on the headland at the southern tip of the great sweep of Torbay. Access is signed from Brixham. From the seaward end of the car park a grass slope is descended until it begins to steepen and a traverse to the right (looking out) along exposed rocky ledges followed by a short drop leads to a sloping platform on the edge of the great cave that penetrates the headland. At the start of the traverse are a set of bolts used to attach a video camera so that the nesting birds can be observed, so the chances of sneaking on in the closed season are slim!

The Route: A long climb with a serious approach, especially for non-swimmers. The route is rather smelly at the end of the nesting season.

Description: The impressive corner on the other side of the cave is reached by a trip into the depths of the cave followed by a traverse back along the other side. This is only possible at low tide and in calm seas.

From a small stance ten metres above the water, head up and right to outflank the bulges and reach a long crack system which eventually leads to overhangs. A short traverse left is taken to a good stance with varied belays. Pitch two climbs the steep but reasonable corner to a small recess which is exited on the left to reach a stance at the foot of the final corner. The last pitch is steep and a couple of bulges make it quite strenuous until a leaning wide crack is reached. This is best laybacked rapidly to reach the walls of the fort and a belay on a big iron pole.

MOONRAKER

Looking across from the sloping platform under the vast roof, the line of MOONRAKER stands out as a great corner system that does not quite reach the sea. Plenty of parties come this far and then find the whole place so intimidating that they run away.

The first obstacle to success is the wide channel between you and the route. Assuming that you have read the tide tables correctly this is bypassed via a traverse into the Stygian recesses of the cave. In the depths of this black hole daylight appears as a distant triangle, and the water laps and gurgles in a most sinister fashion.

The return traverse to the start of the route is tricky, as well as being slippery and strenuous. It is a toss-up whether to put the rope on or not. There are problems keeping the loops out of the water, though these pale into insignificance with the

MOONRAKER: The view out from the sea cave with a climber silhouetted on the steepest part of the first pitch.
Climber: Jeff Carlin. Photo: C.Binks

problems you may have swimming with a rack of gear on and a rope around your neck!

All being well you arrive at a restricted stance marked by the rotting remains of some old pegs. Originally the route went left up the corner now taken by GODDESS OF GLOOM, but nowadays a steep traverse on excellent holds leads up and right to a long crack line falling from the roofs above. This is intimidating but technically reasonable and has plenty of protection. At the top of the crack a short traverse out left leads to a smelly stance at a series of ledges. The belays here need to be selected carefully as there are few real 'bombers'. The rather 'niffy' atmosphere of the stance is at its worst in the late summer just after the birds have gone. In the early spring the route is somewhat sweeter with the cliff having been given a bit of an airing by the winter storms. The second pitch of the route is short and straightforward and leads to a stance below the upper corner. This is steep and mightily exposed, and is best climbed by a combination of wide bridging and rather butch laybacking. The runners drop in with a satisfying regularity and the situations are great, with the ropes curving down from your waist and the quiet hiss of the dark sea far below. A final steep wide crack leads to the grassy top of the cliff below the walls of the Old Redoubt fort.

At the tender age of 16, and under the watchful eye of the old master Peter Biven, MOONRAKER was one of Pat Littlejohn's first new routes. It must have been a stunning experience for the youngster, and he never looked back.

28: MALBOGIES

Situation:	Main Wall, Avon Gorge, Bristol
Aspect:	South-west facing
Grade:	H.V.S. (5a, 4b)
Length:	65m (210ft)
Equipment:	A standard rack, there are also several good peg runners in place.
First Ascent:	C.J.S.Bonington, M.Thompson, 1959
Guidebook:	*The Avon Gorge* by Steve Monks, published by Dark Peak in 1981. A new guide is due out in 1991/2

Approaches: The climbs at the Avon Gorge are reached from the A4 (Portway) that runs between the River Avon and the cliffs. Below the highest section of cliff is a large parking space complete with tea wagons and toilets. Looking to the left along the line of cliffs from the parking place the most prominent feature is the pink wall with a thin diagonal crack near its top, taken by THINK PINK. MALBOGIES takes an ill-defined rightward rising ramp line starting about 20 metres right of the fall line from this wall.

The Route: A two-pitch route with the crux low down. The rock is rather polished but protection is excellent with much of it fixed.

Description: Scramble up easy rock to a belay below and left of the shallow depression that rises rightwards to meet a conspicuous band of overhangs half-way up the cliff. There are two possible starts, either straight up from the stance (5a) or by a line slanting up to the left followed by a traverse back to the right (4c). The routes reunite at 'the shattered wall' which is climbed on polished holds to gain the continuation of the groove which leads more easily to a cramped and shiny stance beneath the band of overhangs.

The second pitch starts by crossing the

---

roof on good holds before climbing right to gain a rib and then back left until a direct line can be taken over an assortment of bulges to the top.

MALBOGIES

In the mid and late 50s climbers were just beginning to nibble away at the vast expanse of terrifying rock that ran leftwards for what seemed like miles from the easy angled slab of DAWN WALK. PINK WALL TRAVERSE skirted along the upper right edge of the wall but the first route to break into this 'Brave New World' was Bonington's MERCAVITY, put up in 1955 and running up the right side of the cliff. This was a serious undertaking on a big cliff with plenty of loose rock and route-finding problems. Thirty-plus years on, it does not see a lot of traffic; people preferring better known and more solid outings.

The next chink in the great sheets of overlapping armour was away at the left side of the wall. MALPRACTICE was another Bonington discovery and again it was a 'character building' exercise, skirting the right side of the big smooth pink wall that towers over this part of the cliff. In the next few years two more routes were added further to the left, but the central part of the wall remained inviolable. From almost all angles it looked steep and loose and the knowledge of the generally unhelpful state of the rock hereabouts was not much of an encouragement to exploration.

At certain times of the day as the cliff comes into the sun a vague scoop can be picked out rising through this hostile area. From directly below it becomes apparent that there really is a major weakness here and in 1959 that man Bonington was back again to bag it.

The route has changed a great deal since those days and there is no need to risk your life on it now. Much of the rock is well polished and a precise technique is a must - shoddy footwork will get you nowhere, except perhaps back at the foot of the pitch. There is still a smattering of loose rock around but it has been tried and tested over the years so unless you are particularly ham fisted it should see you through. A few years ago the British Mountaineering Council shelled out some cash to replace some of the old pegs at Avon and Malbogies came out of the deal very well. (Be warned - some of the less popular routes still sprout

MALBOGIES: Two climbers dwarfed by the Main Wall. The upper climber is crossing the overhangs on pitch 2, the lower one is engrossed in the 'Shattered Wall' on pitch 1. *Climbers: Unknown*

archaic bits of metalwork that would not hold your coat, let alone a fall.) Our route is now equipped with a line of new hard steel pegs, so that if you are confident only a few nuts need be carried. Route-finding problems are much eased by these pegs, and the polish; if the rock turns rough you are probably lost.

Despite the changes the route remains a great one, a superb line bang up the centre of a big cliff. When you top out climb over the fence and belay on one of the park benches. If you are really switched on you will have a few pence secreted about your person so you can nip and buy an ice-cream before you take in the ropes. Climbing in the Avon Gorge really is rather civilised.

PINNOCHIO: "Getting started on the wall is problematical, but once established good holds and good jams lead up into a hanging slot".
Climbers: Chris Craggs and Jim Rubery

29: PINNOCHIO

Situation: Ogmore, Bridgend, South East Wales
Notes: The route is not accessible at high tide. The name is spelt as in the guide cf. Pinocchio.
Aspect: South-west facing
Grade: H.V.S. (5a)
Length: 40m (130ft)
Equipment: A standard rack with some long slings to extend runners and a few extra Friends for the horizontal breaks.
First Ascent: J.Kerry, C.Horsfield, 1974
Guidebook: *Gower and South East Wales* by Mike Danford and Tony Penning, published by the South Wales Mountaineering Club in 1983. A new guide is due out in 1991.

Approaches: From the town of Ogmore-by-the-Sea drive along the coast road towards Southerndown for a kilometre to a grassy parking place on the right. This is a short distance before a farm and is surrounded by concrete posts. Descend a gully towards the sea and bear right along terraces for 80 metres to reach the flat top of a slightly projecting buttress. Either climb down this to the beach (15m and V.Diff in descent) or abseil from the in-situ reinforcing rod. Scramble back eastwards for 100 metres to a flat white wall with many horizontal breaks. A rounded cave at five metres is also a useful landmark. To the right of the cave is a left slanting crack. Scramble up to the start of this.

The Route: A long and quite devious pitch which feels a lot more serious than it looks from below.

Description: Follow the slanting crack up to the left, then traverse to the left until below the right edge of the large roof high on the crag. Climb the wall awkwardly then more easily to reach a slot at the right edge of the roof. Go up this then swing out left in an exposed situation before continuing up and left to a gap behind a pinnacle. Escape through the gap to belays on the other side.

PINNOCHIO

Ogmore is not a popular crag, visitors from far afield are rare, and even many of the locals prefer to ride up to the more obvious attraction of the Gower or Pembroke. The heavily stratified rock does not look that solid, and the number of recent scars caused by storm damage helps to reinforce the rather temporary feel that the whole place has. The beach is pleasant enough but when the tide comes in the sea is an unsavoury brown colour. A scramble along the sharp limestone pavement at the foot of the cliff reveals little in the way of obvious powerful lines, though there is certainly plenty of mighty steep rock. Despite these initial misgivings the place is certainly a bit different, and when you actually rub your nose against the rock it is surprisingly solid.

PINNOCHIO is as good introduction as any to the cliff, passing through impressive scenery at a pleasantly low grade. The beach scramble takes you past a series of caves and bays to reach a fine white wall; arguably the best bit of rock on the whole cliff. A slanting corner crack starts under the centre of this wall, and wriggles its way leftwards to vanish just short of an impressive band of overhangs.

This crack is climbed on razor-sharp holds until a short traverse leads out left to a good ledge below the more impressive upper wall. Getting started on this wall is problematical, but once established big holds and good jams lead up into a hanging slot at the right edge of some huge roofs. Judging by the size of the cobwebs found suspended across the slot there must be some fairly large spiders lurking in the back of these horizontal breaks, so perhaps it is a good idea not to tarry over-long, just in case they come to see what all the noise is about.

Good protection can be placed before a stride out to the left takes you onto the very tip of the overhang. It is at this point that you begin to hope that the battering by last winter's storms has not undermined this particular piece of rock to any great degree. An awkward pull leads up and left to a bay and then an easier corner is followed until a wide crack is reached. Creeping through this allows you to avoid the rather unstable cliff top and if you want a really substantial belay you can lasso the whole top of the pinnacle.

PINNOCHIO only goes to show that first impressions can be a bit misleading; or am I imitating the wooden puppet with the telescopic nose by telling little white lies? There is only one way you will ever find out.

30: CIMA

Situation: Block Buttress, Mewslade Bay, the Gower, South Wales
Note: The route is accessible for a couple of hours either side of low water.
Aspect: South facing
Grade: H.V.S. (5b)
Length: 40m (130ft)
Equipment: A standard rack with a few more large wires.
First Ascent: J.O.Talbot, R.J.Corbett, R.B.Owen, 1962. Aid was used to pass the overhang and possibly elsewhere.
First Free Ascent: Unknown
Guidebook: *Gower and South East Wales* by Mike Danford and Tony Penning, published by the South Wales Mountaineering Club in 1983. A new guide is due out in 1991.

Approaches: The small village of Pitton lies astride the B4247 about 25 kilometres west of Swansea. Turn down a narrow lane in the centre of the village (towards the sea) and park on the left in a field with a complex entry - honesty box. Cross the lane and follow a track through the farmyard and down a pleasant valley to the beach. A couple of hundred metres to the right (facing the sea) is a fine buttress with a deep recess on its left side and a prominent block overhang towards the top of the cliff. Ten minutes from the car.

The Route: A fine crack pitch with an impressive overhang. Protection is perfect throughout though the rock is a bit loose on the final moves.

Description: Start in the back left corner of the recess and climb the crack to a niche, thread. Continue up the wide awkward crack to a larger niche (a belay is possible here if the tide threatens) then step right and climb the steep corner to the roof. This is passed by jamming and bridging to gain the final corner which is quitted on the right. The rock on the last couple of moves requires care. Iron pipe belay a little further up the bank.

CIMA

In the late 1950s and well into the 60s, Jeremy Talbot had pretty much a free-hand in the development of the Gower. He ranged far and wide, putting up over a hundred routes with a variety of partners, all along the coast. Names such as MARMOLATA, KAMIN and CIMA suggests that they saw these routes as practice for greater things, but perhaps the climbs and the cliffs just reminded them of mighty Dolomite towers.

The settings of many of the routes are exceptionally 'un-alpine', rising as they do from magnificent unspoilt sandy beaches. This is in stark contrast to the cliffs of nearby Pembroke, which are often much more difficult of access, and it is this contrast that probably accounts for the early development of the Gower.

CIMA is just one example of a collection of fine single pitch routes that are to be found rising from the beaches between Fall Bay and Mewslade Bay. The route is found in the back of a deep recess and the state of the start depends upon the work the tide

CIMA: The rather slippery nature of the start to the route can be seen, as can the quality of the rock above.
Climber: Chris Craggs

and the rollers have been doing. On some occasions there is fine flat sand to start from and on others a deep pool has to be skirted around.

The rock on the first few moves is green with algae and smooth with wave action, so several slippery moves have to be made to reach cleaner and rougher rock. A wide crack then has to be addressed and gives an odd mixture of strenuous and precarious climbing to a good niche and possible stances. From here the route rears up and the rock turns rough. A rugged rib is climbed to reach a crack and this is followed in turn to an impressive roof. Here are to be found some rotting relics of the original ascent. Dubious mild steep pegs are now replaced by superb nut protection, while solid finger jams and high

left footholds allow you to power over the roof into the final corner. A good crack in the back of this means that it is a lot less fierce than it looks from below. Bridging and laybacking leads to an exit on the right wall over rather blocky rock and a little higher is an iron pipe hammered into the bank to act as a belay. The Gower may not be the Dolomites but then again, in the Dollies you can't go for a paddle after you have finished your route!

31: ORIGINAL ROUTE

Situation:	High Tor, Matlock, Derbyshire
Aspect:	West facing
Grade:	H.V.S. (5a, 4c)
Length:	39m (130ft)
Equipment:	A normal rack.
First Ascent:	P.Hassell, P.Biven and 'Darkie', June 1953. The right-hand exit was climbed a week later by J.Brown and P.Hassell.
First Free Ascent:	S.Read and S.Hunt, 1958
Guidebook:	*Peak Limestone, South.* Published by the British Mountaineering Council, 1987.

Approaches: High Tor towers over the valley just to the south of Matlock. There are two possible approaches to the crag.

Firstly just south of the cliff there is limited parking at either side of the iron bridge that leads to the cable-car station. Cross the river and pass behind the buildings to find steps and a path leading back towards the cliff which is ten minutes away. An entrance fee may be charged at the cable-car station or at the café on top of the crag.

Secondly and more expensively take the A615 from Matlock towards Alfreton for one kilometre then turn right up a minor road signposted Starkholms. After another kilometre turn right (by the phone box) up a narrow track that leads to the café on top of the cliff. A fee will definitely be charged if this approach is used.

The Route: A long steep pitch on good rock and with excellent protection. Rather strenuous.

Description: To the right of the highest part of the main wall is a steep open groove running almost the full height of the cliff. This forms the substance of the route and is further identified by a small tree at the base of the groove.

From a belay on the tree traverse left for three metres to reach a ramp that leads back into the main groove line. This gives steep sustained climbing to a roof which is passed on the left. The easier groove above leads to a superbly situated stance with bolt belays. Pitch two traverses to the right for eight metres and then climbs straight up the steep and rather friable wall past an old peg to gain the summit meadows. A tree belay is found some distance back from the edge.

ORIGINAL ROUTE: On the main pitch a tricky ramp has to be climbed to gain access to the soaring groove line.
Climbers: Ian Smith and his dad

ORIGINAL ROUTE

As the most striking feature on the cliff the groove line was an obvious contender for an early ascent by chaps looking to improve their aid technique in preparation for the annual summer visit to the Dolomites or Chamonix. High Tor Bastion ,as it was initially known, did not last long and within five years the route had been free-climbed to give a magnificent main pitch. In 1958 it must have been a major undertaking, though nowadays it is just another great route that has to be ticked off at some time in every climber's career.

The upward view from the bottom is very impressive, with the open groove cutting up the cliff looking far too smooth and steep to be 'only Hard V.S.'. A short scramble leads to the stout little tree sprouting from the rock. From here a rather grassy but easy traverse leads left to the foot of a hidden ramp slanting back into the main groove line. The ramp is initially easy but just short of the groove it clams up. The footholds are slippery, the runners rather distant and the moves all out of balance. With a touch of cunning the groove is reached and suddenly the picture changes as the rock bulges and the climbing becomes strenuous. At this point you may come up against one of the great conundrums in climbing, whether to hang on and get gear in while your strength evaporates, or take a deep breath and press on in the hope that things will ease. Most of us opt for the former course of action and this is definitely the best bet here because things don't ease for a considerable distance. Bridging and the odd rather reckless-feeling layback move gain height at a steady pace and once the obvious roof is passed things do get easier. Jugs appear and you can romp on to the stance.

There used to be a large iron spike hammered down the back of the ledge for belaying and this was backed up by a couple of fiddly but sound nuts in the horizontal breaks in the wall behind. Recently a couple of good bolts have appeared, though these have probably been placed to remove the need of climbers doing the hard routes to the right of ORIGINAL ROUTE having to go to the top of the crag, rather than out of any sense of duty to folks doing the Hard V.S.

The final pitch of our route is rather an anticlimax after the classic climbing below, but it has to be done to earn your tick. An easy traverse to the right leads to an old peg. Directly above this the wall is steep and some of the holds are a bit rattly, formed from fossil-encrusted blocks and sprouting bits of grass, so a judicious approach is required. With care the top is reached safely and just down the bank is a café. If you have remembered to bring your cash a celebratory brew is in order. On the other hand, if you have avoided paying the entry fee so far it is probably best to sneak off into the bushes on the right to find the path back to the bottom of the cliff.

KIRKBY WALL: Climbers dotted along the line of the route show the way it weaves through bands of overhangs
Climbers: Dave Gregory, Jim Rubery, Dave Spencer and Mick Horlov

32: KIRKBY WALL

Situation:	The Right Wing, Malham Cove, Yorkshire
Aspect:	South-west facing
Grade:	H.V.S. (5b, 4c)
Length:	30m (100ft)
Equipment:	A standard rack with a few extra slings.
First Ascent:	J.A.Austin, R.B.Evans, 1961
Guidebook:	*Yorkshire Limestone*, published by the Yorkshire Mountaineering Club in 1985.

Approaches: Park in Malham village, a large National Trust car park being available on the left just before the first buildings. The footpath to the cove is well signed and immensely popular. From the foot of the cliff a path leads up to the right to a great block in the grass which is a good place to dump the gear.

The Route: After a desperate start the route gives varied climbing on great rock. Difficulties are both delicate and strenuous in nature.

Description: The Right Wing is directly above you and in the main part is undercut, this rather restricts access. There is a prominent weakness through these overhangs towards their right-hand side starting from a shallow cave. Scramble to the cave and take a belay. Climb the short but polished and technical wall on the left to a jug, swing right and climb to the overhangs, passing a thread and then make a delicate traverse to the left to reach a good small ledge with thread and peg belays. Continue along the traverse line until below a corner. Climb up to a stump then move rightwards up the steep wall to get into a second corner which leads to the cliff top.

KIRKBY WALL

In the late 50s and early 60s there was a growing realisation among a few climbers in the know that there were some ripe plums to be picked at Malham Cove, especially on the steep and impressive Right Wing. Alan Austin, of WALL OF HORRORS fame, and Brian Evans, accounted for about 20 routes of which KIRKBY WALL is the best.

The rock on the Right Wing is exemplary in its solidity and roughness and for climbers largely brought up on gritstone, there was not too much of a culture shock when they started climbing on the 'white stuff'. The first tentative steps were taken on the far right where the wall is very short, but soon they started probing further to the left. The problem here was, and still is, that the good grey rock is undercut by a band of very ungritstone-like stuff. This is a layer of shattered material that even after 30 years of traffic requires careful handling.

A belay in the little starting cave is definitely a good idea as the bank below the route is both steep and stony. From the cave a step left gains the rib. The first couple of moves are the crux of the route and involve difficult moves on small, loose and polished holds; not a nice combination. Fortunately a couple of good wires are available. This 'trial by grot' is short-lived and a good jug allows a swing right onto much better rock and then easier, but still steep, climbing leads to a bulge that stops upward progress. A traverse to the left is the key to the upper wall and this is protected, at least for the leader, by a couple of good threads. The traverse is very delicate, involving a precarious sideways shuffle on good but hidden footholds, with only the poorest of dimples for your fingers. It is at this point that you realise all the time spent doing pull-ups and fingery problems on the climbing wall last winter was a waste of time, at least for this style of climbing.

The stance is small and not very comfortable but the belays are good (threads, a peg and nuts) and the outward views are superb. The second pitch continues the traversing theme a little further by stepping up and back down until a small ledge is reached and it becomes necessary to start climbing upwards. A short wall leads to a small but stout stump, then moves out right and up via a hidden hold gets you into a fine little corner. This can be laybacked

or bridged, depending on your confidence and state of fitness, to a sudden exit onto the billiard table top of the cliff.

So that's KIRKBY WALL, a great little route, offering a couple of fine meandering pitches, full of contrasts, and still no pushover even in these days of big numbers.

33: KING KONG

Situation:	The GO Wall, Wintour's Leap, the Wye Valley
Aspect:	West facing
Grade:	H.V.S. (5b, 5b, 4a)
Length:	90m (300ft)
Equipment:	A standard rack.
First Ascent:	T.Taylor, C.F.Tanner, June 1965
Guidebook:	*The Wye Valley* by J.Wilson, D.Hope, T.Penning, M.Ward, published by Cordee in 1987.

Approaches: Wintour's Leap overlooks the River Wye two kilometres north of Chepstow, but is invisible from the road. From the M4 follow the Chepstow bypass and then the B4228 into the village of Woodcroft. Almost opposite the Rising Sun is a road running uphill with a large steel gate across it. Park sensibly here then walk up the road to reach a high wire fence and warning sign. Pass around the right side of the fence and follow the track that winds down through the quarry. At its end descend the slope until a path branches right into the trees. The GO (Great Overhanging) Wall is in front of you and KING KONG takes the massive continuous corner system towards the left side of the wall.

The Route: A long climb on a big cliff. Both cruxes are strenuous but fortunately the protection is exemplary.

Description: The base of the corner system is guarded by an overhang. Battle round this to reach a clean cut corner which is climbed to a rightward exit. Climb slightly left then follow the corner without incident until it begins to steepen (peg). There are several ways of reaching the belay ledge, the best being the steep finger crack running straight up the wall. The second pitch follows the huge corner then crosses the roof to an easier groove beyond which is a large tree-covered terrace. A straightforward corner on the right leads to the cliff top.

KING KONG

A legendary monster, a giant lurking amongst the primeval forests of some far-flung realm. Despite his great size, the beast is no man-eater, in fact he is a retiring and timid creature - much admired and wholly misunderstood. Are we talking about the route or the monkey? The description fits either of them equally well!

As to the route, the line is one of the finest around, a great corner system cutting up one of the largest limestone walls in the country. The climbing is mostly straightforward with only a few tricky moves, all of which are well protected.

The initial problem is an evil bulge a short distance from the ground which guards access to the obvious delights just a little higher up. The attraction of the soaring crack line and the big groove unimaginable far above you is too much to stand, so let 'the battle of the bulge' commence. A couple of tricky moves leads to cold clammy jams under the overhangs. By craning your neck round the corner it is possible to peer into the depths of the crack and poke a good runner in. A strenuous layback move with your feet on slippery rock gains a big

KING KONG: A view up the first pitch shows the soaring line with the crucial chimney hidden far above.
Climber: Chris Craggs

spike and a sudden sense of commitment. Another stiff pull on the rather rattly spike and you are in the base of the corner, where an in-situ thread gives you the chance of a breather. The rest of the pitch is classical climbing, wandering up the corner to a final steepening where a stiff little finger crack, complete with perfect protection, leads to a grand bivi-style ledge.

The outward views are superb, with the tree-tops already far below, the muddy meanders of the Wye in the middle distance, and beyond the white scar of the Wyndcliffe. Over all this hangs a rare pastoral tranquillity that has changed little in the past century.

Unfortunately the upward view is rather less prepossessing. The corner is obviously no great problem but it is capped by a big bad overhang. Just round the lip is an old bent peg (back it up), much used and abused over the years. A big hold is available, just out of reach, and once it is grasped a short sharp struggle is needed to haul your carcass over into the easier groove above. The rest of the route is mild by comparison. The groove you have just entered leads by a rather dusty exit into a small lost world, beyond which a polished corner deposits you suddenly back into the world of day trippers and cream teas.

The climb is a great one, impressive and intimidating, but on closer acquaintance it proves to be rather more friendly, perhaps a little like its hairy and much maligned namesake.

34: ROCK IDOL

Situation:	Mother Carey's Kitchen, Lydstep, South Pembroke *Note: The start of the route is only easily accessible below half-tide.*
Aspect:	South facing
Grade:	E1 (5a)
Length:	40m (130ft)
Equipment:	A normal rack supplemented with a few larger Friends and a selection of longer slings.
First Ascent:	P.Littlejohn, R.Harrison, May 1976
Guidebook:	*Pembroke* by Jon de Montjoye and Mike Harber, published by the Climbers' Club in 1985. A new guide is due out in 1991.

Approaches: Mother Carey's Kitchen is the most important of the many cliffs scattered along the coast at Lydstep. There is a car park on the top of the headland that is reached by turning seaward off the A4139 and passing through Lydstep Bay Caravan Park until the road turns left and rises steeply to the downs. Park as far eastward (towards Tenby) as is possible. There is also a direct track from Lydstep village to the headland but this involves going the wrong way round the caravan park's one-way system. Pass through the bushes and follow the track to the left, almost immediately there is a small track to the right that leads through the gorse to meet the coastal path. Turn left along this for ten metres or so until level with twin towers on the right; this marks the top of the cliff. It is quite common to overshoot the crag but if you keep glancing over your right shoulder you will recognise the black gash of Deep Space.

It is normal to make a 40 metre abseil from the left-hand tower (looking out to sea) but care is needed in case there are

---

people below as there have been deaths here - you have been warned!

The Route: A steep sustained and intimidating pitch on perfect rock and with excellent protection.

Description: ROCK IDOL basically follows the great corner system that bounds the left side of the main wall of the cliff. Easy climbing leads to sloping ledges and a possible belay beneath the imposing corner system. The wall to the right of the corner leads to a bulge which is passed to get into the corner proper. Continue straight up the leaning groove, resisting any temptations to move out right into a series of peculiar tubes. Steep rock is followed to reach a ledge at the foot of a crack which eases as height is gained.

ROCK IDOL

A grade of E1 (5a) suggests that the route in question must be very sustained, possibly with some loose rock and most probably a little dangerous. ROCK IDOL is certainly sustained, but the rock is as solid (and as rough) as you could wish for, and as to danger - it is as safe as houses. So why the rather odd grade? All you need to do is go and stand under the corner that the climb follows and things will become a little clearer. Once embarked on the pitch things become clearer still, and bridged on the lip of the last bulge it is suddenly as clear as daylight!

The first section of the route climbs a vertical wall on wonderfully rugged rock to get you established in the corner. The upward prospect is one of tier upon tier of overhangs, forever heading outwards. If you do not let this view intimidate you and bridge on upwards you will be rewarded by a rare experience. There are jugs galore to aid progress, along with solid threads and good nuts to allow you to savour the whole experience. Undeniably the route is steep, very steep in fact, and a series of grooves out on the right wall offers the chance of escape onto rock of a saner angle but do not be tempted, otherwise you will find yourself on a rather inferior route and will have to come back another day to collect the real prize.

Above you the corner continues to bulge and lean to the right and the whole thing becomes quite strenuous, though fortunately the protection remains as good

ROCK IDOL: A downward view gives some idea of the intimidating nature of this stupendous pitch.
Climbers: Rhydian Williams (Age 14¹/2) and his dad.

as ever. With a steady approach enough energy can be conserved to relish the situations as you are pushed ever-further outwards until you suddenly pull round a larger-than-average bulge to the foot of a short ramp. This is still very exposed and no pushover, but the spell has been broken. You are no longer roofed in, trapped by a vaulted ceiling of rock, and although the climbing is a little tricky, it is not too technical. There are no route-finding difficulties and you can return to the ledge for a rest if required. The rope drag is now something to worry about and care is needed to reach easy rock and assorted belays in a small outcrop some distance back.

Doubtless your second, with the comfort of a snug top rope, will cruise the route and declare it "Only H.V.S.", to which you can reply, "Oh sure, and I'm a rock idol".

35:
THE ARROW

Situation:	St Govan's, South Pembroke
Aspect:	South facing
Grade:	E1 (5b)
Length:	40m (130ft)
Equipment:	A standard rack, with a couple of long slings for spikes and threads.
First Ascent:	P.Whillance, D.Armstrong, 19th February 1977
Guidebook:	*Pembroke* by Jon de Montjoye and Mike Harber, published by the Climbers' Club in 1985. A new guide is due out in 1991.

Approaches: A minor road leads from Pembroke, via Bosherston, to a large car park and the flat ground above St Govan's Chapel. From here walk eastwards towards the prominent coastguard's lookout on the headland. The descent to the base of the cliff is down a chimney between a large pinnacle and the mainland and is marked by a cluster of spikes and often a scattering of rucksacks. The descent is slippery and steep; if in doubt use a rope.

The Route: A long pitch with good protection. The climbing is strenuous low down and more delicate towards the top. The exit is rather loose.

Description: THE ARROW lies up the centre of the largest and most prominent buttress at St Govan's and is to the right of a huge flake system, CUPID'S BOW. The route starts from a big ledge and is nontidal, except when heavy seas are running. Climb steep rock on good but unusual holds to reach the crack line above. This leads to an open groove which is followed to a slabby area which is climbed rightwards to outflank an overhang. An easier groove is climbed slanting left to the top and stake belays.

THE ARROW

In early 1981 we finally decided to go to Pembroke to see what all the fuss in the climbing press was about. We camped at Bosherston but as almost all the information we had was about Mother Carey's Kitchen we travelled around to Lydstep each day. We did have a bit of 'gen' about a route called DIEDRE SUD and another called THE ARROW but it hardly seemed worth going to cliffs with so few routes on. Then on the Thursday before Easter more people began to arrive including Ken Wilson with a car boot full of shiny new guidebooks. In a blinding flash we suddenly realised what we had been missing right on our doorstep. The rest of the week was spent running around like scalded cats, in the never-ending sunshine, ticking classics galore until fingertips were reduced to tender pink patches and we were forced to rest.

On the first day we did THE ARROW along with five other routes: all excellent. Despite the quality of the climbs THE ARROW stood out as one of the best, a great natural line on perfect rock and with pro-

tection to match. The start is steep and easy if you are feeling strong. It is the kind of terrain where it is possible to climb fast and watch the ground recede at an alarming rate. The horizontal breaks are contorted and knobbly in the extreme, they provide plenty of holds but are a real fiddle to get solid runners in. A little higher the rock changes to smooth white limestone and there are runners a-plenty. Sustained and

THE ARROW: The route takes the centre of the largest buttress at St Govan's and offers superb sustained climbing.
Climbers: Unknown

intriguing climbing leads up the crack using an odd collection of holds, both in the crack and stuck on the walls with flowstone in a most random fashion. A final delicate move leads to a change in angle and in the style of climbing. An ominous-looking roof is skirted around and much easier rock leads away left to a slightly unstable exit and the top.

Sat on top of the cliff later in the day I was talking to 'Nipper' Harrison who had just completed his third new route of the day. I asked how long he had been visiting Pembroke, and he replied five years or so. The next question was obvious, why had they kept it so quiet, and the answer was even more obvious as he slowly gazed around the bay: "Well, wouldn't you?"

36: SIRPLUM

Situation:	Plum Buttress, Chee Dale, Derbyshire
Aspect:	North-west facing
Grade:	E1 (5a, 5b, 4a)
Length:	77m (250ft)
Equipment:	A normal rack and at least one long sling.
First Ascent:	R.Dearman, R.D.Brown, 1964 (a little aid was used)
Guidebook:	*Peak Limestone, Chee Dale,* published by the British Mountaineering Council in 1987.

Approaches: Plum Buttress is close to the western end (the Buxton end) of Chee Dale and is best approached from the lay-by on the A6 at the top of the hill above Topley Pike. Cross the wall and descend steep grass into the valley bottom. The crag is five minutes walk away to the right along

SIRPLUM: "..until you are directly below a shallow groove which offers some prospect of sanctuary from the drop clawing at your backside.."
Climbers: Mike Riddings and Dave Spencer

the (at present) disused railway line.

The Route: Strenuous climbing on big holds in a terrifying situation.

Description: The centre of the lower wall of the buttress has a shallow groove in it. Start six metres to the right of this and climb up and right keeping just above the vegetation to reach a short wall and scoop. These are quite tricky but short-lived and soon lead to a comfortable ever-dry terrace with a giant block belay and a sitting stance. Pitch two pulls over the roof at the left end of the terrace and then goes up and left to a good ledge in the centre of the face. From here climb up to the roof (large thread) then continue up and left over steep rock to gain a shallow groove which is followed to a large terrace and tree belay. The final pitch follows the crack in the arête to the top. Descend to the left down a steep gully.

SIRPLUM

SIRPLUM is easy - everybody knows it is a piece of cake climbing on big holds and with perfect protection. So what is the big deal? It can be summed up in one word, exposure. On the second critical pitch every move carries you further and further away from security and out over that yawning void.

In the 1950s Plum Buttress was just that, the biggest ripest plum in Derbyshire just waiting to be plucked (or should that read pegged?). After Graham West bashed his way up the centre of the cliff in September 1960 to produce the classic BIG PLUM, it was all eyes right to the terrifyingly situated right wall of the buttress. To the eye of faith there was certainly a line there, but unfortunately a great flake sat in the niche that was to prove the key to the route. The offending monster was persuaded to leave its resting place by the judicious use of a crow bar, and it was heaved, groaning and protesting into the void. What a trundle! With this gone and five pegs in place the route came into being, and continuing the plum theme it was called SIRPLUM, a corruption of the French for overhanging.

Today the route is no big deal but it still demands a little respect and the use of a sit harness. The first pitch is a formality and leads to a dusty, dry terrace where your second can lash himself down to a huge cubic block while you steel yourself for the trip ahead. When you are suitably composed, shuffle left to where the ledge vanishes and clip an old dangling piece of string that is attached to God-knows-what before powering over the roof onto rock that is only vertical. With the crux done the rest of the pitch should be a mere formality; in truth the fun is only just beginning. Climb straight up and then left to gain the niche left by the long-gone flake, now you can rest awhile and ask yourself what the hell you are doing here.

The longer you look at the next section the more ridiculous it appears, so it is best to press on before you run out of steam altogether. A tricky wall leads to a band of roofs where jams can be slotted in and a huge thread is available for protection if you can hang about long enough to put it on. Many years ago there was thick steel cable shackled around this thread. It was painted bright orange and had the words 'the ring of over confidence' emblazoned on it. This was easy to clip and caught several shooting stars on their way Earthwards. I wonder which miserable sod went to the trouble of removing it?

Once you have the thread on and clipped you are immortal. Any mistakes on the final steep section and the welcoming air will break your fall. Swing down and left into ever-more ridiculous positions until you are directly below a shallow groove, which offers the prospect of some sanctuary from the drop clawing at your backside, and fingers that are determined to uncurl and drop you towards the nettles 40 metres below. A few of the holds look distinctly temporary, but that is the least of your worries - it is time for a bit of forceful climbing, so go for it!

Once established in the groove good nuts give you a chance to calm down a little before bridging your way to glory, grassy ledges and a big tree belay. It is possible to traverse off at this point along a narrow grassy shelf, but the straightforward crack in the arête above provides a pleasant way to the top of the highest buttress in the Peak District, and the end of a peach of a route.

37: SEALHUNT

Situation:	The West Face, Mowing Word, South Pembroke *Note: There is an access restriction on this cliff, it is closed to climbers from 1st March to 31st July.*
Aspect:	West facing
Grade:	E1 (5b)
Length:	40m (130ft)
Equipment:	A standard rack.
First Ascent:	R.Burns, J.Jones, April 1976
Guidebook:	*Pembroke* by Jon de Montjoye and Mike Harber, published by the Climbers' Club in 1985. A new guide is due out in 1991.

Approaches: From the large car park at Broad Haven cross the beach and then head up to and straight across the downs to skirt around the deep narrow rift of Raming Hole. The path bears away to the right to reach the top of Mowing Word. Twenty minutes from the car. Towards the far end of the cliff an easy grassy ramp descends towards the tip of the headland. From the upper end of this a 30-metre abseil leads to non-tidal ledges.

The Route: A fine pitch with a difficult wall leading to a well-hidden groove. Protection is good.

Description: From the left end of the ledges climb up and left across the slab to reach the arête. Move up to a series of horizontal breaks and follow them around the corner. Thus far the route is the same as the classic traverse HEART OF DARKNESS, which continues along the breaks for two pitches to reach DIEDRE SUD. Move along the break for two metres then climb straight up the wall on a series of less than obvious holds to ledges. Move left again to reach the main groove line and follow it throughout on excellent holds.

SEALHUNT: "The downward views are superb, the ropes arching away and the sea far below."
Climber: Jim Rubery

SEALHUNT

Climbing guidebook writers have a lot of power at their disposal. They can produce a workmanlike volume (mundane some might say) or a lighthearted one full of anecdotes and humour (flippant some might say). However these souls attempt to pitch their literary endeavours, there will be a fair percentage of the climbing world ready to criticize their best efforts. The critics are usually folk who have never been to a guidebook committee meeting, and don't usually buy guides anyway.

The use of good photos in a guide can bring instant popularity to a climb. A great (but not classic) example being the shot of JOLLY SENSIBLE ARETE on the back cover of the last Pembroke guidebook. The route is pleasant enough, though it is a short, unremarkable and over-graded piece of climbing. Despite this the photograph has ensured its popularity. People walk past many an unsung classic to get at this climb even though it gets no stars in the guide.

It is in the use of the now well known 'star system' that the real power of the guide author becomes apparent. In the days before the star system the great classics were well enough known, but once you had done them, you had to do a bit of research and reading between the lines to find the 'almost classics'.

Nowadays, if a climb does not get at least two stars most people ignore it, where does that leave the routes with one or even no stars? SEALHUNT is a perfect example of this neglect. It is one of the best routes of its grade in Pembroke (I can hear the cries of "cobblers" ringing round the climbing world already). To justify my point I would claim it certainly offers a much finer climbing experience than, for example, the ever-popular B-TEAM BUTTRESS DIRECT*** CLEAN HAND BLUES BAND*** and ULTRAVIXENS*** (the stars are the guidebook's, not mine).

The abseil approach and sea level ledges are a great way to start any sea cliff route; there is an instant feeling of heightened anticipation and a sense of isolation. A slab of perfect rock leads to an arête, from where a blind swing takes you round the corner, instantly out of sight of the second, and directly above the sea. A difficult wall protects the base of the main groove line, though a brown streak containing some small flat holds weathered out of the fine white rock allows a way through it. A quick couple of moves on these and you reach small flat ledges below and right of the corner. A shuffle to the left reveals another short and quite difficult wall which has to be crossed before you finally gain access to the main corner system. It looks steep and imposing from below but there are some great hidden flake holds in the back, and the walls are rough and bubbly. You can bridge your way upwards by practising some fancy footwork, or you can layback on the flakes and steam ever-onwards. The downward views are superb, the ropes arching away, and the sea far below. The corner is long but, as always, not quite long enough, and suddenly you are back at the cliff top, with perhaps one thought uppermost in your mind - "That's what I call a three-star route".

THE EARL OF PERTH: Great climbing up the centre of the buttress and overlooked by Brunel's masterpiece. The second has taken the optional stance half way up the route. *Climbers: Derek Carter and Chris Craggs*

38: THE EARL OF PERTH

Situation: Suspension Bridge Buttress, Avon Gorge, Bristol
Aspect: West facing
Grade: E1 (4c, 5b, 5b, 4a)
Length: 65m (210ft)
Equipment: A standard rack is adequate unless you intend to run some of the pitches together. Don't forget your best lycra for the crowds.
First Ascent: E.Ward Drummond, H.Ward Drummond, 1965
Guidebook: *The Avon Gorge* by Steve Monks, published by Dark Peak in 1981. A new guide is due out in 1991/2

Approaches: Suspension Bridge Buttress is easily identified from the structure that provides its name. There are two possible approaches to the base of the buttress.

Firstly, when driving alongside the River Avon there are a couple of small lay-bys on the left 100 metres or so before the tunnel that protects the road from rock falls from Suspension Bridge Buttress. These are best reversed into but *great care* is needed with fast-moving traffic. From here a short scramble to the left of the road leads to the roof of the tunnel.

There is a second approach which is slightly longer but has the advantage that you end up back at the car after completing the route. Park anywhere in the open area around the Bristol side of the Suspension Bridge then walk a short distance down to the left (facing the river) to pick up a steeply descending footpath that reaches the valley bottom just to the east of the road tunnel. Scramble round behind the fence and up onto the roof of the tunnel.

The Route: An interesting and varied route in an unusual setting. The lower section is strenuous but protection is good.

Description: Slightly left of the centre of the buttress are some prominent black bulges containing a series of large pockets. Start below and left of these bulges. Climb directly up the white wall to get to the ledge that crosses the lower part of the face. Traverse right and climb through the bulges (threads) until you are forced to swing out right. Climb straight up the wall to a possible stance at a horizontal break (pegs) then continue up the shallow groove above to reach a major ledge system cutting across the top of the face. Belay on wired nuts. Move five metres left to a bush then climb straight up the wall on good holds to reach the bridge parapet.

THE EARL OF PERTH
Suspension Bridge Buttress is the odd man out in the Avon Gorge. The rock has not been quarried to any great extent and the holds and style of climbing are reminiscent of many a cliff hidden away in a quiet

Derbyshire dale. The buttress is not popular among Avon devotees, perhaps due to this difference in the style of climbing, but this is a pity as it houses some excellent routes.

The crag used to be a horribly noisy place to climb, with a fast section of road squeezed between the rock and the river. The roar of the traffic made thinking difficult and communication impossible. A few years ago the council decided there was too much of a danger of rocks falling onto the road so they did some stabilising work on the cliff and then built a bridge, (or is it a tunnel?) over the road. The top of this construction has grassed over and provides a remarkably tranquil grandstand for watching climbers at work on the routes far overhead. The most bizarre aspect of climbing here is the Suspension Bridge hanging high above your head. It was designed by Isambard Kingdom Brunel (with a name like that he was bound to be famous) and was completed in 1864, 101 years before Edwin Ward Drummond (with a name like that ...) put up our route. The crest of the buttress formed the ideal place for the take-off point for the bridge. There was no such natural feature on the other side of the river so a huge sandstone plinth was built. It is worth paying your two pence and having a walk out onto the bridge, to ponder awhile on the problems associated with spanning this massive rift, the Avon Gorge.

The route can be split into as many as four pitches, though with confidence it can be done in a lot less than this. The first pitch is a pleasant V.S. wall that leads to a ledge below the foreboding black bulges. There are a couple of threads here for use as runners or to belay on. The holds on the initial steepest part of the bulge are massive crystal-lined pockets, a couple of quick pulls on these will see you bridged under a rather blank groove, hanging strenuously from jams in a short spiky crack. As the upward view is not very encouraging the best policy is to outflank it. On the right are some large flat holds which are gained by a long reach and a distinctly committing swing. Once on the front face things ease and steep climbing on good holds leads to a diagonal break. It is possible to belay here on old pegs backed up by wires and Friends in the break, but if you have enough kit left it is perhaps worth pressing on.

A shallow groove is quite tricky to enter and gives sustained climbing with good protection to eventually reach a cleaned ledge. At this point you are sure to have gathered a large audience hanging over the edge of the bridge. Comments like, "You wouldn't catch me climbing up there", are worthy of a well rehearsed witty reply on the lines of "This rock's been here a damn site longer than that bridge", or "If you could see what's holding that bridge up you wouldn't be so sure!"

The last pitch is steep but easy and lands you right under one of the great cornerstones that surround the towers of the bridge. A pull on a flat sandstone hold gains the top edge of the rampart and then you can throw a loop of rope over the pillar to form one of the finest and most substantial belays you will ever get. Hats off to 'Issey', he was some engineer!

39: GEORGE

Situation: Tissington Spires, Dovedale, Derbyshire
Aspect: South facing
Grade: E1 (5b)
Length: 40m (130ft)
Equipment: A few extra middle-sized wires might not go amiss plus a couple of long slings to extend some of the runners.
First Ascent: S.Read, R.Leeming, D.Carnell, P.Brown, S.Hunt, (aid), 1956
First Free Ascent: Possibly P.Nunn, J.Morgan, 1969
Guidebook: *Peak Limestone, South.* Published by the British Mountaineering Council, 1987.

Approaches: Tissington Spires is a set of ridges and pinnacles hidden in the depths of Dovedale. They are approachable from either end of the dale in about 30 minutes, the approach from the south (Thorpe) being slightly shorter than that from the north (Milldale). On the other hand parking at Milldale is free if somewhat restricted, whereas at Thorpe there is plenty of space but it will cost you - decisions, decisions!

Seen from below, the crag appears as a confusing set of gullies and faces. Our route lies on the John Peel wall, which is the largest face. It is approached up a steep unstable gully: in high summer it bristles with man-eating nettles.

The Route: A long and strenuous pitch which fortunately is very well protected.

Description: From below the most obvious feature on the rather flat wall is a rightward curving overlap, which is the line of JOHN PEEL, another great route. GEORGE reaches the left end of this overlap from directly below and then swings out leftwards onto the front of the impressive buttress, before following the crack line to the top.

GEORGE
Dovedale is a beautiful place, almost too beautiful for its own good. On a fine summer's day the car park and minor roads at each end of the dale are choked solid with traffic and there is a constant stream of trippers up and down the valley. A few years ago the footpath through the dale was being churned into an ever-widening morass. Drastic action was needed and the National Trust took it. Mechanical diggers moved in and a good path was pushed right through the dale. At the time there was a lot of complaints about the mess, the rock scars and the felled trees, but time has healed things and now it looks as if the path has been there forever.

At the time the path was being built a lot of the trees that shrouded the cliffs were cut down to allow the public to view the splendid rock architecture. The spin-off from this has been that the cliffs now get more sun and therefore dry more quickly, but most important of all you can actually find them relatively easily.

Once you have found the start of GEORGE the fun begins. Climb the rather floral groove to a stubborn little bulge (the

GEORGE: Passing a peg runner to gain the upper crack line is generally regarded as the crux.
Climber: Brian Rossiter

SURPRISE ATTACK: Once the crux slab has been overcome the groove that forms the main substance of the route gives superb climbing at a much more reasonable standard.
Climber: Jim Rubery

crux?) to reach the traverse of JOHN PEEL which is followed up into the corner. There are plenty of good nuts here but make sure you extend them or rope drag will become a real problem later on. From the corner an awkward move down and left leads out onto the steep exposed face; fortunately the holds are huge and there are some old pegs to clip. Climb up and left to the crack line that soars upwards. This give sustained and interesting climbing with as many runners as you want and is nowhere very difficult, (well, apart from one move). Gradually things ease and a final blocky corner leads to the crest of the ridge; don't fall down the back. A large tree provides a suitable belay, and a possible abseil anchor, or follow the narrow ridge back to join the hillside and slide down the gully back to your gear. When asked by your mates what you thought of the route tell them the truth, "By George, it's a corker".

40: SURPRISE ATTACK

Situation:	Mewsford Point, Range East, South Pembroke
Aspect:	South facing
Grade:	E1 (5a, 5c)
Length:	50m (170ft)
Equipment:	A standard rack backed up with a set of R.P.s for the slab and a couple of larger Friends for the upper groove.
First Ascent:	S.Lewis, C.Heard, 10th October 1979
Guidebook:	*Pembroke* by Jon de Montjoye and Mike Harber, published by the Climbers' Club in 1985. A new guide is due out in 1991.

Approaches: Mewsford Point can be approached from the car parks at either end of Range East, that is at St Govan's Chapel or at Stack Rocks, though the latter is rather shorter. The headland is easily recognised as it has a large coastguard's lookout building on top of it and a huge tiled rock platform in front of it. The crag is rather too high to abseil down so follow a grassy ramp down to the right (looking out to sea) for a short distance to a large block. A 30-metre abseil from here reaches the edge of the platform running below the cliff.

NOTE: The approach (and escape!) is cut off soon after the tide turns.

The route takes the most prominent vertical groove in the centre of the cliff. This is directly beneath the coastguard lookout.

The Route: A great route up a big cliff. The crux is a short, delicate slab, the rest of the climbing is much easier.

Description: Direct access to the groove is cut off by overhangs. To avoid these a start is made a short distance further right. Climb straight up the steep wall to a break which is followed to the left to a beak and a small ledge then press on directly up a steep shallow groove to a good stance. Move left then cross a smooth slab slightly rightward to gain the main groove line which is followed all the way to the coastguard lookout.

SURPRISE ATTACK

Mewsford Point is a huge crag, a massive barrel-shaped piece of good quality limestone with remarkably few strong natural lines (ignoring the numerous horizontal bedding planes). If you have a few minutes to spare it is worth a scramble up to the tip of the great tilted rock platform that lies between the cliff and the open ocean. From this elevated vantage point it is possible to gauge the size of the cliff and get a grasp of its geography. On the far left are alternating shallow grooves and steep walls terminating in an enormous hanging flake cutting diagonally across the crag, the line of IDLE THREATS. To the right of this, roughly in the centre of the cliff is the great bottomless groove of our chosen route, the best line on the cliff, while further away to the right a sea of slanting slabs, ribs and bulges disappears into the distance.

The obvious problem with the central section of the cliff is that it is severely undercut throughout its width, and so a devious approach is needed on all the routes in this area. To get to SURPRISE ATTACK a short steep wall to the right of the base of the groove leads on encouragingly big holds to one of the many bedding planes that cut across the cliff. From here it is possible to sneak out left, passing over the lip of the largest overhang to get established below the main line. The wall above is steep but the holds are good and a bit of bridging is possible to ease the strain. A comfortable sitting stance is available either at the point of arrival or a little further left at the foot of a short grey slab.

The slab that forms the crux of the route lies between you and a groove that is the main feature of the route soaring upwards out of sight. This slab is all a bit strange - the rock is smooth, grey and compact and good runners are notable by their absence. This is in complete contrast to 99.9% of the rock on this coast. The rock here may be a welcome relief to fingertips flayed a bright shade of pink by a week on the cheese grater textured stuff elsewhere, but the footholds are sketchy and slippery and upward progress is strangely insecure. The odd small wire can be fiddled in but the chance of a slip landing you back on the belay ledge is a very real one.

The saving grace of this slab is that it *is* a slab (obvious really) so you have time to work out your moves in advance, and there is no need to do anything too rash. Immediately above the crux the rock returns to its usual reliable roughness. Rugged cracks and flakes make for rapid progress and the odd bulging section has big 'biffos' so you can storm on in confident fashion. Your second will be well impressed until he feels the holds for himself. Just short of the cliff top the rock deteriorates a little and so care is needed until you pop out a short distance from the coastguard lookout. The great flag pole held up with steel hawsers 50 times thicker than the miserable wires you put in lower down the cliff provides one of the world's better belays. Tie on, take a seat and take in the rope - in fact sit back and take everything in, a great route on a great cliff; mellow.

41: MACHETE WALL

Situation:	Chudleigh Rocks, South Devon
Aspect:	South facing
Grade:	E1 (5b)
Length:	30m (100ft)
Equipment:	A standard rack
First Ascent:	E.Rayson and party 1961 (with some aid on the bulge).
Guidebook:	*South Devon and Dartmoor* by Pat Littlejohn and Pete O'Sullivan. Published by Cordee in 1985.

Approaches: Chudleigh Rocks lie just to the south of Chudleigh village, a short distance off the A38. When approaching the village from the south take the second right turn (by a rather inconspicuous police station) down a narrow lane. Park at a widening and go through the iron gate on the right. A narrow path is followed for a couple of hundred metres to a flat area in the wood. A slippery descent to the left leads to the foot of the rocks. MACHETE WALL is to be found towards the left side of the cliff. It starts at a rib to the left of a cave recess and eight metres to the right of the base of the prominent crack line of WOGS.

The Route: An intimidating pitch. A well-protected, fingery crux leads to easier but bolder climbing above.

Description: Climb the rib to the left of the recess then move up and right to a niche (pegs). Climb steeply to gain better holds on the wall above then trend boldly left onto easier angled rock. Step back right and pull (carefully) onto a large flake. Step left into a groove which is followed until it is possible to finish up the wall above.

MACHETE WALL

The name speaks volumes for the state that many of today's limestone classics were in before they became 'squeaky clean' from the passage of folks in search of a bit of adventure. The lime-rich, freely draining soils that formed on the ledges and in the many solution pockets on the cliffs were colonized by a great proliferation of lime-loving plants. As each generation died the organic matter was recycled and the cliffs became ever-greener. Even today on the most popular limestone cliffs there are small patches of greenery and the occasional flowering plant sprouting from the rock. These can add to the pleasure of the ascent, as long as you do not tread on any of them and end up with low friction plant juices all over your high friction boots.

There is quite a collection of rare plants that live only on these dry limestone cliffs and in the past over-zealous gardening has led to conflicts between conservationists and climbers. In reality there is plenty of room for both the plants and the climbers. This is because the plants tend to occupy the easier angled or ledge covered parts of the cliffs. Most of these have been cleaned and climbed at some time in the past by glory seekers, but are returning to well-earned floral obscurity. Where climbs end up running into steep vegetation at the cliff top e.g. in some of the deeper Derbyshire dales and at Cheddar there is a case for fixed anchors to belay to and lower off at the end of the clean rock. This removes the need to 'jungle bash' to safety and leaves the vegetation undisturbed.

Nowadays the once overgrown MACHETE WALL offers a fine, clean pitch up steep rock. An easy rib offers a way past the undercut start, then a couple of steeper moves leads to a niche containing two good pegs. A fingery pull (or a metal handhold, tut, tut!) is required to reach better holds on the wall above. From here the climb trends left on surprising pockets to a good resting place below bulges. On the right is a rather dicky-looking flake. From a standing position on its tip (don't put a sling on it) a stride to the left reaches an easier corner, and the remainder of the climb proves to be much more straightforward. Thanks to the passage of people and time, nowadays you can leave your machete and pith helmet at home and concentrate on enjoying the climbing.

MACHETE WALL: Above the crux niche, the wall is climbed first right and then left by sustained moves.
Climber: Chris Craggs

42: CORONATION STREET

Situation: High Rock, the Cheddar Gorge, Somerset
Note: Climbing in the Cheddar Gorge is not allowed between 1st April and the end of September, and the Easter weekend, this is because of the danger to tourists. If you ignore these restrictions you had better have a good third party insurance policy.

Aspect: North facing

Grade: E1 (4b, 4a, 5a, 5a, 5b, 5a)

Length: 120m (385ft)

Equipment: A standard rack with a few extra large wires and mid-range Friends.

First Ascent: C.Bonington, J.Cleare, A.Greenbank, March 1965. A little aid was used but this was soon dispensed with.

Guidebook: *Cheddar* by Richard Broomhead, published by Cordee in 1977. A new guide is due out in 1991/2

Approaches: When driving up the Cheddar Gorge a vast wall soars up from the tarmac of a car park on the right side of the road - don't park too close to the cliff!

The Route: A magnificent varied expedition, safe and a little on the strenuous side. If in doubt about your ability start early.

Description: From the back of the car park an obvious corner crack rises between the ivy fields. This is followed for two straightforward pitches. The third pitch continues up the crack system and over a roof to reach a belay on a rather tottery pedestal. Follow the crack to the big roofs and then traverse left in an ever-more spectacular position to a small stance beyond the nose. Move back right and climb the deep groove to a bulge that is passed on the right to reach a steep crack that leads to a small ledge in the middle of nowhere. The slab above is taken to a sapling, and then easier rock leads to the top.

The best descent is found by turning right at the top of the route and descending grass slopes towards the village before returning by way of the road.

CORONATION STREET: The view down the last pitch to the final stance, and the car park far below. Who said the route is not exposed?
Climber: Colin Binks

CORONATION STREET

The Cheddar Gorge has some great routes in a dramatic and spectacular setting. Unfortunately the place has one major drawback. For the whole of the summer as well as Easter time, almost all of the gorge is closed to climbers. This gives time for ivy and other herbage to grow back and so most of the routes have a scruffy unkempt air about them. Added to this is the fact that nowadays most people are not too interested in climbing on north-facing cliffs in the depths of winter. This is all a bit of a pity because with more reasonable access the cliff could be cleaned up properly and would doubtless become one of the most popular limestone climbing areas in the country - there is certainly no shortage of rock to go at. With correct management it would also give the grockles something else to look at when they had 'done' the various attractions in the village.

As things stand, all these acres of rock only contain one mega classic that all serious climbers have to do at some point in their career (don't get me wrong - there are plenty of brilliant climbs, but the names Coronation Street and Cheddar go together like cheese and Cheddar).

To call CORONATION STREET a rock climb is almost to belittle what is perhaps the finest outcrop route in these islands, perhaps 'expedition' is a more fitting title. For climbers used to a one or occasionally two-pitch route this really is something rather special; there are not many roadside outcrops from which retreat is really rather problematical especially when you are only half-way up it.

I remember watching the first ascent on TV as an enthusiastic teenager, and being very disappointed at the end of the broadcast when they chose the name of the new route. I felt that such an epic ascent at least deserved a grand title rather than that of a decidedly boring television series. On the other hand 'Quatermass and Godzilla meet the Creature from the Black Lagoon' doesn't quite have the same ring to it.

The route starts off amenably enough with two pitches of pleasant V.S. bridging nicely protected by the enshrouding ivy. It is possible to run these two pitches together, but the idea behind the exercise is to maximise the experience and so there is no point in rushing it. Pitch three is made of sterner stuff as steep bridging and jamming leads onwards and the exposure begins to bite. The next pitch is a bit of a gripper as you approach the big roofs and then are faced with a semi-hand traverse out left over the void. The moves are technically reasonable but the rock is undercut and the holds are slippery. It is perhaps best not to look down, and as to what is actually holding the shield of rock onto the face, your guess is as good as mine.

The stance at the far side of the shield is superb, small but comfortable and with perfect belays. A vague nagging thought crosses your mind: will the ropes actually reach the ground from here? Let's hope you don't need to find out! The next pitch is the crux and elsewhere would only be graded H.V.S., but up here it is a different matter. Luckily you can hide from the awesome drop by burying your head in the back of the groove and there are plenty of runners to calm shredded nerves as you bridge your way upwards. Then the groove closes and you are forced out into a real 'fly on the wall' situation. A glance between your feet reveals the car park filled with dinky toys surrounded by swarming ants, many of which have strange white faces craning up towards you.

Perhaps this sums up why we all climb, to put ourselves a bit above the average 'ant in the street', to add just a little spice to a humdrum world, to live and not just exist.

From the magnificently-positioned final stance the last pitch is almost a formality, a gentle cruise to cap a truly great route. I still think it deserves a better name.

43: GREAT CENTRAL ROUTE

Situation:	Chee Tor, Wye Valley, Derbyshire
Aspect:	West facing
Grade:	E1 (5a, 5c)
Length:	45m (150ft)
Equipment:	A standard rack, with a couple of extra mid-sized Friends for Pitch 2 should be adequate.
First Ascent:	R.Brown, A.Wright, winter 1963 using a considerable amount of aid. This was reduced to two points by 1970 and probably freed a short time later.
Guidebook:	*Peak Limestone, Chee Dale*, published by the British Mountaineering Council 1988.

Approaches: Chee Tor lurks in the central part of Chee Dale and is reached from parking places at either Topley Pike, Millers Dale or Wormhill. All of these routes require a 20-minute walk and although the latter approach is the shortest it is also the most complicated and leaves a bit of an uphill hike at the end of the day. With reliable friends a pleasant day's outing can be had by being dropped at Topley Pike on the A6, walking down to Chee Tor and then after doing the route continue down the valley to Millers Dale.

The Route: A long first pitch leads to a short, sharp safe crux, followed by more good climbing above.

Description: As the name suggests the route takes a central line on Chee Tor. The flake crack taken by the second pitch of the route is the most conspicuous feature on the cliff, above the horizontal break of the GIRDLE. Start below and left of the upper flake at a prominent shallow groove containing a small tree at ten metres.

The first pitch gives good H.V.S.

GREAT CENTRAL ROUTE: The lower pitch gives fine HVS climbing, with the bulge that protects the upper groove visible high above.
Climber: Ian Adamson

and a selection of new-fangled nuts. From a good belay on solid threads the crux of the climb can be addressed. The bulge is tough but perfectly protected and once over it the upper crack line gives sustained and quite strenuous climbing, until you pull up to safety in the trees at the top of the cliff.

GREAT CENTRAL ROUTE

Chee Tor is a bit of an odd spot. It is immensely popular, and a good summer weekend sees the cliff littered with teams all getting stuck into their own particular thing. Unfortunately this popularity means that the bottom of the cliff has become heavily churned and is somewhat reminiscent of an allotment vegetable patch. In high summer the whole dale sprouts giant rhubarb plants (butterbur) and if the air is at all humid there is more than a passing resemblance to the more remote parts of the East Indies. Add to this the fact that the vast majority of the routes only go halfway up the cliff, and you realise they must be pretty damn good to get all that attention. In reality the climbing is of exceptional quality and the few routes that manage to make it the full height of the cliff are real treats, especially if sampled on a spring evening when the dale is quiet and the sun shines full on the tor.

Of these GREAT CENTRAL is the easiest and perhaps the 'most classic' in a traditional sense, taking a strong central line and having an interesting history. It was chosen as the line of the first assault on the wide white wall of the tor and plenty of aid was used to ensure success, including a rudimentary bolt.

The first pitch would be a classic H.V.S. on a lesser cliff, but here it serves as a lead into and a warm-up for the technicalities of the second pitch. The line is obvious, a long sweeping curve up the crag, marked by a stout little tree and a long ragged flake crack. The stance is small and comfortable and the belays are true confidence givers. The grade of the second pitch reveals all, if it is both E1 and 5c then it must also be short-lived and with perfect protection. It is true to form. The problem is manifest, above beckons the half-hidden delights of a bridging groove with a juicy flake in its depths. Between you and this Shangri La is a little pig of a bulge (a piglet), a nasty, smooth and altogether unhelpful critter. On this occasion though there are abso-

climbing following the obvious line that climbs straight up for ten metres and then trends to the right to reach the base of a large flake, which leads to the bedding plane. The climbing is quite fingery and steeper than it looks (a common phenomenon on Chee Tor) but there is plenty of protection from a few old-fangled pegs

lutely no excuses. Your second is at hand, the protection is rather better than perfect, and this really is a one move wonder. If you are confident then you can ignore the old wilting bolt and any other bits of rotting crap that still hang from the bulge. If you are attempting your first 5c, then clip everything and add a few extra back-ups. Either way just do it, start on the right then make a difficult pull up and left. Once bridged past the offending animal, the world opens out before you. Steady progress is guaranteed up the groove, onwards and upwards into that rarely visited 'garden' on top of the cliff. You can sit amongst the spring flowers and ponder on the name of the climb, it is undeniably a 'great central route'.

44:
MANZOKU

Situation:	Stennis Head, Range East, Castlemartin, South Pembroke
Aspect:	South-west facing
Grade:	E1 (5b)
Length:	40m (130ft)
Equipment:	A standard rack with extra mid-range wires.
First Ascent:	K.Wilkinson, S.Jones, 27th August 1978
Guidebook:	*Pembroke* by Jon de Montjoye and Mike Harber published by the Climbers' Club in 1985. A new guide is due out in 1991.

MANZOKU: The climbing is sustained, the rock wonderful and the setting superb; Pembroke at its best.
Climbers: Dave and Christine Hall

Approaches: From the car park for St Govan's Chapel pass over the stile into the range, providing the red flags are not flying, and follow the coastal path westwards. Pass the impressive inlet of Stennis Ford then turn left and head out towards the sea. Rather to the right of the tip of the headland is an easy rocky ramp that gives a scrambly descent to ledges below the cliffs.

The Route: A steep strenuous pitch that is well protected. The rock is nothing short of magnificent.

Description: At the foot of the descent rake is a shallow, rounded cave at five metres. Start below and right of this and climb rightwards to ledges. Continue up the wall until the groove filled with overlaps on the left can be gained. This is followed to the top and is very sustained.

MANZOKU

Stennis Head is a very popular venue when the weather in Pembroke is out of sorts. It is non-tidal, though the odd rogue wave occasionally surprises folk with a cold shower, and the whole place is well sheltered from winds that blow out of northern skies. The crag is also useful when the range is closed during the day but open in the evening. It is possible to scoot in for a couple of quick routes in the rays of the setting sun before nipping off to the St Govan's Inn for a coffee or whatever takes your fancy.

MANZOKU is the best route on the left side of the cliff and it gives a long sustained pitch on superb rock and with protection to match. In these days of 'E big numbers' it is easy to forget that the E stands for extremely severe, and that not too many years ago some of these lowly E1s were amongst the hardest routes in the country. MANZOKU is a route that reminds you that E1 routes can still be substantial undertakings.

The start is up and at you straightaway, no easy lead-in for this boy. Steep moves on sharp holds take you rapidly up a leaning wall and into a situation of instant seriousness. It would be nice to press on, but runners have to be placed at regular intervals to guard against the possibility of a ground fall due to one of the multitudinous razor-edged holds snapping. Undercut ledges arrive and it is possible to take stock. A short wall leads to a groove bearing away to your right. This is COOL FOR CATS, another fine route but not quite in the mould of MANZOKU. Left of this is another groove that appears to be brimming over with small overhangs. Access to the groove is awkward and once ensconced it proves to be very sustained. The expected jugs fail to materialise and progress is via a sustained series of moves on layaway edges, undercuts and small fingerholds. Fortunately there is plenty of protection, always assuming that you have not used all the required runners lower down. The rock on this wind-blasted and wave-battered headland is fantastic stuff, a filigree of razor-edged pockets and flakes. It is so rough that if you fell you would probably suffer 'the death of a thousand cuts' and would need to be peeled from the rock like so much Velcro.

When you finally reach the good holds in the easy groove at the top of the cliff you know you have not done just any old E1, this is an Extremely Severe rock climb and it certainly feels like it.

45: LIGHT

Situation:	Gordale Scar, Yorkshire
Aspect:	North facing
Grade:	E1 (5c, 5a)
Length:	35m (120ft)
Equipment:	A standard rack with an extra couple of large wires.
First Ascent:	E.Wallis, D.Hadlum, with a little aid on the initial crack, 1964.
Guidebook:	*Yorkshire Limestone* published by the Yorkshire Mountaineering Club in 1985.

Approaches: From the village of Malham a minor road is signposted to Gordale Scar, two kilometres to the east. There is limited parking by the old bridge and the path to the cliff is obvious. Once inside the gorge scramble up the side of the lower waterfall and turn right to reach the base of a huge black chimney. LIGHT takes the crack and groove line in the right wall of the chimney.

The Route: A tough but safe crux is followed by much easier climbing in a dramatic setting.

Description: Climb the initial leaning crack with considerable difficulty and perfect protection to a small stance. Access to the big corner is barred by a bulging wall (actually the front of a huge flake), but once gained it gives good jamming to a roof. Traverse to the left into ever-more impressive territory and escape into the chimney which is followed to the top and a steep grassy exit.

LIGHT

Gordale Scar is a geological marvel, a great ragged gash slashing into the hillside, the towering walls leaning together in a conspiratorial attempt to cut out the daylight. In all but the kindest of weather it is a really

LIGHT: The initial crack is tough when dry, and its gloomy setting means it is often damp. In these conditions it becomes a real battle.
Climbers: Nigel Baker and Graham Parkes

grim place to climb, dark and foreboding with the thundering of the waterfall and invariably a keen wind seeking out every corner of the gorge. Further into the gorge the setting becomes ever-more bizarre. A natural tufa ladder leads up between cascades and overhead the walls appear almost to touch, while water spouts from a great hole in the rock; the whole atmosphere is like caving, with the roof taken off.

LIGHT takes an impressive line in the eye of this geological maelstrom, starting at the foot of a slippery slope that leads up into an awesome chimney. This great black rift (DARKNESS) is one of the few routes in the present guide that gets the dreaded Black Spot, an indication that the climb is to be avoided at all costs. When we did the route a few years ago (in a drought) it proved to be a fascinating blend of caving and climbing, but no doubt the Black Spot will ensure it never gets done again, such is the power of the guidebook writer.

The lower section of LIGHT hardly ever sees the sun and is often damp. Under these conditions the start is truly desperate and a traditional aid nut may be justified. In the dry, a couple of fierce but very safe moves reach good holds and a stance just a little higher. It is the kind of climbing that is best done speedily, but a rapid approach ensures that the runners get left a long way behind very quickly, and the possibility of a long ground fall must be borne in mind.

Compared to the start, the rest of the route is easy, but it does not feel it. A short leaning wall, best tackled on the left (3 peg runners) leads to a long corner system. The rock is steep, the climbing a touch strenuous and the whole place extremely gripping. When I first did LIGHT in 1972, (then graded Yorkshire H.V.S.) we were having our own mini epic on this second pitch when a wild-haired bespectacled figure came winging around the corner on the end of a rope. "Ah do", said Livesey, for it was he, the super hero we had all heard about. "Yu'd better take care, somebody was killed there last week. Fell all the way to the ground," he said before shooting back off round the corner to work on the first (almost) free ascent of DELIVERANCE. That was all we needed! The ascent of the rest of the route was marked by extreme slowness and the great number of runners we felt justified in placing. In the event we survived the experience, and felt that we had done our bit of character building for the day. On emerging from the darkness we definitely felt we had seen the light.

46: SHAPE UP

Situation:	Huntsman's Leap, Range East, Castlemartin, South Pembroke
Aspect:	West facing
Grade:	E2 (5b)
Length:	40m (130ft)
Equipment:	A normal rack.
First Ascent:	A.Sharp, P.Lewis, S.Lewis, 17th June 1978
Guidebook:	*Pembroke* by Jon de Montjoye and Mike Harber published by the Climbers' Club in 1985. A new guide is due out in 1991.

Approaches: From the car park at St Govan's Chapel, cross the stile and walk westwards into the range. After a short distance comes the impressive inlet of Stennis Ford and just a little further is the narrower inlet of Huntsman's Leap. Access is by a 35-metre abseil from a cluster of spikes at the point of arrival.

The Route: A long sustained pitch, technically reasonable and with great protection.

Description: The abseil takes you down a steep smooth slab. The first feature to the right of this is a shallow groove leading into a deeper corner near the cliff top. An awkward start gives way to easier climbing until the groove steepens. A bulge is passed with difficulty, then good cracks are followed into the corner. This is bridged past solid threads to a grassy exit. Stake belays.

SHAPE UP

Aficionados of 'the Leap' are dismissive of SHAPE UP, considering it unworthy of so grand a setting. In reality it is one of the most popular routes in this glorified hole in the ground, and it would be the classic of many a lesser cliff. Part of the route's popularity stems from the fact that on the first visit into Huntsman's most folk can't wait to get out again, and so they have a quick look round and then shoot up the route as fast as they can. In reality it deserves better treatment.

The base of the groove is slightly undercut and the best way to get started is to layback the right edge of it rapidly to better holds. Easier climbing and the odd loose block lead to where things steepen up. Fortunately there are plenty of good run-

SHAPE UP: At the top of the initial groove a series of difficult moves lead up and left to reach deep cracks and easier climbing.
Climber: Pete Anderson

ners to protect a precarious series of moves up to a big undercut hole and a swing left onto the face above. This looks tough but is seamed with deep cracks that provide good holds and perfect runner slots. A little higher you climb into the base of a water-worn groove which gives straightforward bridging protected by some solid threads.

From the other side of the Leap the exits to all the routes on this side look horrendous, as rock gives way to grass with no perceptible change in angle. On closer acquaintance things are rather more friendly, though care is needed, especially in the wet. Good steps have been created in the grass from the passing of many hands and feet and you can exit easily leftwards, back to the cliff top. There are some rather corroded iron stakes in the grass to belay on and it is worth using at least two of them, and sitting well back from the edge unless you have an 'undying' faith in your second's ability.

SHAPE UP is quite a straightforward undertaking for the grade but it is a great introduction to climbing in Huntsman's Leap. If it is your first route down there, savour the experience, and have no doubts, it will not be your last.

47: A TOUCH OF CLASS

Situation:	Craig Arthur, the Eglwyseg Valley, Clwyd, North Wales
Aspect:	West facing
Grade:	E2 (5b, 5a, 5a)
Length:	70m (230ft)
Equipment:	A standard rack is adequate.
First Ascent:	S.Cathcart, P.Stott, 13th October 1980
Guidebook:	*Clwyd Limestone* by Stuart Cathcart, published by Cicerone Press in 1983. A new guide is under preparation.

Approaches: From the town of Llangollen a minor road, starting just to the east of the Bridge End Hotel, runs up the Eglwyseg Valley. This is followed for six kilometres to the ford at World's End; park here or just down the road on the grass verge. A short distance below the ford a path crosses a stile and heads into the forest. This is followed through the trees and out onto the open hillside beyond. A little further on the edge of the cliff appears up on the left, and a steep path leads up scree to the cliff. Twenty minutes from the car.

The Route: A wandering climb taking the easiest line up the left side of the cliff. Protection is good, though some of the rock on pitch two requires careful handling.

Description: Near the left side of the cliff is a prominent clean cut corner leading to a flat roof. Start directly below this and climb easily onto a ledge. Follow the ledge rightwards until it ends then make steep moves up the wall to a peg. Traverse the thin break to the right until it is possible to step down onto a slab, which is climbed to a foothold stance and peg belay. Move right and climb into the hanging corner, passing a thread. Swing right onto the rib then climb direct to a tree belay. Traverse out

left onto the exposed rib and finish up easier rock. Belay well back.

A TOUCH OF CLASS

Craig Arthur is a massive rambling cliff, and it has always been rather neglected. Back in the early 60s a few of the more impressive parts of the cliff were pegged and later in the same decade, a few of the easier lines were climbed largely free. Throughout the 70s and early 80s Stuart Cathcart had the crag to himself and picked off a fine set of routes. Even today in the crowded and rock-hungry 90s it is unusual to see another party on the cliff, which, when you consider it is as extensive as Kilnsey Crag for example, is rather strange. The setting is high and wild with a dramatic outlook and although some of the rock is a bit rattly most of it is fine compact limestone. The reason for the neglect is in fact quite simply one of fashion. There are a number of routes of a variety of grades that are well worth the walk up, either on a day when you fancy getting away from the crowds or perhaps to salvage something out of a wet weekend in Wales on your way home.

A TOUCH OF CLASS provides a good introduction to the cliff and starts conveniently at the point where the approach path meets the rock. The route skirts away to the right to avoid the band of overhangs directly above. A ledge is followed out right and where it ends a steep and quite bold wall is climbed to an old peg complete with a bunch of grey tatty string. Above are more overhangs but a fingery seam continues the traversing theme and it sprouts a good solid peg a couple of moves away. An intricate series of moves leads out past the peg until it is possible to step down onto a hidden slab. At the top of this is an excellent (though solitary) peg for a belay, which can be backed-up by large nuts behind a flake. Although only 15 or so metres from the ground, the tiny stance and the steep grass below the cliff accentuate the exposure; you really feel a long, long way up.

To the right of the stance a groove finally breaks through the band of overhangs that have barred upward progress thus far. It is entered by a strenuous pull on holds that could really do with gentle treatment. A good thread is reached and a pull out right on more 'wobblies' leads to a bent and battered tree. A little higher is a fine stance below yet more overhangs and another tree that forms a solid belay.

The final pitch traverses out left via a couple of tricky moves (small wires in a thin vertical crack) until it is possible to step down onto a minute ledge on the edge of all things. At last the upward view is not hemmed in by frowning roofs and a juggy wall leads to the well-cropped grass on the cliff top. The climb is a classic very much in a traditional mould, with a little loose rock to add spice and a devious but natural line. It well deserves its name.

A TOUCH OF CLASS: "The final pitch traverses out until it is possible to step down onto a ledge on the edge of all things."
Climber: Chris Craggs

48: CHIMES OF FREEDOM

Situation:	West face of Mowing Word, South Pembroke. *Note: There is an access restriction on the cliff. It is closed to climbers from 1st March to the 31st July to protect nesting sea birds.*
Aspect:	West facing
Grade:	E2 (5b)
Length:	40m (130ft)
Equipment:	A standard rack with a few long slings to reduce rope drag.
First Ascent:	P.Littlejohn, J.Garner, May 1976
Guidebook:	*Pembroke* by Jon de Montjoye and Mike Harber published by the Climbers' Club in 1985. A new guide is due out in 1991.

Approaches: The nearest car parking is at Broad Haven just to the south of Bosherston. Cross the beach and then head eastwards until past the deep slash of Raming Hole. The long wall of Mowing Word is visible further to the east and is reached in about 20 minutes from the car. The simplest access is to abseil down DIEDRE SUD in the centre of the cliff though great care is needed if there are parties below. From the base of DIEDRE SUD traverse to the left for ten metres (or walk along the beach if you are really lucky) and take a stance below a double overhang in a corner, half-way up the cliff.

The Route: A superb pitch, steep and intimidating but well-protected and not too hard.

Description: Follow a thin crack and then a corner up to the roofs. Climb over the first overhang then swing right to a prominent block foothold. Step up and make difficult moves back left to the base of a hanging groove. This is awkward to start but soon

CHIMES OF FREEDOM:
Alone on the west face of Mowing Word, a calm sea, the hot sun and stupendous climbing.
Climbers: Chris Craggs and Colin Binks

leads to a fine face crack and the top.

CHIMES OF FREEDOM

Mowing Word is a fine cliff with an excellent selection of mid-grade routes. Unfortunately the crag is closed for the spring and early summer to allow sea birds a little peace and quiet. It is also very tidal, a calm sea and low water being required to get to the foot of many of the routes. Finally it faces due west and receives any incoming bad weather 'full frontal'.

Despite these problems, and a relatively long walk in (at least, by Pembroke standards) there are several routes that are an absolute must. CHIMES OF FREEDOM is the best of the half a dozen or so routes in the E1/2 category, though don't take my word for it, they are all well worth doing.

From the bottom of DIEDRE SUD an undercut traverse around the corner to the left on soft crunchy rock leads to a fine grey wall directly below the roofed-in corner the route follows. If you happen to snap a hold off and fall in, the water is not too deep and it is only a short wade to the beach, though how you are going to get back to the cliff top with soaked boots and chalk bag remains to be seen.

It is necessary to set up a hanging belay below the groove and find a way of keeping the ropes out of the water, as there is not a lot in the way of sizable ledges. Once organised it is time to get stuck into the real climbing. The lower section of the route is as good as it looks, wonderful grey rock equipped with both sharp-edged holds and superb friction allows you to make rapid progress up into the hanging groove. Easy bridging takes you ever-higher towards the great flat roof that totally blocks access to whatever delights (or horrors) lie hidden above. From right under the overhang it is possible to lean around the first roof and make a rapid hand traverse out to the right onto a wedged block. The second band of overhangs are a little trickier to overcome, especially if you are long in the legs. The wall you have to traverse is less than a metre high and totally undercut. A rather reckless layback, in a position of some exposure, is the best way to get into the foot of the continuation groove. The second has now disappeared below the roof and you are faced with a leaning corner that narrows as it rises. The exposure is becoming considerable and it is still a long way to the top. The crack in the back of the groove is a bit of a disappointment in that it takes runners but not fingers, so precarious bridging is required to make progress. As the corner fizzles out completely you are squeezed onto the hanging face on the left. The upward view is now more promising, a good crack that takes any number of runners and has good holds runs all the way to the cliff top.

Relish these last few steps. Below you is just a little rock and far beyond that the pale blue sea. Above you lies the 'real world' and all its worries, but for a little while you have heard the chimes of freedom carried on the west wind. You will be back.

49:
CRACKED
ACTOR

Situation: Trowbarrow Quarry, Carnforth, North Lancashire
Note: Access to the quarry is occasionally restricted. Be discreet and leave graciously if asked to do so.
Aspect: South-west facing
Grade: E2 (5c)
Length: 35m (115ft)
Equipment: A standard rack.
First Ascent: A.Evans and party 1975
Guidebook: *Lancashire and the North West* by Phil Kelly and Dave Cronshaw. Published by Cicerone Press in 1989.

Approaches: Trowbarrow Quarry is four kilometres to the north-west of Carnforth. A minor road is followed until just before Silverdale Station where a right fork is taken. A kilometre along this road is a wood; park in one of the lay-bys and pass through the trees on the left into the quarry, five minutes away. At the far right-hand side of the quarry is the crack seamed Main Wall.

The Route: A fine face crack with perfect protection.

Description: The wall is split by three main cracks. Rising leftwards from the wide left-hand crack is a thin seam. Climb up to the base of the wide section of the main crack then head left up the much thinner crack. The lower section is the crux and offers sustained finger jamming. Despite the upward view the holds get better as height is gained.

CRACKED ACTOR

Trowbarrow used to be very much the preserve of a few local climbers, there being nothing there worth travelling any distance for. It did contain a great rippled sheet of rock, peppered with fossils and on the right side of vertical but it was blatantly protectionless and was dismissed as unclimbable. The owners of the quarry are required by law to remove a quantity of rock on a regular basis to maintain the quarry's working status. In 1970 they duly blasted the base of the blank wall and when the dust settled it had been transformed. The whole sheet of rock was riven from top to bottom by a series of cracks. It looked as if the whole thing was on the point of collapse but 20 years later it is still standing. Initially the crack lines were loose and dusty but time and traffic have cleaned them up and nowadays they offer a fine set of climbs across a range of grades.

The present surface of the rock was once the muddy floor of a shallow tropical ocean, where a wide variety of creatures crawled and burrowed. Some catastrophe befell this community (perhaps a volcanic ash eruption that buried them all) and they all died, but instead of rotting they were preserved as fossils. As time passed the mud turned to rock and much later it was bent and buckled, slowly being forced up to its present angle. The quarrymen came and first unearthed the sheet of rock and finally filled it full of cracks - many thanks to all involved! The fossils now provide good footholds but are rather inclined to part company with the face - be warned.

CRACKED ACTOR takes one of the thinnest crack lines on the face and actually starts almost half-way up the cliff. This thin crack is approached by the easy lower section of ALADDINSANE. When the main

CRACKED ACTOR: Engrossed with the main difficulties of the pitch, sustained but well protected finger jamming.
Climber: Ed Wood

50: XIMENES

Situation:	Boulder Ruckle East, Swanage, Dorset
Aspect:	South facing
Grade:	E2 (5b, 5b)
Length:	35m (115ft)
Equipment:	A standard rack.
First Ascent:	G.Smith, R.J.Crewe (5 points of aid), 4th September 1971
First Free Ascent:	K.Turner, N.Buckley, D.Over, Summer 1977
Guidebook:	*Swanage* by Gordon Jenkin, published by the Climbers' Club in 1986.

Approaches: From the car park at Durlston Head Country Park to the south of Swanage, follow the tarmac road to the lighthouse then continue westwards along the coastal path. The least complicated method of access to XIMENES is via the abseil down Marmolata Buttress. This is the prominent square pillar of rock that protrudes from the cliff face 450 metres west of the lighthouse. Abseil down the east face of the buttress and scramble back eastwards for 65 metres (not at high tide or in heavy seas) to a prominent hand crack splitting the right edge of a massive double roof.

The Route: An intimidating route offering strenuous well-protected climbing up a very steep piece of rock.

Description: Climb a narrowing chimney crack to the first overhang and cross this with difficulty on painful jams to reach a restricted stance. Pull over the second roof on good holds and climb the corner to a third roof. Either pull over this or climb rightwards up a flake then trend back left. Easier climbing leads to the top of the cliff. Belay amongst blocks a short distance back.

XIMENES

Sea cliff climbing is perhaps one of the more bizarre aspects of our sport. The logic

climbing is sustained and hard. When all looks lost good face holds appear out on the left. A quick swing on these and the situation eases, a ladder of good jugs leads all the way to the crest of the wall.

This is a man-made route in every sense of the expression, but remains a great climb in spite of its dubious origins. Do it and do it quickly, for it may not be there tomorrow.

crack turns wide and nasty-looking it is time to get out left onto the face. The upward view is distinctly intimidating as the rock looks smooth and the crack is difficult to pick out from below. Protection is excellent which is a good job because the

XIMENES: The crux involves difficult moves on painfully knobbly jams to get established in the crack.
Climber: Graham Parkes

going down to deliberately seek out a difficult way back to the top, most observers would shake their heads in disbelief and wander off muttering something about madmen. In reality sea cliffs can offer climbing as good as any in more 'normal' settings. One minute you are at the cliff top, with walkers and day trippers, and a holiday atmosphere and the next you are cut off in your own private world with only one way out. For me this instant contrast is one of the great attractions of sea cliffs.

Swanage has a lot of rock to go at and the base of the cliffs is a very private place. The convexed and rather unstable cliff top means that no one can peer over and see what you are up to. Added to this, the generally flat fronted nature of the face means that there are no projecting buttresses to act as vantage points. This privacy is great - that is, as long as you don't need rescuing.

XIMENES is a fine route, a well-hidden sea cliff classic that is only visible from close quarters. A straightforward chimney leads to the first and biggest overhang. There are excellent jams available in the vertical crack around the lip but they are very knobbly and a high resistance to pain is an asset. Gradually it is possible to work the jams up the crack, but eventually your feet have to follow. The simplest method is to use your knees (tut tut), though this is far from elegant. It is perhaps a good job you can't be seen from above at this point. A little higher an uncomfortable stance is available squatted within a horizontal break, below the second roof. An assortment of belay nuts can be placed in the crack in the roof of the slot.

The overhang that blocks the upward view is passed on good holds, to reach a groove below yet another overhang. By now the downward view has become quite impressive, though the upward one is rather more worrying. Fortunately more good holds are available for the stiff pull into the short finishing groove. Some distance up the bank are large solid blocks to tie onto. The tourists continue to wander along the coastal path (where are they all going?), and occasionally one of them will attempt to peer over and see where your ropes are disappearing to before giving you a disbelieving look and wandering on. Madmen? Maybe, but what a fine kind of madness.

of wanting to climb a piece of rock 'because it is there' can be seen by the more adventurous members of the general public, but to abseil down a cliff just so that you can climb back up again is stretching things just a bit too far. If they knew you were

51: DEEP SPACE

Situation:	Mother Carey's Kitchen, Lydstep, South Pembroke
Aspect:	East facing, though the route does not see a lot of sun.
Grade:	E2 (5b, 5a)
Length:	45m (150ft)
Equipment:	A normal rack and a good selection of long slings.
First Ascent:	P.Littlejohn, D.Garner, May 1975
Guidebook:	*Pembroke* by Jon de Montjoye and Mike Harber, published by the Climbers' Club in 1985. A new two-volume guide is due out in 1992.

Approaches: DEEP SPACE is to be found on Mother Carey's Kitchen, which is the premier cliff at Lydstep. There is a car park on the headland which is approached through a caravan site. The cliff is to be found five minutes away from, and slightly to the east of the car park. It is quite common to accidentally walk past the cliff though the top is recognisable by a prominent tower, from which a 40m (130ft) abseil takes you to the foot of the cliff. This is inaccessible at high tide or in heavy seas.

If you do overshoot the cliff as you walk along the coastal path, a quick look over your right shoulder will reveal the huge black chimney of DEEP SPACE.

The Route:

A thrilling trip to the gates of hell and back. Technically reasonable climbing with good protection, but strenuous and intimidating.

Description: From the foot of the abseil you will encounter a great archway leading into the depths of the cliff, passing through this and turning right you come back to daylight inside a massive towering chimney that narrows as it rises to become blocked just short of the surface. The route ascends the landward wall of this cleft (yes, the side with a huge overhang half-way up it) and starts where the wall becomes undercut, just before the chimney opens out.

The first pitch starts by pulling left onto the wall and then trending slightly rightwards following discontinuous crack systems, until level with a shallow cave on the right. This is reached by a short strenuous traverse and offers a restricted stance complete with excellent thread belays. The intimidating second pitch crosses the roof to get into the chimney which is followed in an impressive setting to the cliff top.

DEEP SPACE

Classic climbs take many forms. Often it is the attitude of the climber that makes a route great experience, as much as the actual quality of the climb itself.

There are folks who would describe Cloggy's GREAT SLAB as a total 'bag of rubbish', with a wandering line, too much easy climbing and a smattering of loose rock and vegetation to cap it all. This same person would probably choose a short vicious Cheedale pitch as his current classic. The pitch would probably have bolt protection, excavated holds and a chain to grab for and lower off from, just below where the rock turns to grass. Doubtless there are plenty of people who would argue the opposite, and both schools of thought are entitled to their points of view. Despite this variance of ideas there are some routes that are, and always will be, true classics, whether you claw your way up them by the skin of your teeth or treat them as a pleasant solo at the end of a hard day's climbing. The overwhelming quality shines through, they are routes that quite simply just have to be done, and DEEP SPACE is one of these.

The position of the route is pure Gothic brilliance, as sinister and sombre a setting as any Boris Karloff film, like the gateway to hell flanked by mighty portals that strain together in an effort to keep the sun out of this gloom-ridden world. When the tide is out and the day draws to an end, a hush falls over the cave and you can almost hear the soft flapping of leathery wings as the bats prepare to release themselves onto an unsuspecting world.

DEEP SPACE:
"The first pitch looks damp and often is though this is offset, at least in part, by the exemplary roughness of the rock."
Climber: Jim Rubery

The first pitch always looks damp and often is, though this is offset, at least in part, by the exemplary roughness of the rock. The climbing is steep and intimidating rather than technically difficult, and good layaways mixed with rugged jams and the odd jug allow steady progress. Many of the fluted pillars have holes through them and so plenty of good solid threads are available to bolster your morale if it starts to flag. A short strenuous traverse out to the right gains an odd scooped cave whose inside resembles the convoluted interior of a skull. Once again there are good thick threads to allay any fears you may have about the possibility of being pulled backwards into the void below you.

The second pitch looks ludicrous for the given grade of 5a. An almost horizontal roof runs out for about three metres and round the lip, hidden from view, lurks the chimney which you have to gain. The far wall of the chimney helps to cut out the light and accentuate the position you are in as it drops towards the sea. When you are suitably fired-up the roof has to be addressed. Good holds lead out slightly leftwards passing a couple of solid threads, whether you try to stop and put them in or press on (in blind panic?) is up to you. The moves are all straightforward but the inverted position will soon start to tell on your arms. As you pass the lip the far wall comes within reach and you can drop across into a back and foot position, from harassing strenuosity to a no-hands rest in a matter of seconds - unless you miss the opposite wall of course!

The remainder of the route is classical backing and footing up the parallel sided cleft. It is a technique that appears in every climbing textbook but this is the only place I have ever used it in earnest. There are not many runners but the climbing is only about V.Diff, (try telling your legs that) and the situations are dramatic, the ropes dropping in a great loop to your second hidden somewhere below the roofs and the sea far below that in the shady depths. The final obstacle is a great block wedged in the chimney, it is tricky and exposed to pass it on the outside, though if you have had enough you can continue the backing and footing in the gloom and step onto it from the back. Above this a short corner leads to golden sunshine, sweet-smelling flowers and the land of the living - blessed salvation.

52: CARNAGE

Situation:	The Right Wing, Malham Cove, Yorkshire
Aspect:	South-west facing
Grade:	E2 (5b, 6b or 5b with one aid peg)
Length:	46m (150ft)
Equipment:	A standard rack with a few extra small and mid-range wires.
First Ascent:	R.Barley, T.Barley, 1966 (one point of aid)
First Free Ascent:	R.Fawcett, 1979
Guidebook:	*Yorkshire Limestone* published by the Yorkshire Mountaineering Club in 1985.

Approaches: Park in Malham village and follow the signed and well-made footpath to the Cove. Cross the stream and scramble up the foot of the right wing. A narrow path leads back leftwards and the route starts behind the largest tree standing a short distance away from the rock. About 15 minutes from the car.

The Route: A two-pitch route of increasing interest and quality. The top pitch is usually considered to be the crux and is fingery but well-protected.

Description: From the tree (which may be used as a belay in case of a tumble) scramble up grass to the base of the wall. Up this steeply to ledges then trend slightly to the right to a shallow depression. From here traverse to the left, with hands above the bulge until it is possible to climb straight up to vegetation and then a cave stance with a tree belay. For pitch two move right to find a peg over the lip of the roof. Use this (or spit on it) then climb straight up the wall to a prominent horizontal break. Swing right and move up to gain a small ledge then step right to finish.

CARNAGE

When *Hard Rock* was published in 1975 it contained seven free routes on British limestone and CARNAGE was one of the chosen few. This was recommendation enough and immediately the route was on every hot rocker's hit list. In the intervening years the grade has gone up from H.V.S. to E2 (if only we had known we were that good) and the route's reputation for quality has remained undiminished. CARNAGE'S sister route CARNAGE LEFT HAND, which starts far away on the right!! has gained something of a reputation as a bit of a classic, but in reality it is definitely the poor relation of the pair, blessed with a wandering line and with the best climbing belonging to the parent route.

There must be a reason why the route is such a gem and as with all classic climbs it is an amalgam of features that makes the outing an all-time great. The line is a natural weakness up an impressive part of the cliff, the climbing is sustained and continuously interesting, and protection is good enough where it matters to allow the route to be enjoyed. Perhaps most important of all is the way the route increases in interest and quality as height is gained with a superb climax high up in an ocean of wonderful grey rock.

The start of the first pitch is a bit of a gripper as from the tree a short bank of steep grass leads to the foot of the rock. The wall is slightly bulging and is peppered with small flat fingerholds. Unfortunately there are no runners hereabouts so a modicum of courage is needed. It used to be traditional to carry a large screwdriver from the car and push it down the back of the grassy ledge then drape a sling over it. Nowadays strong fingers deal with the wall quickly and better holds soon arrive. The rest of the pitch is interesting as it finds a sneaky way up the wall. It climbs up right first (peg) and then heads away with a cunning leftwards traverse on a set of most unusual fingerholds (peg to the left). A steep (and sometimes wet) wall then leads to a big tree and a long, low cave where you can sit for a while and hide from the snarling exposure.

The second pitch of CARNAGE is the one to write home about. If you lean out of the cave you catch a glimpse of a steep, light grey wall capped by a big black overhang. Individual features are difficult to pick out from here so it is down to work.

climbing elsewhere and certainly should not clip the peg as a runner!

The wall gives sustained climbing on small, sharp fingerholds on perhaps the best quality limestone in the country. The rock here is so good it is used as a benchmark for other areas, ("Ah, but is it as good as the top of Malham?"). There are plenty of small wire runners available if you can stop to place them. If not, press on to a long reach for a good horizontal break where Friend runners and a rest of sorts are available. If you make a mess of these moves you might fall a long way and will certainly give yourself and your unwitting second a hell of a fright, but you can rest assured that you won't hit anything. From the break the LEFT HAND sneaks away into the prominent corner but such an easy option is not for us. A move up and right gains a tiny corner with a small ledge at its top. This is the famous (or should it be infamous) mantelshelf. If you really want to, you can do the move as a mantelshelf, I suppose you could also do it blindfold and with one hand tied behind your back if you really want an epic. If you don't fancy any of these options a long reach for a good finger jam in the back wall and a high step will see you through, crouched below the capping roof. A couple of tricky moves out right gets you into a final easy corner which leads to the putting-green-quality grass on top of the cliff. Large threads are available in a rock wall a short distance back.

When your second arrives it might be worth a walk down to see exactly what all those folks are doing on that little wall above the stream. They all appear to be involved in a funny blend of aid and free climbing, but whatever they are up to, I am sure they are not having as great a day out as you are!

CARNAGE: The crux moves where gaining a standing position on a small ledge proves problematical. The photograph shows that the title "mantelshelf" is something of a misnomer.
Climber: Dave Spencer

The superb wall has an access problem all of its own in the shape of a continuous overhang that forms the roof of the belay cave. A short traverse to the right should find a peg lurking around the lip. The first good holds are some distance above so it is usual to stand in a short sling. A bit of thrashing is traditional until you find the jug (hint: it's up and left) and cut loose to get established on the wall. If you do these moves free at 6b you should really be

53: DIEDRE

Situation: Kilnsey Crag, Wharfedale, Yorkshire
Aspect: East facing
Grade: E2 (5a, 5b)
Length: 50m (165ft)
Equipment: A normal rack with a few extra large wires and a couple of longer slings is adequate.
First Ascent: J.Sumner, D.Adcock, 1956 (aid)
First Free Ascent: P.Livesey, J.Sheard, 1971
Guidebook: *Yorkshire Limestone*, published by the Yorkshire Mountaineering Club in 1985.

Approaches: Kilnsey Crag is in upper Wharfedale about ten kilometres (seven miles) north of Grassington and almost overhangs the B6160. Access is limited to weekdays because of weekend 'gawpers' blocking the road to essential services. Permission to climb must be sought from the farm opposite the northern end of the crag (North Cote). Please park sensibly, a large lay-by is available just north of the cliff. PLEASE leave no litter and leave the dog at home as there are occasionally farm animals below the cliff.

The Route: A two-pitch climb up a major natural feature. The rock is good as is the protection. The top pitch is strenuous.

Description: DIEDRE takes the obvious right-angled corner that runs the full height of the crag. The first pitch gives straightforward if rather floral bridging, with good protection, to a small stance below the bulging upper section of the corner. The second pitch continues up to the bulge which is passed awkwardly to reach better holds and a solid thread runner. The corner above looks uninviting so make difficult moves out left to reach a crack and a tree. More tricky climbing leads back into the main corner which is steep to start but eases rapidly. There are peg belays hidden in the grass bank above the route, but if you cannot find them, nuts in the small outcrops that litter the area will have to do.

DIEDRE: The crux moves involve escaping out left from the corner to gain easier rock and then a stout tree. a traverse along the upper break then leads back into the corner.
Climbers: Chris Craggs and Graham Parkes

DIEDRE

The great right-angled corner that soars up the right side of Kilnsey Crag is one of the biggest natural lines on British limestone. From a distance it appears as if two huge sheets of clean grey rock meet in a great blank corner, but on closer acquaintance the first impressions are a little disappointing. Being such a major feature the corner is slow to dry out and the whole thing appears to be a bit of a vertical herb garden, with a variety of plant life sprouting from the walls and the bed of the groove. Don't let these initial doubts cloud your judgement; as soon as you get on the pitch the greenery slides out of focus and the good rock grabs your attention. As you absorb yourself in the pleasant bridging the ground recedes, the runners drop in with satisfying regularity and gradually you realise the whole pitch is pretty steep. A neat little footledge arrives with a selection of belays to suit all tastes. The outlook from the stance is 'Herriot country' to perfection: rank upon rank of stone walls, with little grey buildings that look as if they have been there since the dawn of time. Beyond the flat bed of the valley the rolling tops of the high Pennines cradle the villages and farms, a glorious backdrop to a piece of real England. Long may it remain so unspoilt.

Enough of the poetry, your stalwart second has arrived and it is time to address the main course of the day. A couple of moves and the corner begins to bulge. A tatty old thread on an elder tree stump protects a blind grope over the offending pot-belly of rock where large holds and a solid thread, as well as a bridged rest, give you time to collect your thoughts. The next few moves out left are the crux of the route and if the thread does not instil total confidence (though it should) a high wire can be fiddled in a short distance up the corner. With such perfect protection the moves are a formality, and a little higher you can wrap your arms round a hunky tree. From this arboreal jug a finger traverse leads back into the main groove and things feel a bit harassing until you can get into a bridging position across the corner. Suddenly you realise it's in the bag, so linger on those final few exposed moves soaking in the situation before you top out. Now there is time to relax, take a seat on the soft springy turf and get back to the poetry.

54: LUCKY STRIKE

Situation:	Rusty Walls, Range East, South Pembroke
Aspect:	West facing
Grade:	E2 (5b)
Length:	40m (130ft)
Equipment:	A normal rack with perhaps a couple of thin tapes to drape over small flakes.
First Ascent:	P.Littlejohn, C.Heard, 11th May 1980
Guidebook:	*Pembroke* by Jon de Montjoye and Mike Harber, published by the Climbers' Club in 1985. A new two-volume guide is due out in 1992.

Approaches: The Rusty Walls are a little tricky to find on first acquaintance. The usual approach is from the large car park at St Govan's Chapel. From here walk west past the inlets of Stennis Ford and Huntsman's Leap. The next promontory is the well-named Saddle Head (with a wire enclosure on top) and the one beyond this is Quarry Point. The Rusty Walls are on the far side of this, before the next cliff-top building, but are invisible from directly above. Scramble down a steepening stony bank and then abseil down the centre of the slab and over the bulges onto a huge boulder (low tide only). So as not to detract from the route, it is useful to get a third party to pull the rope back up again out of the way.

The Route: Delicate and sustained climbing in a 'hairy' situation. Protection is adequate, but falling off is not advised.

Description: Step across on to the wall and then climb up and left into a groove which skirts around the overhangs. Once past the bulges follow the line of good (but small) holds up across the slab, until just short of its right edge. From here climb straight up on mostly good holds to the top.

LUCKY STRIKE

On our first visit to Pembroke we had heard about a fabulous route crossing an apparently blank slab hung above the boiling ocean, giving technically reasonable climbing in stunning situations. It sounded like a must.

The initial trip into the Range to pick this gem was a bit of a disaster as we failed to locate the cliff and spent some time mooching around The Castle and The Fortress before we saw the light. As the light was in fact disappearing we had to do the same.

On the second visit we knew exactly where to head for and had a good look at the route from a little further west. The rock was red rather than the usual perfect concrete grey, and looked distinctly uninviting. Added to this and rather more important was the fact that there was a big sea running and the starting boulder was being periodically submerged as waves slapped and gurgled in a sinister fashion under the overhangs. We ran away.

It was third time strike lucky. Late one August day we ambled through the Range, the short grass and gorse shimmering in the afternoon heat and Lundy just visible squatting on the horizon far away to the south. We kitted up above the route, chose a varied selection of belays and tied in the 200ft caving rope that we use for long abseils (when we can be bothered to carry it). Down at sea level it was hot as the sun hammered into the sheltered recess. The sea slopped about in a comforting lazy fashion as we sat on top of a large boulder and watched the end of the rope disappear back up the cliff to leave us a little committed and very happy. What a superb place to be, the sea, the rock and the sun; no man could wish for more.

The climbing started with a stride across back onto the mainland followed by easy climbing on a wonderful rock, sharp-edged jugs and excellent friction, better than the best French limestone. The bulges that cross the wall forced me across to the left into an easy groove which was followed until I was abreast of the slab. If the distant view was disconcerting then the close-up one was inviting. A line of small flakes ran across the slab keeping just above the lip of the bulges, the rock was rough and covered in small holds and the protection was, shall we say 'adequate'.

The climbing was at least as good as it

LUCKY STRIKE: "The climbing is as good as it looks, intricate, sustained, and in a most dramatic setting - certainly no place to fall from."
Climber: Bob Bradley

up on the crab-wise motion and I headed straight for the blue horizon a short distance above. The belays were already in place so I quickly tied on and took in at the same time as soaking up the last few rays from the golden disc as it slid silently into the sea. By the time we had reunited the sun was gone and a chill in the air heralded the coming of the cool of night.

We wandered back through the scrub each wrapped in our thoughts. The experience was gone; like a shooting star, brilliant but oh so transient. It might never have happened except for the small matter of a few memories that will stay with us forever, always drawing us back to try and recapture those few precious moments.

55: FIRST BLOOD

Situation:	St Govan's East, Castlemartin, South Pembroke
Aspect:	South-east facing
Grade:	E2 (5c)
Length:	40m (130ft)
Equipment:	A standard rack.
First Ascent:	P.Littlejohn, H.Clarke, 30th April 1982
Guidebook:	*Pembroke* by Jon de Montjoye and Mike Harber, published by the Climbers' Club in 1985. A new two-volume guide is due out in 1992.

looked, intricate and sustained, and in a most dramatic situation - certainly no place to fall from. The sun, now low in the sky, burnt into my bare back as I cruised upwards, dancing on tiny holds, suspended above the burnished ocean. At the top corner of the slab the climbing finally gave

Approaches: From the car park for St Govan's Chapel, walk east along the tarmac road to the coastguard lookout, and continue toward the distant Caldey Island for 150 metres, about ten minutes from the car. A large stake allows a 30-metre abseil to non-tidal ledges. Scramble back westwards for 50 metres to an undercut brown slab with a prominent finger crack up it.

The Route: A non-tidal route in a sheltered setting. A strenuous start leads to a thin crack which has one very hard move. Protection is exemplary.

Description: Begin below the right arête of the slab and climb steeply leftwards until a difficult move gains easier angled rock. Follow the crack on its right side then step left and make thin moves to better holds. Continue up flowstone into a hanging corner and exit to the left over a giant perched flake.

FIRST BLOOD

Named after a Rambo film in which he single-handedly destroys a small town, this route is rather less of a battle than you might expect. The climbing is much more subtle than Rambo's treatment of the town, with only one move requiring an aggressive approach.

Admittedly the start is a bit on the butch side, being a leaning wall that is fortunately furnished with a series of massive knobbly holds. These are common at the base of many Pembroke routes, but very rare elsewhere on British limestone. They allow very rapid progress, often up alarmingly steep rock and can present real problems when you try to place protection. Friends tend to walk into the crack and open out whereas nuts often sit unhappily, rocking to and fro in a most disconcerting manner.

Near the top of the initial wall is a particularly large set of jugs but a short blanker section prevents access to an enticing brown slab. A powerful layaway move facing rightwards is the key to the easier angled rock above. Once the base of the thin crack line is reached all worries about protection are behind (or below) you, it will take as many wires as you can carry, and the vast majority of them are downright perfect.

The holds tend to lead you up and right of the crack to a good bracket where you can shake out a bit and survey the scene. The crack has steepened several degrees and it has become painfully thin. Added to this is the fact that the walls are

devoid of any really decent footholds. The easiest way to climb the crack is to cross awkwardly over to its left side and use a couple of really skinny finger jams (almost fingernail jams) to reach for what looks like a flat hold in the crack. This proves to slope at a horrible angle but all is not lost; the

FIRST BLOOD: A classic piece of climbing following a thin crack up a steep slab. Protection is excellent and there is only one really hard move.
Climbers: Charles Halstead and Alison Riocreux

edge of the crack is sharp and ideally suited for use as a layback hold. One more awkward move and you are back onto sinking finger locks and good footholds. A large patch of slippery flowstone is reached which contains some magnificent jugs as well as a collection of threads and nut slots, take your pick.

From here the rest of the climbing is almost a formality, though it is enjoyable enough. Slabby rock is followed up and right to the base of a steep crack. Either follow this or step round to the right into an easier angled groove. Both ways lead to a huge leaning flake behind which you have to squeeze. It is perhaps best to hold your breath and climb gently until you can step off the tip of the flake into the final corner. A step left at the top avoids the worst of the capping rubbish, and belays are found a short way back in a scattering of rocky outcrops.

A friend of mine reckons that if the single hardest move on the route was a touch easier it would make the climb into a brilliant E1 (5b). That's as maybe, but as it stands the route is a brilliant E2 (5c) with a tough crux and plenty of excellent climbing above and below it, what more could you ask for?

First Ascent:	P.Littlejohn, C.Wand-Tetley, April 1977
Guidebook:	*Pembroke* by Jon de Montjoye and Mike Harber, published by the Climbers' Club in 1985. A new two-volume guide is due out in 1992.

HEAVEN'S DOOR: A steep wall leads to the foot of well protected but strenuous jamming cracks. The route is best enjoyed as here, in the evening sun.
Climber: Graham Parkes

56: HEAVEN'S DOOR

Situation:	West Face, Stackpole Head, South Pembroke *Note: This cliff has an access restriction to protect nesting auks. It is closed to climbers from 1st March to 31st July.*
Aspect:	South-west facing
Grade:	E2 (5a, 5c)
Length:	35m (120ft)
Equipment:	A standard rack with a few extra mid-range Friends or Hexes.

Approaches: Stackpole Head lies roughly midway between the car parks at Stackpole Quay and Broad Haven. Both approaches take about 20 minutes and involve crossing one or other of two superb beaches (Barrafundle or Broad Haven respectively). The former approach has the slight advantage that parking is free.

For two hours either side of low tide in calm conditions descent is possible down the first loose ridge to the west of the cliff. Alternatively abseil in from one of the belay stakes above the routes.

The Route: A strenuous but well-protected crack line gained via a short traverse and a leaning wall.

Description: One of the most prominent features of the left side of the cliff is a huge square cut arête. The route takes the impressive cracks just to the right of this arête. Start a little further to the right at a series of short (and often damp) corners leading to bulges. Climb up a short distance then move left to an uncomfortable ledge where you can take a semi-hanging stance. From here climb up and left towards the arête then head up the difficult leaning wall to reach the base of the cracks. These give easier though strenuous climbing to the top.

HEAVEN'S DOOR

The major problem with Stackpole Head (and Mowing Word) is the access. I don't mean the 20 or so minute walk from the car park, which admittedly is quite long by Pembroke standards, or even the gripping abseil approaches, from glorified tent pegs, that are needed to get to the foot of the routes. I am not even referring to problems associated with the tide or the fact that the cliffs are closed throughout the spring to allow puffins a bit of peace and quiet while celebrating their nuptials.

The problem is those bloody beaches. There you are, tromping down the steps with a great bag on your back and festooned with ropes, while all round you scamper small kids, even smaller dogs, and harassed parents. "Oh, look at the climbers", YUK! In the car park there is usually a cool wind blowing but you can bet as soon as you get on the beach it will be red hot. You stagger across the burning sands like some manic Lawrence of Arabia with that distant look in your eye and wonder why you bother.

Ordinary mortals are getting a tan, paddling in the shallows and eating sand-flavoured butties, while you are off to frighten yourself stupid, not to mention risking life and limb by plummeting from a great height, drowning, or most likely both.

The route is of course worthy three stars (if not more), offering a typical Pembroke experience. Steep strenuous climbing, superb rock, good protection, and magnificent situations. Climbed on a rising tide in the afternoon sun it will provide you with a memorable trip.

Later on in the day when you stagger once again across the beach you can look at those ordinary mortals in a rather different light, now you remember why you bother. And if the route did not do anything for you, the beach will still be there tomorrow.

57: KANGAROO WALL

Situation:	The GO Wall, Wintour's Leap, the Wye Valley
Aspect:	West facing
Grade:	E2 (5c, 5c, 4b)
Length:	90m (300ft)
Equipment:	A standard rack should be enough.
First Ascent:	F.Bennett, P.Lennard, May 1966 (some aid on pitches 1 & 2)
First Free Ascent:	Possibly C.King, 1978
Guidebook:	*The Wye Valley* by J.Wilson, D.Hope, T.Penning and M.Ward, published in 1987 by Cordee.

Approaches: Wintour's Leap is a couple of kilometres north of the pleasant town of Chepstow and is approached from the village of Woodcroft on the B4228. Just beyond and on the opposite side of the road from the Rising Sun is a gated track. Park by this then walk up the track to a high fence with quarry warning signs on the right. There is a way round to the right of the fence, and a good track winds its way down through the quarry to an open slope which is descended to an opening in the trees on the right. The base of the GO Wall is to be found on the right beyond the flat ground. The most prominent feature of the wall is the huge corner system on the left taken by KING KONG. Ten metres to the right of this is a steep roofed-in corner with slings dangling from its lip. This is it.

The Route: A long climb with two short strenuous crux sections and a lot of easier climbing.

Description: Climb the corner to the roof, then move out right and up the wall (first crux). Follow the obvious line without much difficulty and rather less protection to a white flake crack which is laybacked to reach a fine stance. From the ledge move up and right passing fixed gear to reach bulges. These are most easily passed slightly to the left, (second crux) before traversing back to the right to gain the chimney. Amble up this to a good sheltered stance. Continue up the chimney either on the inside (tight) or on the outside (exposed), to a rather dirty exit onto a big ledge. For the final pitch move right to a crack which provides straightforward climbing to a spiky tree and the top.

KANGAROO WALL

The steepest and most impressive wall at Wintour's Leap is always known as the GO Wall. This abbreviation of the original title of the Great Overhanging Wall disguises the fact that this remains a mighty piece of rock. In the days of slow aid ascents, rudimentary harnesses and 150-foot ropes, this was one of the few places in the country where you could almost guarantee an epic quality to most ascents. The lower wall is 160 feet (50 metres) high and once embarked on a passage across the big roofs there was quite simply no easy way down.

The first route to impinge on this piece of rock was the classic KING KONG, but

KANGAROO WALL: The GO Wall is crossed by a barrier of massive overhangs. The route climbs the white flake crack to the left of the climber to a small stance, and then bears rightwards below the largest overhangs to gain a chimney crack which offers a way through the roofs.
Climber: Chris Craggs

this took a continuous corner line in which it was possible to hide and from which escape was relatively straightforward. KANGAROO WALL was the next route to find a way up this piece of cliff (today the total stands at over 50!). This was a rather more serious beast, though it still avoided the challenge of the huge roofs which were breached shortly after by the aid route TECHNICIAN, once again put up by Fred Bennett.

From the ground the upper part of the route is obvious; a big chimney which cleaves the upper wall but does not manage to breach the band of overhangs. The lower section of the climb is less obvious, though once on it, the line reveals itself.

The initial corner gives good bridging with plenty of runners (save a few for higher up) until you can reach a peg. A strenuous layback move enables a second peg to be clipped and then some blind groping around the corner is needed in the hope of finding something to pull on. Life would be a lot easier if you knew there was a good jug up and right of the peg wouldn't it? Now you do, so there are no excuses for not 'flashing' the move. A quick pull gains easier rock which is climbed slightly leftwards heading for the white flake high above. All of this section is very reasonable but there is little in the way of runners and there is still the odd hollow-sounding hold. A careful approach is needed as there are a couple of places where a fall could well see you back on the ground, a long way below. Eventually the beckoning flakes are reached and good runners can be placed. The crack in the back of the flakes is fairly unhelpful so a quick layback on the outer edge is the best way to reach the stance.

The ledge would make a great bivi site, and low pegs give you an excuse for a sitting belay. Above are a band of overhangs and around to the right the upper chimney can be sensed rather than seen. After a tricky move to get off the ledge easy climbing leads to the roof where some archaic aid gear is to be found. The guide suggests that the bulge is climbable rightwards following the old aid line but we found the shallow groove a couple of moves to the left was a safer and easier proposition. A couple of fingery moves up this then you can swing back right past a very skimpy thread to reach good holds and then the chimney. This allows much easier progress to a belay where a great cave opens out on the right. I am not sure what lurks in this dark recess - we managed to curb our curiosity.

The third pitch heads off up the impressive chimney, which is best tackled on the outside so as to maximise the exposure. A final steep couple of moves on rather dirty rock gains a vast ledge with a veritable forest of tree belays to choose from. Direct finishes from here are available but feel a bit artificial after following such a strong natural line below. Move right to the obvious corner and jam up this to an abrupt end to a great route.

58: ALCASAN

Situation: Windy Buttress, Stoney Middleton, Derbyshire
Aspect: South facing
Grade: E2 (4c, 4c, 5b, 5a, 5c, 5c, 5b)
Length: 135m (450ft)
Equipment: A normal rack is adequate.
First Ascent: Various combinations of R.Dearman, B.Moore, C.Jackson, J.Ballard, G.Birtles, spread over several months in 1964 and using a considerable amount of aid to overcome the loose rock. The route was probably free-climbed in its entirety in the early 1970s.
Guidebook: *Peak District Limestone, Stoney.* Published by the British Mountaineering Council in 1987.

Approaches: The start of the route is ten metres from the road at the foot of the largest buttress on the crag. It is possible to park on any one of a number of rough tracks that run below the crag, though if you value your suspension it is probably better to use the large car park 300 metres down the road towards the village.

The Route: A long and varied traverse, with reasonable protection and still possessing a smattering of loose rock.

Description: ALCASAN uses all of the first pitch and most of the second pitch of AURORA to get close to the top of Windy Buttress before setting off crab-wise on one of the country's great girdle traverses. The first pitch climbs the left edge of the lower buttress with meagre protection to gain a large ledge above which a fine steep corner is followed until it is possible to step left to a small exposed stance, the Altar. Now move round the corner and traverse deli-

ALCASAN: The crucial fourth pitch descends 'the naughty bit', a steep wall on rather suspect holds, to reach a hanging stance in the crack line of KINK.
Climbers: ? and Dave Thomas

cately left to a swing down to the sanctuary of the 'OUR FATHER' cave. From here cross into the corner and descend two metres before traversing the wall on 'black crumbly stuff.' A small stance and excellent belays are available just around the corner.

Continue the traverse at the same level on small holds to the lip of an overhang, swing down under this to reach a cramped rest and make a couple of slippery moves out to a superb stance. The break continues at the same level until the rock bulges sharply and a diagonal descent is made on poor rock to gain a hanging stance in KINK. For the final pitch cross into the corner then move up and out on to the wall which is crossed in a fine position to a last couple of delicate moves into a corner, and easy climbing to the safety of a big tree. Scramble to the top or abseil off.

ALCASAN

It has to be admitted that Stoney Middleton is a bit of a rat pit, what with the roar of the traffic, the banging and grinding of the quarry, the deathly white pallor that the dust brings to everything and the general air of squalor - it can't be anybody's favourite crag. Despite all the points against the place it still has some great routes, ALCASAN being one of the best of them.

From the enclosed security of the corner of AURORA it swings out into a wild situation and follows a superb natural line across the face of the biggest buttress in the area. The first two pitches are unusually delicate for limestone, requiring subtle footwork and the use of lots of undercuts and sidepulls. After following the precarious first pitch a friend of mine had nightmares for a week, each one ended up with him falling backwards, arms flailing, into a black void.

Once around the corner things change and the climbing becomes more strenuous. It used to be normal to go down WINDHOVER and back up THE FLAKES but the direct link is much more logical and creates less problems with the ropes. After following the line across the wall it becomes necessary to swing down left under the bulges to join THE FLAKES just in time for its crux, an awkward move down and left again using a poor sloping pocket. At one time this contained an old wooden wedge, more out than in, that was used for aid. No such luxury is allowed these days. From the finely situated stance continue in the

same line to 'the naughty bit', a black crumbling bulge that has to be descended past some ancient aid pegs to get back to decent white limestone. Twenty-five years of passing climbers have not cleaned up this particular piece of rock though it must be more solid than it used to be. Even so, many climbers still swing on the pegs to avoid the possibility of ripping a lump off and falling onto the rusty bits of mild steel.

The final pitch is a joy; you know it's in the bag and it is not too strenuous, with plenty of good gear to protect the nicely delicate finale until you reach the security of a big solid tree belay. If you have not had enough you can now reverse the whole procedure (NASACLA?), at least the tricky bits are uphill going to other way.

59: DEEP THROAT

Situation:	Triple Overhang Buttress, Range West, South Pembroke
Aspect:	South facing
Grade:	E2 (5c, 5b)
Length:	50m (160ft)
Equipment:	A normal rack with a selection of Friends or larger nuts and a couple of longer slings.
First Ascent:	C.Heard, S.Lewis, 16th June 1979
Guidebook:	*Pembroke* by Jon de Montjoye and Mike Harber, published by the Climbers' Club in 1985. A new two-volume guide is due out in 1992.

Approaches: The route takes a long crack line on the right side of Triple Overhang Buttress and access is a little problematical.

Triple Overhang Buttress is easily recognised from the coastal path because of its enormous jutting overhangs. It lies roughly midway between the car parks at St Govan's and at Stack Rocks, about two and a half kilometres from either place.

A descent is possible in calm seas down easy rock to the west of the buttress from where a traverse leads rightwards, easy at first but getting more strenuous (no place for non-swimmers) until small ledges are reached below the impressive chimney line of the route.

It is also possible to reduce the amount of traversing required by abseiling down the corner to the west of the big roof (GALACTIC CO-ORDINATOR). A spare rope is needed for this approach and the abseil line offers a means of escape at V.S., (4c).

The Route: A huge chimney crack offering steep, strenuous and insecure climbing. Protection is adequate and the route is often damp.

Description: Climb up into the bomb-bay chimney, exit right and climb up onto a good belay ledge, gripping stuff. Step back into the crack and follow it without deviation to the top, marginally less gripping stuff.

DEEP THROAT

If you could actually get a good look at it DEEP THROAT would be one of the most outstanding lines on the south Pembroke coast. A 50-metre chimney crack that narrows as it rises and slices straight through three bands of overhangs. As it is, there is nowhere that you can get to see the line, except from directly underneath - from where it looks pretty impressive. (If you try looking down from the top you see a couple of metres of rock and then the sea a l-o-n-g way below.)

To get to the base of the route requires a mini expedition and then kitting up presents its own problems, trying to keep the ropes out of the water, and making doubly sure you do not drop anything (especially the Friends) into the greedy ocean. Once established, organised and psyched up, it is off up a straightforward corner, heading for an evil backside of an undercut chimney that hangs menacingly over your head. This is often damp and the safest way to make progress is to swim up

DEEP THROAT: "If you try looking down from the top you see a couple of metres of rock and then the sea a l-o-n-g way below."
Climber: Jim Rubery

and hurtle blindly round the corner. Relief is instant and easy rock leads to a small stance where it is possible to regain some composure. It is worth pointing out that those long of limb (I believe 'great lanky sod' is the usual term of endearment for such fortunates), can bridge the chimney, with tears in their eyes. The walls are smooth and protection difficult to arrange without recourse to the depths so most people prefer to get well and truly stuck into the route.

From the stance the line beckons onwards as it cuts through another bulge. Thankfully the crack is now a bit narrower and so progress although still strenuous is a little more secure, in addition protection is now more plentiful and easier to place, though the climbing is still no push-over. Once through this bulge there is yet another one cutting across the crack line above you. The downward view is memorable, a little rock and a lot of water, but the upward view is now more important. A distinct roof bars access to the final corner, and although endowed with good holds the moves are committing, strenuous and spectacular. Once over this the route finally gives in and a short corner with a smattering of loose blocks is bridged easily back to the horizontal world above.

Despite the dampness that often pervades the depths of the crack line it is a route worth seeking out, and because of the effect it has on you perhaps it should have been called DRY THROAT.

into the depths of the slot until it becomes too tight to progress further. From here it is necessary to head insecurely out towards daylight, with the chimney trying to spit you out like an irritating fish bone. In a near horizontal position it is possible to grasp a spike on the edge of all things, and then some conviction is required to cut loose

60: MYSTERIES

Situation: Stennis Ford, Range East, South Pembroke
Aspect: East facing
Grade: E2 (5c, 5a)
Length: 50m (160ft)
Equipment: A normal rack plus a few extra slings.
First Ascent: P.Littlejohn, J.Harwood, 13th November, 1977
Guidebook: *Pembroke* by Jon de Montjoye and Mike Harber, published by the Climbers' Club in 1985. A new two-volume guide is due out in 1992.

Approaches: The short walk in starts from the car park above the St Govan's Chapel, which is six miles south of the town of Pembroke. Access is gained through the military range and is prohibited when the red flags are flying. The range is usually open at weekends and Bank Holidays as well as after four o'clock on weekdays. Pass the stile and walk westwards for a couple of hundred metres to the first huge inlet that cuts in towards the path; this is Stennis Ford. The line of MYSTERIES is obvious on the wall facing you. A poor path descends a short way down the back wall of the bay to a small recess where gear can be left. From here a variety of indifferent anchors allow a 30m (100ft) abseil down steep grass to the boulders.

NOTE: The route is inaccessible for a couple of hours around high water.

The Route: A fascinating climb with the crux low down and pleasant climbing beyond. Protection is good.

Description: A steep scoop protects the slanting line that forms the substance of the route. This scoop provides steep insecure bridging protection by small wires until a difficult pull leads to easier angled rock. Amble up and left to a stance with nut and thread belays. The second pitch continues up the scoop and over an overhang to a deep horizontal break, which is traversed to the left around a corner and into the finishing groove. Stake belays will be found some distance back.

MYSTERIES

A great name for a compelling route. From the car park a journey of discovery heads off into the Range, and for a newcomer to the area, actually finding the routes is often a major feat. With MYSTERIES this is no problem. The first piece of rock that comes into view as you walk westwards is the smooth west wall of Stennis Ford, white and dropping sheer into the sea. At the right side of this wall is a line that cries out to be climbed, highlighted by the morning sun. A sinuous groove snakes its way down the wall all the way to the boulder beach, forming a way up a steep and imposing cliff at a remarkably reasonable grade.

The groove must have started life eons ago as a tiny crack in the ground. Gradually rainwater gnawed away at the solid rock and the crack was opened out into a tube in the limestone. All this time the sea was eroding away at the rock, seeking out weaknesses and eating the cliffs away. The crack that the water had initially started down was a suitable place for the sea to work on along, with another similar weakness in the rocks that now forms the other side of Stennis Ford. Over tens of thousands of years the millions of tons of rock between these two weaknesses was reduced to sand by the actions of the waves,

MYSTERIES: The initial groove provides the crux of the route, precarious bridging and strenuous laybacking lead up to and over a bulge. *Climber: Brian Rossiter*

leaving half of the tube suspended in space, awaiting the invention of rock climbing.

The initial ten metre groove is the crux of the route. A nasty precarious sequence of bridging moves protected by flimsy little wire nuts that do not instil great confidence leads to a bulge. This bulge guards access to the obvious delights above and has to be overcome. A few deep breaths and then commit yourself, there are obviously jugs just over the bulge so you go for it. The odd thing is that the expected just don't exist, just a series of dimples and sloping ledges, so you are faced with a simple choice, up or off. Those with sufficient will to succeed will storm over the bulge and will have opened the door to a delightful piece of climbing above, those with doubts will be back on the boulders with clouds of depression threatening on the horizon. Don't let it get to you. Take your time, have a breather and a walk round, you know you can do it! When the vibes are right get back up there and show it who is really boss. Once you reach the stance call down those time-honoured words, "It's easy when you go for it, come on up".

The rest of the route is sheer pleasure, climbing imposing-looking rock on good holds in magnificent situations, with as much protection as you require to enjoy the experience. Pembroke at its best.

61: DARIUS

Situation:	High Tor, Matlock, Derbyshire
Aspect:	West facing
Grade:	E2 (5a, 5c)
Length:	50m (165ft)
Equipment:	A normal rack plus extra mid-range and large wires with plenty of extenders. A few longer slings may also be of use.
First Ascent:	O.Woolcock, C.Rowland, P.Nunn, (aid), 1963
First Free Ascent:	P.Livesey, 1974
Guidebook:	*Peak Limestone, South.* Published by the British Mountaineering Council 1987.

Approaches: Just to the south of Matlock is the very conspicuous cable-car to the Heights of Abraham. The approach to the cliff passes the lower station and this is reached over a bridge with limited parking to either side of it. Pass behind the buildings (you may have to pay for access to High Tor grounds) and follow steps until a path heading back towards the cliff is reached. The bottom of the cliff is less than ten minutes away.

The Route: A very long and sustained pitch with the crux moves a long way up. Protection is good but care is needed with the rope drag.

Description: In the centre of the highest part of the cliff is a sinuous series of shallow grooves. This is five metre right of a large tree at the base of the cliff.

The first pitch is a bit scrappy and leads after a tricky start without further incident to a peg (and Friend?) belay at the level of a band of crumbly rock that runs across the lower part of the cliff.

Pitch Two steps left and pulls over the bulge into a groove which is followed until another groove on the right can be gained.

From the top of this trend up and right to a bulge then back left to gain yet another groove which leads to a surprisingly big bolt with a small hole through it. An excellent and more direct version, avoiding the loop to the right is also possible. From the bolt the easiest way to the top is to climb diagonally leftwards to a final steep groove. One rope will have to be pulled through to reach a large tree belay some distance down the bank.

DARIUS

Pete Livesey once described High Tor as the finest outcrop in Britain, high praise indeed. The main face is criss-crossed by a veritable spiders' web of high quality routes and perhaps the best of these is Darius. As the best route on the best outcrop it has to be something rather special.

The first pitch is indifferent, a rather poor hors d'oeuvre that has to be dealt with before you get down to the main meat of the day. The second is a delight, starting well and improving as height is gained. A stiff bulge to the left of the stance protects the first groove and a couple of powerful layback moves, initially with rather poor protection, are needed to get established above it. The groove thus gained is followed until it steepens and it is possible to escape up and right into a longer groove. This is followed until it opens out and bulges are reached. It is possible and quite popular to belay on the right here on old pegs and good nuts, but there is nowhere to stand and changing places is problematical. Most important though is that a stance here breaks one magnificent long pitch into two good short pitches - it gives a far more memorable experience if you run it out to the top in one go.

Either way the route now swings back leftwards into a third groove that is climbed by laybacking to a series of small ledges (or big holds) and a large bolt. A more direct version of this section avoids the pseudo-stance altogether by climbing straight into the base of the third groove. This then becomes the crux of the route.

The rather chunky bolt has a history all of its own. The original bolt was a golo that was a friction fit into a drilled hole and was placed in 1963 on the original aid ascent of the line. Although the route was free climbed in 1974, many people still used the bolt for aid to bypass one very hard move. In 1977 the bolt was removed

DARIUS: With the protection bolt clipped, the crux moves involve a difficult traverse to reach some thin undercuts which are followed leftwards into the easier finishing corner.
Climbers: Richard Johnson, Richard Hyde and Bill Birch

by a flying Aussie, Jon Chester on his way 'down under'. The route suddenly lost its popularity because those who wanted to free climb the route had a problem; the difficult moves were a lot less well protected. Those who wanted to use the bolt for aid had an even greater problem; it was not there any more.

This situation existed for about a year until I decided to take the bull by the horns and do the public spirited thing, (the fact that I was keen to do the route had nothing to do with it, 'onest Milud.) I abbed down, enlarged the original hole and put a substantial expansion bolt in it, doing the route later the same day. The tale should have ended here but the thread on the bolt was far too long and the bracket rattled about like a pea on a drum. A friend of mine on hearing the news that the bolt was back in, was on the crag the very next day and cruised it until he pulled a hold off the last move. Fifty feet lower down the cliff the bolt arrested his fall but the leverage had bent the bolt like a banana. He finished the route and bought me a pint, and the following weekend I was back with a sawn off nut to complete the job satisfactorily.

Nowadays, the bolt is still there and it protects the three possible finishes admirably, (though you do not have to clip it if you feel it is unethical). The usual and easiest way to the top is to climb leftwards along an overlap into the final steep corner, the most direct and difficult way is straight past the bolt, and a third variation is a couple of metres to the right of the bolt. Unfortunately there is almost always a bit of tatty tape tied through the rather small hole in the bolt. This means that instead of clipping a solid piece of thick steel, you are obliged to use the frayed and bleached tape, unless of course you have your Swiss Army penknife with you!

Whichever finish you opt for you will know as you pull your weary body on to the grassy top of the cliff you have just completed a rather special climb, one of the very best.

62: SCOOP WALL

Situation:	Windy Buttress, Stoney Middleton, Derbyshire
Aspect:	South-east facing
Grade:	E2 (5c)
Length:	27m (90ft)
Equipment:	A normal rack should be adequate though a couple of extra middle-sized Friends can be used in the initial crack.
First Ascent:	R.Leeming (aid), 1955
First Free Ascent:	T.Proctor, G.Birtles 1967
Guidebook:	*Peak District Limestone, Stoney.* Published by the British Mountaineering Council 1987.

Approaches: It is possible to park on the side of the rough tracks that runs below the crag, more space and a safer situation is available 300 metres down the road towards the village. Walk underneath Windy Buttress and scramble up to the narrow ledge that runs across its face. This is followed to the right, past a narrow and exposed section and round a corner to a more friendly spot. SCOOP WALL climbs the obvious bulging crack line in the centre of the bay.

The Route: Strenuous climbing up a powerful line. The crux is fingery and technical.

Description: The crack line is followed in its entirety, with the crux moves entering the final groove. It is possible and quite common to split the pitch with a short traverse out right to a stance in the OUR FATHER cave.

SCOOP WALL

Scoop Wall is a route that provides a classic example of the gradual evolution of many of our modern free limestone routes. To the early pioneers exploring the limestone dales in search of weekend sport this impressive bulging crack line must have been an obvious contender for a bit of 'bang and dangle', (or 'dangle and whack' as some folks referred to it). It is very easy to be dismissive nowadays of the aid used by these pioneers, but protection other than from pegs (mild steel ones at that) would have been minimal, harnesses at best were primitive and belaying methods were rudimentary. Apart from that their overall idea of the game was to have a bit of fun so advanced ethics took a back seat.

On the first ascent Roy Leeming used about fifteen pegs and wedges and doubtless had a great day out. Over the years the loose rock disappeared, the odd peg was left in place and the easier moves were free climbed. By the mid 1960s improvements in equipment and a general rise in standards had reduced the aid to one point on each pitch and a short time later Tom Proctor picked an over ripe plum with the first totally free ascent. Today the pitch gives a classic piece of climbing - perhaps the best on the crag.

A couple of stiff pulls lead into a sentry-box which is left by bridging to reach an intimidating bulge. A droopy old ring peg hangs forlornly from the rock and is best backed up by an excellent Rock 4 a little higher. The bulge looks tough but a quick layback on peg pockets leads to a short deep crack with some good layaways in it. A couple of old threads are available here for protection though I must admit I have never been able to make out what they are threaded around. Steep but delicate moves lead to the break crossed by ALCASAN and a good rest. (If you are really bushed it is possible to traverse but this rather breaks the spell). There is a host of good gear available here so you can dump most of your ballast. A bridging move gains some excellent small finger

SCOOP WALL:
Awkward bridging and some good but small finger holds allow a long reach for finger jams which gives access to the final groove.
Climber: Jim Robbins

holds and a rather bendy peg runner on the left. The next two moves constitute the crux of the route and involve some wild bridging moves to reach good fingerjams in the crack above. From these step awkwardly left to get into the final short wide crack that is followed to the capping bulge. It is worth hanging here a second or two and glancing down the inward sweep of the ropes to the little faces far below. Is it possible that Roy Leeming felt any more chuffed on the first ascent than you do now?

WOMBAT: The final couple of moves form the crux of the route. A steep wall has to be climbed using a couple of mediocre finger pockets. The top is set further back than is evident from below.
Climber: Dave Spencer

63: WOMBAT

Situation:	The Right Wing, Malham Cove, Yorkshire
Aspect:	South-west facing
Grade:	E2 (5c)
Length:	27m (90ft)
Equipment:	A standard rack with an extra couple of larger wires.
First Ascent:	R.Barley, D.Gray 1964
Guidebook:	*Yorkshire Limestone*, published by the Yorkshire Mountaineering Club in 1985.

Approaches: The usual route into Malham is from the south via the minor road that runs northwards from Gargrave on the A65. On entering the village there is a large National Trust car park on the left. From here walk though the village keeping left at the junction until a good gravel path leads up to the Cove. Cross the stream and scramble up a steep path to the Right Wing; 15 minutes from the car. A large flat boulder just beyond the fence is the usual place for kitting up. It also provides a great sunbathing spot and excellent views of the cliffs.

The Route: A strenuous pitch, with an awkward start and the crux right at the top.

Description: Below the fence that protrudes over the cliff top, is a weakness through the barrier of overhangs at the base of the wall. Climb this weakness by laybacking to reach the groove above. Continue up the corner to a bulge and swing right. Climb the wall to another bulge which is passed on the right. Above is yet another corner which leads to a horizontal break. Swing left along this then finish rather boldly up the wall.

WOMBAT
From below one of the striking things about the Right Wing of Malham Cove is the almost total lack of decent vertical lines. There are plenty of features but they consist almost entirely of horizontal breaks and narrow bands of overhangs. The main exception to this rule is the discontinuous series of corners taken by WOMBAT. The route would only be E1 except for the minor detail that the corners fail to reach both the ground and the top of the cliff, leaving the route with a stiff start and a sting in the tail.

The initial wall used to be a reasonable if somewhat rattly proposition. Over the years it has shed most of its decent holds, the ones that have stayed on have become well glossed with the passing of many sweaty hands and slippery feet. It used to be possible to cheat here (it was called "using cunning" in those days) by lassoing a small tree at the top of the initial wall and top roping the offending moves. Sadly the tree is only a shadow of its former self and so such dubious tactics are no longer possible. The only saving grace is the fact that there is a good nut slot available a couple of moves off the ground to protect the precarious and strenuous layback moves that are necessary to reach the base of the corner. Once established things ease and straightforward if somewhat butch moves lead up the corner until it is possible to step out onto the face on the right. The wall is climbed to a roof which is skirted on the right to gain a good resting ledge. There is an ancient ring peg here and it is well worth backing it up before setting off up the final corner. This fizzles out into a steep blank looking wall at a horizontal break and things turn a little tricky. There used to be a fine finger flake here that ran right to the top of the cliff, all that was needed was a deep breath and a couple of quick layback moves, and the route was in the bag. Sadly a few years ago the flake joined its smaller brethren from the bottom wall, on the slopes below the cliff, where it rests to this day.

While hanging from the rather rounded break it is first necessary to fiddle a runner or two in, and then swing left to a large jug and head up the steep wall with an increasing feeling of urgency. The top is not far away but the holds are small and spaced. A quick pull on thin finger pockets may allow you to find the rather retiring finishing hold (having someone spot them from the top is definitely not cricket). Fail and you will soon be back on the resting ledge, when after a quick blow you can show it who's the boss. So that's WOMBAT, a rather battered beast but one with a great pedigree.

64: MYTHICAL MONSTER

Situation:	Huntsman's Leap, Range East, Castlemartin, South Pembroke
Aspect:	West facing, but because of the route's recessed position it only gets the sun for a couple of hours, shortly after midday.
Grade:	E3 (5b, 5c)
Length:	40m (130ft)
Equipment:	A standard rack.
First Ascent:	G.Gibson, A.Hudson, 28th May 1983
Guidebook:	*Pembroke* by Jon de Montjoye and Mike Harber, published by the Climbers' Club in 1985. A new two-volume guide is due out in 1992.

Approaches: From the car park for St Govan's Chapel cross the stile into the Range and walk past the inlet of Stennis Ford to Huntsman's Leap. A 40-metre abseil from spikes in the north-east corner leads to the beach. The route lies on the Monster Face which is the black forbidding buttress to the left of the narrows when looking out to sea. It is only accessible at low water.

The Route: Technically reasonable climbing for the most part, and with good protection, in a sombre setting. Some of the rock is a little loose but this does not detract from the route.

Description: Start at a three metre high flake near the left edge of the face. Climb the flake then trend right into a groove. Up this to its top then swing right and climb the wall following the line of threads until easier climbing leads to ledges and a variety of belays. From here climb up and left steeply to a thread then continue straight up the wall to a slightly unstable exit. Stake belays.

MYTHICAL MONSTER

Huntsman's Leap is an immensely popular climbing venue, due partly to it's proximity to the car park and more importantly, the quality of the climbing. It is a most un-Pembroke like setting; a deep gloomy pit in the ground, the atmosphere being more akin to that in many a grotty Derbyshire quarry. At least it provides a welcome shelter from savage winds and for the few hours a day when the sun shines along the length of the Leap it glows with a friendly golden light. It is a great place to climb.

The Monster Face on the other hand is a really grim spot. The rock is black and the closeness of the west wall means that the whole area is in perpetual gloom. The fact that the base of the wall is very tidal adds to this remote air, and to cap it all there is almost always a cold wind blowing through the narrows and across the face. The place has an evil feel to it.

It is this atmosphere that makes the place worth a visit. The climbing on its own is good, though nothing spectacular by Pembroke standards, but the setting turns an average route into a memorable trip.

The start is only accessible at low water and is almost always damp. Thankfully the rock is sharp and the barnacles encrusted on the rock make for good friction. At the top of the flake you can dry your boots, chalk up and get on with the real climbing. A steady groove leads to a bulge which is passed on the right to give access to a wall containing some decaying old threads. (If at this point the setting has got you questioning your ability to climb 5c, it is possible to traverse right and do HONEY

MONSTER, another three star route at the more amenable grade of E2 5b. You can't get lost - just follow the threads.) At the top of the wall is an area of shattered ledges with a variety of belays. There used to be a shell (and I don't mean seashell) jammed here which you could thread, to really put the willies up your second. It has gone now, perhaps it fell out or perhaps its disappearance explains the state of the ledges!

The final pitch is steep but there are only a couple of hard moves, again with in-situ threads, and then a juggy wall with

MYTHICAL MONSTER: "The final pitch is steep but there are only a couple of hard moves followed by a juggy wall of mud filled cracks."
Climber: Christine Anderson

mud filled cracks leads you back to daylight. While you sit there in the sun thawing out, spare a thought for your lost and lonely second, still down there. He is probably shivering by now, and not just because of the cold!

65: LAST SLIP

Situation: The Sea Walls, Avon
Gorge, Bristol
Aspect: South-west facing
Grade: E3 (5b, 5c)
Length: 45m (150ft)
Equipment: Not a lot! Two large rocks
for Pitch 1, four quick
draws and a rock three for
Pitch 2. Anything else will
definitely be ballast.
First Ascent: E.Ward Drummond,
C.Woodhead, 1966
Guidebook: *The Avon Gorge* by Steve
Monks, published by
Dark Peak in 1981. A new
guide is due out in late
1991.

Approaches: Driving towards Bristol city
centre along side the river Avon the first
piece of rock is the towering yellow face of
the Unknown Wall. Just beyond this the
cliff falls back as a series of grey slanting
walls set back from the road. A huge barred
cave on the left acts as an unmistakable
landmark. It is possible to park on the
grass, on the road side (care required) or in
a small layby a little further towards town.

A large tree on a ledge to the right of
the centre of the cliff marks the end of the
route. The start is to be found down and left
at an open corner with characteristic smooth
walls.

The Route: A good first pitch leads to a fine
stance. The second pitch is delicate and
very poorly protected.

LAST SLIP: "a glance down the curve of the
rope suddenly brings the name of the route to
mind, your first slip will probably be your ...."
Climbers: Chris Craggs and Derek Carter

Description: The corner has a slippery start,
then solid finger locks and laybacking leads
to a good stance and bolt belay. Pitch two
starts with a traverse down to the right
until under the obvious smooth groove
(wire in horizontal break). Move up to a
bolt in the rib then step down and traverse
right to reach a peg under the roof. Now
enter the groove and follow it with sustained interest to a peg just below the top.
Exit and traverse right to the big tree which
provides shade, a belay and an abseil point.

LAST SLIP
With the advent of modern protection the
vast majority of traditional 'necky' routes
have been tamed. At one time the age old
adage that the leader must not fall, was
strictly adhered to because to ignore it was
to risk serious injury (and that was if you
were lucky!) With the proliferation of wired
nuts and then camming devices, times have

changed. As long as you can hang on long enough to get the gear in (not to mention affording it in the first place) most routes can be made quite safe. LAST SLIP is one of the few routes that has changed not a jot since it was first put up a quarter of a century ago.

The first pitch is traditional H.V.S. with a horribly slippery first move and then an easy romp to the stance. The pitch has always been graded 5a but if the first move was further from the ground it might be thought of more highly. From the stance you get an excellent view up the second pitch. It is not too steep but the rock looks woefully smooth and there is not the slightest suggestion of a crack in the back of the groove. A short traverse to the right leads to more ledges and the one nut slot on the pitch. A couple of mantelshelves into the base of the groove allow a bolt high in the rib to be clipped. A step down and a short easy traverse to the right leads to a rather old peg under the roof and with this clipped it is time to steel yourself. If you intend to fall off the pitch this is the place to do it!

A sharp edge allows a layback move up into the groove and a couple of poor shelving footholds let you bridge up a few more moves. A scar marks the spot where a small sharp flake used to be. This provided a good finger and foot hold but alas it is no more. Above, but some distance out of reach is a blade peg and it suddenly dawns on you that the last moves were probably irreversible. At ground level the high step required to get to the peg would be a cinch but a glance down the curve of the rope suddenly brings the name of the route to mind, your first slip will probably be your ....

There is no easy way out, all that is needed is a little courage allied to a touch of delicacy, and the peg is within reach. Now you can breath again and enjoy the rest of the route, padding upwards with a broad grin spreading across your face. The great feeling of a challenge faced and overcome, simply unbeatable.

66: OCEAN BOULEVARD

Situation:	Boulder Ruckle Far West, Swanage, Dorset
Aspect:	South facing
Grade:	E3 (5b)
Length:	40m (130ft)
Equipment:	A standard rack.
First Ascent:	K.Turner, N.Buckley, S.Bartlett, March 1979.
Guidebook:	*Swanage* by Gordon Jenkin, published by the Climbers' Club in 1986.

Approaches: From the car park at the Durlston Head Country Park to the south of Swanage follow the tarmac road to the light house then take the coastal path to the west. This is followed for approximately 900 metres to a wall and stile which form the western boundary of the park. Directly below this are two stakes in a shallow gully. A 40m (130ft) abseil from these will take you straight over the impressive leaning wall climbed by OCEAN BOULEVARD.

The Route: A very strenuous though technically reasonable pitch, protection is excellent always assuming you can stop to put it in.

Description: Follow the steep flake/crack system towards the left edge of the wall throughout. Beefy.

OCEAN BOULEVARD

On my first visit to the western section of Boulder Ruckle we wanted to do the classic route of OCEAN BOULEVARD and so intended to use the abseil approach described in the guide down the line of a rather scruffy severe called the RAMP. When we arrived at the appropriate spot above the cliff there was already an abseil rope in place though this was a little further to the west than described in the guide book. We kitted up and I set off down. The edge was rather blocky and required a

careful approach but soon I was drifting downwards in slow spirals getting ever further away from a huge leaning wall. The party that the rope belonged to were doing battle with a fiercely overhanging flake system right under me, so I apologised for using the rope and then enquired what it was they were on. You have doubtless guessed the answer already; OCEAN BOULEVARD.

From below the thing did not look any less impressive. To someone brought up on the gritstone edges of the Peak District this particular route looked like three RASPS stacked one on top of the other - a fairly daunting prospect!

We soaked up the hot sun while the second stripped the route and Graham even went in for a dip. He pronounced the water "lovely" but I managed to restrain myself from taking the plunge, I had other things on my mind. All too soon it was our turn to address the main activity of the day.

The lowest section of the wall is avoidable by a slanting slab on the right that allows you to sneak in to the very base of the flake system, though doubtless purists will tackle the whole thing direct. A sling on a substantial spike, a couple of deep breaths and it was time to let battle commence. The only really prominent feature of the wall is a major horizontal break cutting across it at about half height so I decided to make that my first objective and to worry about the upper wall later. Despite the angle of the rock the holds were large and juggy and I followed them rapidly to where the flake system split into two. The lefthand crack was eminently jammable and so I "plugged in a unit" to use an Americanism and sprinted to the halfway break. On the first ascent the leader set up a hanging stance here. This was certainly a crafty way of getting a good rest part way up the pitch but changing over must have been a bit of a gripper, to say the least. Without actually hanging on the runners the break does not offer much of a rest, the rock is bulging and the holds are generally a bit on the poor side.

I was not getting any fresher and the sun was beating down on my shoulders so it was onwards and upwards. The next couple of moves proved to be the technical crux of the pitch, a long reach from an undercut and a difficult layaway led to better holds. This was followed rapidly by a quick swing to the left to a distinctly

OCEAN BOULEVARD: The leaning nature of the wall is evident, especially when you consider that the abseil rope is run from the top of the route.
Climbers: Carol MacDermot and Mark Phillips

better resting place. Here there was a good set of footholds and a couple of solid jugs, so it was possible to shake out and survey the upward scene through eyes stinging with sweat. The wall continued to lean in the same menacing fashion but I could sense that the top was near. After a good blow it was back to work, fine but spaced holds led out to the right and then back to the left to the long awaited easing in angle. All that remained was a short dusty wall and I was back at the spikes. I untied and dropped the ropes, before setting off back down the abseil. It was Graham's turn to do the route but first I had a long overdue appointment with the Atlantic.

67: THE STAR GATE

Situation:	Mother Carey's Kitchen, Lydstep, South Pembroke *Note: The start is only accessible at below half-tide.*
Aspect:	South facing
Grade:	E3 (5c)
Length:	40m (130ft)
Equipment:	A few extra medium and large wired nuts and the means to extend them might prove useful.
First Ascent:	P.Littlejohn, R.Harrison, March 1977
Guidebook:	*Pembroke* by Jon de Montjoye and Mike Harber, published by the Climbers' Club in 1985. A new two-volume guide is due out in 1992.

Approaches: Mother Carey's Kitchen is the most important of the many cliffs scattered around the headland at Lydstep. There is a car park on the top of the headland that is reached by turning seawards off the A4139 and passing through a cara-

THE STAR GATE: From the other side of the bay the black rift of DEEP SPACE is the most prominent feature. Further to the right is the impressive Space Face and between the two a climber can be made out on THE STAR GATE, about to start the traverse to the hanging stance.
Climber: Graham Parkes

van park until the road turns left and rises steeply to the downs. Park as far eastwards (towards Tenby) as is possible. There is also a direct track from Lydstep village but this involves going the wrong way round the caravan park's one way system.

Pass through the bushes and follow the track to the left. Almost immediately there is a small track to the right that leads through the gorse to meet the coastal path. Turn left along this for ten metres or so until level with twin towers on the right; this is it. It is quite common to overshoot the crag but if you keep glancing over your right shoulder you will recognise the black gash of Deep Space.

It is normal to make a 40 metre abseil from the left hand tower (looking out to sea) but care is needed in case there are people below, as there have been deaths here. You have been warned!

The Route: Strenuous and intimidating climbing up steep rock. Protection is good throughout.

Description: The right side of Mother Carey's Kitchen is an astounding leaning wall that is known as the Space Face. It is one of those pieces of rock that abounds with optical illusions; the slabs are walls, the walls overhang and the overhangs don't bear thinking about. The left side of this wall is a groove line that stabs skyward with only a kink rightwards to interrupt the purity of line. From below it looks pretty steep and this is no optical illusion. Follow the groove for 20 metres until it ends in overhanging rock. Traverse right to gain the continuation of the groove (possible belay) and follow this upper section to a recess. Step right to gain the top.

THE STAR GATE

Named after the black obelisk in '2001 A Space Odyssey' that allowed access to the far reaches of the Universe, this route is a gateway to the stuff that dreams are made from, with perhaps the ingredients of the odd nightmare thrown in for good measure. It is best climbed, if you are confident in your ability, on a rising tide with a bit of a sea running and in such conditions will provide a trip to carry you through a week or two of sessions on the wall.

An initial easy and often damp groove leads to a bulge. At this point you want to be cruising upwards but the bulge gives a

battle, being fingery and technical, requiring a thoughtful and steady approach in an attempt to conserve energy because of the daunting upward view. All runners need extending to cut down on rope drag otherwise you will be brought to a halt long before the top. Once over this problematic start the holds improve and upward progress becomes more rapid. The only snag is that all the good holds are either layback edges or on the lips of the various overhangs, so slowly but surely the pitch wears you down.

At about 20 metres all roads end in a maze of leaning rock, it is possible to rest, (or at least half rest, you can't exactly take your hands off), and work out a strategy. The only way on is to cross the leaning wall on the right, the holds are large but the angle is well the wrong side of vertical. A rapid approach is the only way and if you hit it right you will find a recess that provides sanctuary and brief respite from this cruel world. If you get it wrong the air will welcome you with open arms and gentle breezes will caress your tortured brow as you scream seaward.

Most teams belay in the niche on a variety of chunky threads - only strong climbers who have really spaced out their protection will be able to run it out 'in one'. By the time the second arrives the tide will be well in and the die has been cast, there is only one way out! It is vastly easier, and safer, to lead through and so the second will have to get stuck into the fearsome layback that beetles overhead. Fortunately the holds are big and the protection is exemplary so you can afford to press on; things soon ease and a cave recess is reached. A steep step right leads to much easier ground and you know it is in the bag. At this point the clever dick who did the route in one pitch will be laying pineapples as the rope locks up and the second is squawking about the waves getting ever nearer. You can cruise on with the comment in the guidebook singing through your mind, perhaps it is the best route in the world after all.

68: TRANSFORMER

Situation:	The Yellow Wall, The Gower, South Wales *Note: This cliff is subject to an access restriction from the 1st of March to the 10th of August.*
Aspect:	South-east facing
Grade:	E3 (5c, 5c)
Length:	50m (165ft)
Equipment:	A standard rack with a few spare large wires should be adequate.
First Ascent:	(As Lap of the Gods) E.Pardoe, M.Hogge, 1969 (aid)
First Free Ascent:	P.Littlejohn, A.McFarlane, 1973
Guidebook:	*Gower and S.E.Wales* by Mike Danford and Tony Penning, published by the South Wales Mountaineering Club in 1983. A new guide is due out in 1991/2.

Approaches: In the centre of the small village of Pitton (B4272) turn left down a minor road and park on the left in the farmer's field (honesty box). Cross the minor road and go through the farm yard and down a narrow valley to the sea. If the tide is well out, walk along the beach for 400 metres until the prominent Yellow Wall appears in the back of Boulder Cove. If the tide is in walk along the cliff top for a similar distance to find a discrete bird ban sign. The top of the cliff is visible from here. Either abseil over the cliff top from a stake (nut back up), or descend the ridge opposite the cliff by slanting diagonally down towards the sea, and then doubling back above the lower steep section.

The Route: A fine, strenuous and well protected groove line.

Description: Gain the right hand of the two main groove lines on the cliff via a

TRANSFORMER: The leaning nature of the wall and the steepness of the first pitch are evident. The stance is on top of the sunlit prow and the upper pitch continues the theme of the lower one.
Climber: Colin Binks

TRANSFORMER

In the sixties Yellow Wall was the preserve of the aid climbers, the great steepness of the rock reduced free climbing possibilities, and so the two main groove lines on the cliff were hammered into submission. In *Sea Cliff Climbing in Britain,* published in 1973 John Cleare and Robin Collomb described Yellow Wall as having 'the most classical artificial climbing in the Gower'. Virtually before the printers ink was dry Pat Littlejohn had nipped in and free climbed the two major aid lines on the crag, typical!

Judging by the lack of fixed gear that remains to this day, LAP OF THE GODS (as it was then known) was never a very popular aid route. The rather more imposing and central line of YELLOW WALL was the one to do and so it is the climb now well equipped with its quota of decaying garbage. The strange thing is not so much the neglect of the route as an aid climb, rather the continued neglect of what is now a great free climb. I have never met anybody else that has climbed on Yellow Wall and yet every weekend climbers stream along the motorway Pembroke bound, little realising that there are a couple (or more) routes here well worth a short detour.

The base of the groove of TRANSFORMER is guarded by a considerable overhang. This can be laybacked or jammed round, either method protected by a thread, proves to be very strenuous. Once established in the groove, it is followed on good but spaced holds, the climbing being easy apart form the slight problem of the angle of the rock. As the groove kinks to the left easier angled rock leads to a fine small ledge perched in the middle of nowhere.

The second pitch is rather more technical than the first one, unfortunately it is not much easier angled. The groove is followed in an ever more impressive situation to a final steep crack sprouting an old peg that appears to be made out of pieces of Meccano. The crack can be followed steeply to the top or if you have had your fill of overhanging rock the easier groove on the left can be gained and bridged to safety.

The climb may have been a reasonable aid route but the free version is brilliant - that is a real transformation.

difficult overhanging start. Follow the groove steeply until it bends to the left and continue with more delicacy to a good small ledge, thread and Friend belays and a sitting stance. Gain the left hand groove in the corner and follow it to a bulge. Cross this with difficulty and continue steeply to the base of a ragged crack. Climb this until it is possible to swing left into a final groove (old peg), or follow the crack throughout.

69: MOONCHILD/ LUNATIC

Situation:	Chapel Head Scar, Cumbria *Note: This cliff is a nature reserve. Access is restricted March 1st to July 31st.*
Aspect:	South-west facing
Grade:	E3 (5c, 5c)
Length:	40m (130ft)
Equipment:	A standard rack of wires.
First Ascent:	MOONCHILD - R.Fawcett, 1974 LUNATIC - P.Livesey, J.Sheard, 1974
Guidebook:	*Rock Climbs in Lancashire and the North West* by Phil Kelly and Dave Cronshaw, published by Cicerone Press in 1988.

Approaches: The crag is reached from Witherslack Hall. From the A590 (Levens to Barrow Road) turn north following the signs for Witherslack. Continue through the village for a couple of kilometres to the hall where there is adequate parking in a short lane on the right. Go through the gate and follow the path past the football pitch into the woods. A well made path soon rises up the scree to the cliffs. Ten minutes from the car.

The Route: Two fine technical groove pitches with good protection once the bold start is overcome.

Description: At the point the path reaches the rock there is a steep shallow groove. Gain this with difficulty and follow it to a peg. Continue steeply to another peg then more easily to saplings, move right to a ledge and tree belay. Step right again and follow another groove to the top of the cliff. Descend to the right or by abseil.

MOONCHILD/LUNATIC

Chapel Head Scar was developed in a new route gold rush in the mid Nineteen Seven-

MOONCHILD/LUNATIC: Starting the committing leaning wall that guards access to the groove that forms the main substance of the first pitch of the combination described.
Climber: Colin Binks

ties. In the stampede for fame and fortune trees were felled, great shrouds of ivy were ripped down and some monster trundles occurred. It never occurred to most of the climbers involved (or if it did they ignored the fact) that the crag was being systematically raped, sod the wild life get your name in the history books.

Pretty soon the place was closed to everybody, this story has a strangely familiar ring to it don't you think? Fortunately due to the efforts of the B.M.C. (who says they never do anything) the main sections of the cliff were reopened outside the nesting season. Good sense has prevailed ever since and some fairly grotty bits of rock have been allowed to return to nature while the biggest and best buttresses are now available for climbing. Of course things have turned full circle and the cliff is out of vogue at the moment so you usually have the place to yourself, accompanied only by

woodpeckers, tree creepers and their feathered friends.

The Great Buttress has a fine selection of modern bolt protected test pieces, but the traditional classic of the crag is MOONCHILD. When combined with the top pitch of LUNATIC a great outing is guaranteed.

The start of MOONCHILD is the crux, perhaps not technically but if you are going to fail anywhere rest assured it will be here. A peg winks tantalising at you far too far from the ground to boulder up to. Some distance below it is a hole that obviously contains a big jug. Reaching this is committing and strenuous, too high to jump too gripped to press on is the usual scenario. It used to be usual, at least for those in the know, to carry a big meat hook to sit in this pocket so guaranteeing rapid safety. Not so nowadays, there is a crack in the back of the pocket but getting a nut in it is a real fart. The crack opens out again lower down so as often as not, the nut pulls through when you try to bed it in. Once happy with the gear a quick move in a state of some 'pumpedness' allows the relative safety of the first peg to be gained. A precarious and gripping step up and out right into a niche is the next obstacle, and provides a real contrast to the lower section as handholds are distinctly lacking. No real rest is possible here but just a little higher jugs and another peg are reached and at last the route begins to relent. It is possible to continue up ever more floral rock to a stout tree from which lowering off is usual.

A better alternative is to prolong the experience by heading up and right to a tree belay on a ledge before swinging into another hanging groove. This gives more fine sustained technical and well protected climbing before the cliff top is reached. A fitting finale to a fine combination of pitches in a flawless setting or just a touch of moon madness?

70: BLACK GRUB

Situation:	Beeston Tor, The Manifold Valley, Staffordshire
Aspect:	South facing
Grade:	E3 (5c)
Length:	35m (120ft)
Equipment:	A selection of mid range and large wires, plus a couple of slings for threads.
First Ascent:	J.Yates, B.Dale, S.Dale, 1974
Guidebook:	*Peak Limestone* published by the British Mountaineering Council in 1987.

Approaches: Beeston Tor is situated in the secluded and sheltered Manifold Valley. It is best reached from the small village of Wetton which is reached from the A515 via Alstonfield. A minor road to Grindon leads down into the valley where a sharp left turn gains a narrow track which leads to

BLACK GRUB: Climbing on Beeston Tor makes frequent use of the solution pockets, on the lower section of BLACK GRUB these are small and well spaced making for fingery climbing.
Climber: Neil Cumyn

the cliff. Parking is available in a field just before the farm and a small fee is usually levied; please smile as you cough up.

From the parking place the rock is three minutes walk via a gate and the (usually) dry river bed. The normal spot for kitting up is the sheltered area at the foot of the great groove of THE THORN.

The Route: Fingery pocket pulling at its best. Protection is adequate.

Description: To the right of the corner system and large roofed cave in the centre of the cliff are a series of white smooth looking walls. The BLACK GRUB takes the largest of these centrally via a prominent dark streak. The route starts from a small ledge equipped with a monster peg belay, below and right of the foot of the streak. This can be reached from the left by doing the first twenty metres of THE THORN and then crossing vegetated ledges, from directly below up a gardened path, or by a short traverse from the foot of BETRAM'S CHIMNEY on the right. None of these approaches is particularly pleasant and in damp conditions they are downright dangerous.

From the belay trend left up easy angled and rather polished rock to the base of the streak (ring peg). An awkward first move gains better pockets that lead to a thin in situ thread. A back up wire is available a little higher to protect the moves out left into a scoop where a rest is possible. Swing right to reach good pockets which are followed past a number of tatty and archaic threads to a big hole. Pull out of this then follow easier rock up and left to another giant peg belay in a corner.

BLACK GRUB

On the first ascent of the Black Grub (or so the story goes) John Yates placed a peg runner, hit it twice and pressed on in search of fame and glory. Hardly surprisingly it fell out when the second arrived, but was replaced later. This second and supposedly 'better' peg also fell out a few years later so some public spirited soul put a couple of thin threads in below the peg hole. These now provide something to 'go for' up the initial steep wall and protect you as you fiddle a good nut (Rock 4) in where the pegs used to be. From here it is possible to continue straight up the streak but this is bold and strenuous, so most

mortals head left into a shallow scoop in the hope of finding a little sanctuary. An odd cross hands move is needed on a small flake to ensure that you can reach into the base of the scoop. Once you have stepped up, the hoped for rest materialises, though it would be very easy to fall backwards out of here, as there is not a lot in the way of good holds.

When suitably recovered, a bit of a teeter out right reaches some superb pockets that head straight up the wall to a big black hole. There are some fixed threads in this section that hardly merit the title 'tat', but the climbing is not too hard. The aforementioned hole provides a squatted rest before the final steepening. No matter how bushed you are, any urges to crawl into the hole and have a lie down must be curbed as there is no turning space inside and reversing out would be tricky to say the least. One steep move reaches good holds, and the top is not far away. The title BLACK GRUB is rather derogatory for such a fine pitch, perhaps BLACK GOLD would have been nearer the mark.

71: ADJUDICATOR WALL

Situation:	Watchblock Buttress, Dovedale, Derbyshire
Aspect:	West facing
Grade:	E3 (5c)
Length:	40m (130ft)
Equipment:	A standard rack of wires and extenders.
First Ascent:	J.Street, G.Birtles, May 1969. (One peg for resting)
Guidebook:	*Peak Limestone, South* published by the British Mountaineering Council in 1987.

Approaches: ADJUDICATOR WALL is to be found on the rather retiring Watchblock Buttress which is on the left bank (facing down stream) of the River Dove. The nearest parking is at the northern end of Dovedale, at the hamlet of Milldale. There is also an excellent cafe here. The crag is about 20 minutes walk down stream, past the Dove Holes and Ilam Rock. A short distance beyond Ilam and Pickering pinnacles (which face each other across the river) is the cliff we are seeking. If the foliage is not too dense it can be recognised by the great perched block stood on top of the crag. If the trees are in full summer raiment it is best to continue to Lion Rock right by the water, and head up the next gully down stream. The crag is recognised by the tunnel, that doubles as a toilet, at its left side.

The Route: A long and sustained pitch, both delicate and fingery. Protection is excellent.

Description: Start at the lowest point of the buttress and climb easily up leftwards to a ledge. From here the line is marked by a series of in-situ threads, which are followed left along the lip of the bulges by sustained technical climbing to reach a shallow groove. This is climbed to an exit leftwards at the old resting peg. From here a series of flakes lead strenuously to easy ground and a grand old yew tree.

ADJUDICATOR WALL

"Puritanically hard despite bastard origins", was the comment in the initial guide book description of this route and in the early seventies it was a real stopper. All the big names of the day came to try it and many of them floundered. One up to Jack Street and his mighty finger strength.

The style of climbing in the lower half of the route is very traditional, as it is all quite delicate requiring subtle foot work and sneaky cross hands moves, always with superb protection from the threads already in place, interspersed with perfect wired nuts. A committed feeling swing lands you in the base of a shallow bottomless groove and things begin to get a bit steeper. Although the holds are good here the undercut nature of the rock means it is no place to tarry so it is onwards and upwards. The groove is furnished with good but small holds and they are well

ADJUDICATOR WALL: Making the fingery and rather committing swing into the shallow groove half way up the pitch, with the crux still to come.
Climber: Colin Binks

before the final push. Passing the peg is difficult and suddenly the route has a much more modern feel about it. Strenuous and committing laybacking is needed and the rope drag is beginning to build up, the second is far away and the upward view offers no prospect of an easy exit. It is time to grit your teeth and keep going. If you can keep it together for a couple more moves jugs appear and the angle relents, an easy romp remains into the shade of a huge yew tree. Here you can tie on and relax, happy in the knowledge that the wall has been your judge and you have not been found wanting.

spaced. At the top of the groove it runs out into a bulge and you are forced out left to reach the old resting peg (if the truth be known, it is still used for resting far too often). If you are beginning to get pumped it is worth reversing back into the groove to semi-rest where you can recover a little

---

72: YELLOW WALL

Situation:	The Yellow Wall, The Gower, South Wales *NOTE: This cliff is the subject of an access restriction and is closed to climbers from the 1st March to 10 August.*
Aspect:	South-east facing
Grade:	E3 (5c, 5b)
Length:	50m (165ft)
Equipment:	A standard rack with extra large wires or small Friends.
First Ascent:	J.O.Talbot, R.J.Corbett (aid) 1962
First Free Ascent:	P.Littlejohn, A.Houghton, 1973
Guidebook:	*Gower and S.E.Wales* by Mike Danford and Tony Penning, published by the South Wales Mountaineering Club in 1983. A new guide is due out in 1991/2.

YELLOW WALL:
Approaching the
crux groove by
climbing a short
bulging wall, " a
magnificently
varied outing up
the centre of a
very impressive
cliff".
Climbers:
Graham Parkes
and Colin Binks

Approaches: In the centre of the small village of Pitton on the B4247 turn left down a minor lane and park on the left in the farmer's field (honesty box). Cross the road and go through the farmyard and down a small valley to the sea.

If the tide is out walk west along the beach for 400 metres until the unmistakable Yellow Wall appears in the back of Boulder Cove.

If the tide is in follow the cliff top path for the same distance until a discreet bird restriction sign is found. The top of Yellow Wall is visible from here a little further to the west. Either abseil in from an iron spike (nut back-up) directly above the wall, or scramble diagonally down the ridge opposite the wall then slant back above a lower steep section to arrive in the cove.

The Route: Powerful and well protected climbing up an impressive line. The rock is excellent.

Description: Gain the left hand groove line by swinging in form the right and follow it to a band of overhangs. Pass these on the left then climb back to the right (peg runner) to gain the base of the main corner. This gives superb finger jamming to a big ledge. The groove behind the stance is followed in complete contrast to the pitch below.

YELLOW WALL

Yellow Wall (the cliff as opposed to the route) is a bit of an enigma. It obviously belongs in Pembroke with its big brothers, rather than lurking here in the Gower amongst the small fry. If you first approach the crag via the abseil described above you will get an interesting insight into angles and perspectives. You reverse carefully off the grass and descend a small slab before slipping over the edge of a huge leaning wall. Slow spirals take you further and further away from the cliff and the boulders are still far below. There is a sudden realisation Yellow Wall is both fairly big and mighty steep.

From below the whole crag towers steeply overhead and the abseil rope appears to defy gravity by slanting away from the cliff. On closer inspection the wall is split by two superb slanting grooves, the route YELLOW WALL following the left hand groove throughout. It was an obvious challenge to the men of steel and there

are many remnants of the early aided ascents in the form of rusting pegs, rotting wedges and decaying bolts.

In its free form the route gives a magnificently varied outing up the centre of a very impressive cliff. The initial groove is gained from the right by a hand traverse and followed without incident to a large band of roofs. These are skirted on the left passing a thread and an odd cave which disappears horizontally into the bowels of the Earth. A short tricky wall with a good peg runner leads back into the main groove line. This forms the highlight of the route and it gives well protected strenuous finger jamming and laybacking that both overhangs and slants to the right. The positions are impressive especially the downward view. Above the groove is a superb large ledge where you can have a lie down and soak up a little sun.

The top pitch is a fine counter point to the grossly leaning territory below. A slabby groove is awkward to enter and is followed with considerable delicacy, (a real shock to the system) around a small roof to a sudden exit on to the grassy top of the cliff. In terms of quality YELLOW WALL is a twenty-four carat route.

73: BRAVE NEW WORLD

Situation:	St Govan's East, Castlemartin, South Pembroke
Aspect:	South-east facing
Grade:	E3 (5c, 5b)
Length:	35m (120ft)
Equipment:	A standard rack with a few extra wires if you intend to do the route in one pitch.

First Ascent: P.Littlejohn, H.Clarke, 30th April 1982

Guidebook: *Pembroke* by Jon de Montjoye and Mike Harber, published by the Climbers' Club in 1985. A new two-volume guide is due out in 1992.

Approaches: From the car park at St Govan's Chapel walk eastwards and pass behind the Coastguard lookout to reach in 150 metres a grass slope with a couple of substantial stakes in it. This is ten to fifteen minutes from the car. A 30-metre abseil from these leads to non-tidal ledges below the centre part of the face. BRAVE NEW WORLD takes the roof, finger crack and groove that splits the highest part of the face some distance to the west of the abseil.

NOTE: The start of this route is inaccessible at high water, or in rough seas.

The Route: A strenuous piece of climbing up a very impressive line. Protection is good throughout.

Description: A strenuous pull over a bulge leads to an easy but often damp corner which is climbed to the impressive roof. This is passed by a combination of jamming and undercutting with a couple of layback moves around the lip. The crack gives straightforward but strenuous finger jamming to a small ledge, and a possible belay. The groove at the back of the ledge gives steep sustained bridging to the top. Stake belay.

BRAVE NEW WORLD

St Govan's East was largely overlooked in the hectic scramble for new routes at the start of the Eighties. A few of the easier lines on the central and right sides of the cliff had been done but the impressive tidal section at left end of the cliff had been ignored. Pat Littlejohn paid an exploratory visit in early spring 1982 and had a productive day, cracking off three first ascents of three of the best lines on this section of cliff. BRAVE NEW WORLD was not the most difficult route put up that day, but the impressive nature of the line, up the centre of the biggest wall on the cliff makes it perhaps the best of the bunch.

The cliff is best visited early in the day so as to catch any sun that is going. It is also well sheltered from westerly gales and so

can be a calm haven on blowy days, though if there is much spray about the whole cliff becomes damp and greasy.

The start of the climb is under water twice daily and is found behind some gigantic blocks that must have fallen from the crag at some time in the (distant?) past. These two factors mean that the initial overhang is nearly always a bit damp, and although this is a bit of a nuisance it at least gives you a ready made excuse if you do not like the look of the big black overhang blocking out the sky not very far above you. If on the other hand you are made of sterner stuff a couple of quick pulls gains the easy juggy corner that leads to the roof. This is split by a thin hand crack that is full of nasty knobbles, giving excellent if somewhat painful jams and plenty of protection possibilities. There is a real danger of major rope drag problems here and so a thoughtful approach to the way you rig the runners is required.

The overhang is as bit easier than it looks through it is distinctly uphill work and passing the lip is somewhat of a struggle. Once out on the open face the route shows a fairer countenance. Gone are the grim black overhangs and you are faced by a superb thin crack up a smooth white wall. This is no big deal to the aficionado of this style of climbing (gritstone H.V.S.!!!) but steel finger youths, well honed to high standard face climbing, after a season on the climbing wall, might find it a bit of a thrash. Eventually an excellent little ledge arrives and you can take a breather or use it as a belay stance. The open groove above the ledge looks innocuous but is sustained and technical. Fortunately the rock is good and there is enough protection to allow you to keep your cool. A couple of steeper moves lead to good jugs and a final pull on to the grass bank. As you wait for your mate to arrive it is worth pondering on how many other bits of rock like this one remain to be discovered along this coast. Once he arrives, the question is what to do next? Perhaps there is just time for a cup of tea and a plate of cakes at Mrs Weston's before the next objective on the sports plan.

BRAVE NEW WORLD: The initial overhangs are passed with difficulty to gain the superb finger crack splitting the white wall.
Climber: Colin Binks

74: SUNLOVER DIRECT

Situation: Trevallen Cliff, St Govan's, South Pembroke
Aspect: South facing
Grade: E3 (5c)
Length: 30m (100ft)
Equipment: A standard rack with perhaps a set of R.P.s.
First Ascent: N.Colton, D.Hall, 5th April 1980
Guidebook: *Pembroke* by Jon de Montjoye and Mike Harber, published by the Climbers' Club in 1985. A new two-volume guide is due out in 1992.

Approaches: From the car park at St Govan's Chapel walk eastwards towards the prominent Coastguard lookout on the headland. After 400 metres you are above Trevallen cliff and access is from one of several abseil stakes. The best approach is a forty metre abseil from a pair of stakes, starting down a rounded dirty gully, the lower section of the abseil is steep.

From the foot of the abseil the route is eighty metres back towards the car park past some gigantic blocks. SUNLOVER takes the left edge of the crack riven white wall.

The Route: A superb wall pitch, technical low down and strenuous higher up. Protection is rather fiddly and a bit spaced in places.

Description: Start a couple of metres to the right of the arête and pull over the roof into a horizontal crack. Move left then climb up the wall using the arête when needed, until better holds lead steeply rightwards to reach a 'lying down' rest. Move right and climb the steep wall to a bay. Scramble off to the right.

SUNLOVER DIRECT

Trevallen cliff contains a fantastic set of routes, mostly pretty hard, but non-tidal and on wonderful rock. The first time you abseil into this arena is a memorable experience. White walls and big roofs, with line after line, disappearing off in both directions. If you turn one way the roofs get ever larger and are eventually terminated by

SUNLOVER DIRECT: Pembroke at its very best, perfect white rock, a dazzling blue sky, and only five minutes from the car.
Climber: Steve Williamson

the fine buttress of TREVALLEN PILLAR, if you choose to go the other way, the walls get ever more impressive until you reach SUNLOVER.

It is difficult to choose from such a collection but SUNLOVER is perhaps the archetypal Pembroke pitch, stunning white rock, a superb setting with the sea close by, (but not too close), and only five minutes from the car.

The start is quite butch; a skip, and perhaps the quick use of a knee along with some knobbly hand jams and you are stood in the break. Up and right are a collection of well scoured slots where everybody (well almost everybody) tries to get a runner. Despite appearances to the contrary the placements are unhelpful and without a touch of cunning you may be forced to press on protectionless, though ever hopeful. Fingery technical moves lead to a slight easing in angle at a horizontal break and a collection of much better gear. The next section is steeper and although the holds are generally good they are well spaced. A forceful approach is the best way, drop in a couple of solid nuts and then press on, the holds keep appearing as long as you have got the 'umph' to used them. A wide horizontal break beckons and it is possible to crawl onto it and have a lie down. (Now that is what I call a rest!) In the roof of the slot is a good thread so you can do something useful while you get your breathing back to normal.

Once you are refreshed there is the slight problem of the bulging wall above your head. The guide book indicates that this is attacked directly, but most folks step a couple of moves to the right where the angle is marginally more amenable and there are some decent holds. A rather committing first move leads rapidly to easier rock and a small embayment in the cliff, a perfect little sun trap from where to belay and survey the scene.

The guide sums up SUNLOVER rather well "A brilliant route, a Pembroke classic".

75: DREADNOUGHT

Situation:	Berry Head, Torbay, South Devon

Note: There is a local bye law protecting nesting Auks on this cliff from 15th March to 15th July with a standard fine of £1,000 for disturbing them. Ignore it at your expense.

Aspect:	East facing
Grade:	E3 (5a, 5c, 5b, 5b)
Length:	95m (310ft)
Equipment:	A normal rack with a selection of extra Friends for use in the horizontal breaks that the cliff abounds with.
First Ascent:	F.Cannings, P.Littlejohn, 4th April 1969 although the crucial traverse pitch had been climbed 18 months earlier by F.Cannings and P.Biven (5 points of aid).
First Free Ascent:	P.Littlejohn, 1977
Guidebook:	*South Devon and Dartmoor* by Pat Littlejohn and Pete O'Sullivan. Published by Cordee 1985.

Approaches: (NOTE: The base of the route is only approachable for a couple of hours around low water and not at all at neap tides or if a swell is running.)

The top of Berry Head, at the southern tip of Torbay, is a country park and the route to it is signposted from Brixham. From the eastern end of the car park and to the left of the fort, a grassy slope descends towards the sea using a set of 'foot prints'. As this steepens and the cliff edge is approached head to the right (facing out) to reach a straight forward but exposed traverse (Moderate) that is followed for 15 metres until big holds lead straight down to a large sloping rock platform. The view of the route on the other side of the water is impressive and it is worth the trip this far

even if you intend to go no further. It is also possible to reach the start of the traverse of Dreadnought by abseiling 40 metres (130ft) down the line of MOONRAKER, but this spoils the completeness of the trip.

The Route: A long and serious trip in a dramatic setting. Protection is adequate but don't fall off.

Description: From the sloping platform spend a few minutes ogling the various futuristic lines hanging above you (many of which have been done already) then head off into the gloom. At the back of the cave cross to the other side and head back towards daylight along a series of narrow slippery ledges that overhang the water. Eventually it is possible to climb up and left to small ledges and the odd old peg ten metres above the sea. Pitch one is as for MOONRAKER and heads back to the right to skirt under the next band of overhangs and reach a long crack which is followed until a traverse out left leads to smelly ledges. The next pitch reverses the traverse and then continues in the same line across the lip of the great roof to reach a corner that leads up to another roof. Traverse right again (crux) and swing round the corner to reach better holds and a little higher a tiny stance and mixed belays.

From the stance climb up and left to pass yet another roof then continue straight up to a flowstone filled cave which it is possible to belay inside. For the last pitch step out left and climb straight up the wall, over a small roof and up the corner above to reach the fort.

DREADNOUGHT

Colin has always been a stout partner to climb with especially on sea cliffs. He has a morbid fear of drowning, (or is it man-eating sharks?) and can be guaranteed to get up the first pitch of any route near the water faster than a ferret up your trouser leg. I had been down to do DREADNOUGHT a couple of times before but the sight of the traverse over the roof had left my partners frothing at the mouth and with rolling eyeballs so we escaped up MOONRAKER.

I thought we had blown it again this time as we slipped and slithered inches above the gurgling and slopping briny in an effort to get to the start of the real climbing. One belly traverse along a nar-

DREADNOUGHT: The third pitch offers steep climbing on large holds in an audacious position. With the crux already completed the upper section of the route can be savoured to the full.
Climber: Chris Craggs

Colin tied on and was gone, and in what seemed like 30 seconds the rope was pulling in and it was my turn. He had led the pitch with two runners and I pointed out that a fall would have been a very long one straight in to the sea.

"Ah, but I wasn't about to fall off", came the reply. It must be nice to be confident!

After re-racking the gear I reversed the traverse to the band of steep rock that leads out to the right over the void. After some poking about I eventually settled for a flexible Friend 1, a lot of which stuck out of the rock and an old peg a short distance across the wall on the right. A fleeting thought crossed my mind, wondering if the peg was an original, now well over twenty years old, and on a sea cliff to boot, but I fended it off. This was no place for worrying about things I had no control over.

A strange brittle hold, like a piece of fossilised wood, stuck out of the wall and allowed a committing cross hands move to reach an undercut finger pocket, I was started on the traverse. A short distance further and good jams materialised along with a perfect Friend 3, then jugs led up to a roofed-in recess. From here a quick look out to the right revealed that the wall I had to traverse narrowed down to less than three feet in height, which is no fun for a six foot three inch 'lanky sod', as I have often been called. I headed out and ended up lying almost horizontal, hanging from a break which was slick with red mud. A quick clip of another old peg and a grope around the corner revealed a good jug, I cut loose and swung around to reach rock of a slightly saner angle and a little higher a tiny stance and three pegs, two rusty and one stainless steel. The pitch had been brilliant, totally absorbing and in an outrageous position and now the stance matched it. The tide was right down and I was 45 metres directly above the only rock showing in the whole cove. If the belays ripped there would be no soft landing.

After examining the area of the stance closely the only decent break was designed to take a Friend 3 and of course that was otherwise employed elsewhere. I called Colin across and told him not to fall off - he cruised it, I plugged in the unit and we relaxed and took it all in. A tourist ladened boat chugged into view and we were celebrities for a couple of minutes. When it

rowing ledge with the runners dangling in the water and the feeling you might soon follow was especially memorable, particularly for Colin. Eventually we reached the safety of the initial stance, dropped in a couple of nuts to hang off and neatly racked the ropes to keep them out of the water.

became obvious that we weren't about to do anything silly they sailed off out of sight and left us to our private world.

Colin led off over more roofs in an ever more exposed situation and vanished from sight. The ropes ran out steadily and soon I was summoned upwards. I was quite sad to leave the little oasis in a leaning world, but duty called. The climbing was great, steep but on large holds, then a nice technical wall leading to our lad squatted in a small cave like an oversized owl.

I swung on to the front of the cave and climbed straight up the wall on good rock to a small roof which was passed on large but spaced holds to the final corner and the top, to be greeted by pop and butties. Colin was soon there and I asked for his opinion of the route.

"Great, what's next?"

PLEASURE DOME: The line of the upper part of the route is clearly visible with the crux wall below the climber and the hand traverse disappearing away around the corner.
Climber: Malcolm Smith

76: PLEASURE DOME

Situation:	Stennis Head, Range East, Castlemartin, South Pembroke
Aspect:	South facing
Grade:	E3 (5c)
Length:	45m (150ft)
Equipment:	A standard rack with plenty of extension slings.
First Ascent:	P.Littlejohn, J.Perrin, 6th April 1980
Guidebook:	*Pembroke* by Jon de Montjoye and Mike Harber, published by the Climbers' Club in 1985. A new two-volume guide is due out in 1992.

Approaches: From the car park at St Govan's Chapel cross the stile and walk west into the Range. Immediately beyond the impressive inlet of Stennis Ford turn left and go out to the headland. Rather to the right of the point, an easy slanting rake allows a scrambling descent to non-tidal rock ledges below the cliff. The route starts on the far right side of these.

The Route: A long pitch with a strenuous hand traverse and a fingery and exposed crux. Protection is good though care is needed with the rope work.

Description: At the very bottom of the ramp is a narrow inlet. Cross this and climb the rib on 'the roughest rock in the world' to a possible stance. Climb the steep groove on the right then follow a swinging hand traverse out towards the centre of the wall. A bold move gains a ramp, above which is the crux. Step right and climb the wall on small holds until it is possible to swing left then climb straight up to the foot of the final corner which leads easily to the top.

PLEASURE DOME

From the foot of the rock ramp that runs under Stennis Head you get a good view of a huge smooth wall of beautiful white rock out to the right. It is undercut by a big sea cave but access is provided by a step across a narrow sea-filled rift and a rugged rib. From the top of the rib a thin overhanging crack runs straight up the wall forming the substance of the well named, and best avoided, MEAN STREAK. To the right a rather more inviting line heads slightly rightwards into the middle of nowhere.

This shallow groove is also pretty steep but has excellent holds and some brilliant nut slots. At the top of the groove a step right finds a line of fine flaky handholds and a good foothold from which to survey the scene.

To the right a horizontal hand traverse runs out towards the centre of the wall. It is both overhung and undercut but proves to be technically straightforward, as the handholds are good. Sadly any footholds are conspicuous by their absence so a rapid approach is best. Some distance along this break you realise that this route is not going to be a pushover, when the hand traverse ends suddenly and a difficult move is made to span across to the next decent hold. From this an awkward finger change and another long reach gains the edge of a steeply sloping ramp. A committing swing is needed to get onto the ramp, which unfortunately is not the longed-for safe haven. The wall above bulges and a 'shake out' is the best the spot has to offer. The positions are dramatic and the upward view is not overly encouraging, access to the obvious corner being barred by a short smooth wall; the crux.

On my first foray here I tried to climb straight up past some prominent undercuts, and was faced with a 'slap' for a hold. I called for slack, made the jump and missed. Not surprisingly I set off seaward at a rate of knots and had just picked my landing spot in the water when the rope pulled me up short. Getting back to my high point proved problematical due to the undercut nature of the wall, and a little craft and cunning was needed. The second attempt was more successful as a good look round revealed some excellent small finger holds to the right of my first attempt line. A pull on a sharp edge allowed me to reach an excellent 'stuck on' flake from which it was possible to swing back left to better holds. A couple of quick moves and I was in the final easy corner. Sat on the top I mulled on the name, PLEASURE DOME came from a Frankie Goes to Hollywood L.P., but at this moment I felt another track from the same record was more appropriate: RELAX.

77: THINK PINK

Situation:	Main Wall, Avon Gorge, Bristol
Aspect:	South-west facing
Grade:	E3 (5a or 5b, 6a, 5c)
Length:	80m (260ft)
Equipment:	A standard rack, with a set of R.P.s if you intend to start up KRAPPS LAST TAPE.
First Ascent:	F.Bennett (aid), 1965
First Free Ascent:	R.Harrison, 1977
Guidebook:	*The Avon Gorge* by Steve Monks, published by Dark Peak in 1981. A new guide is due out in late 1991.

Approaches: The cliffs lie above the A4 (Portway), and there is a large parking area complete with a mobile tea wagon and public toilets (with in-situ bouldering) below the highest wall. THINK PINK takes the smooth looking wall of the obvious colour several hundred metres to the north (left) of the car park. Walk leftwards and climb over the fence. Scramble up to scrubby ledges below the face then trend left and back right to get to a small ledge with a groove rising from it directly below the right edge of the pink wall.

The Route: A varied trip, the lower pitch offering delicate, poorly protected climbing, the upper two being more strenuous but safer.

Description: There is a choice of starts. By far the easiest is to climb the first two pitches of MALPRACTICE. For this traverse left from the stance then climb a wall to a ledge, head up left and pass under a downward pointing spike, with a possible belay further to the left. Step right above the spike then climb the rib to a roof from where it is possible to move left and up to gain ledges with an assortment of belays, or move right to a mighty iron spike.

A rather harder, much better and considerably more serious start is to do KRAPPS LAST TAPE. This provides a great contrast to the strenuous climbing above and gets you an extra tick in the book. Climb the groove behind the stance moving out left at the top to a small ledge. From here move right, up to and over a roof (first half decent runners). Traverse rightwards and cross another roof to reach the biggest overhang. Traverse left to a belay on the iron spike or further left. The rest of the route is much easier to follow.

Move left and climb the difficult wall past bolts to a flake line which is followed to ledges and a tree belay. Move left to gain the prominent short crack which is entered with difficulty, then step left and climb the steep wall to the top.

THINK PINK

The large smooth pinkish wall at the left end of the Main Wall at Avon was an obvious challenge to the 'men of steel' in the sixties. Fred Bennett drilled a couple of bolts in the lowest part of the wall to give access to a fine flake line above and named the route THE PINK LINK. Tony Willmott reduced the aid to three points and renamed the route THINK PINK, then six years later 'Nipper' Harrison free climbed the route and thankfully left the name unchanged.

The best start is by the devious and serious KRAPPS LAST TAPE, put up by Avon devotee Ed Ward Drummond. Most of the original peg runners have fallen out to leave a serious piece of climbing that requires a cool head rather than any great technical brilliance.

From the thick iron rod belay, the second pitch is blatantly a whole different ball game. Three bolts protect a fine bit of face climbing with the crux being the final long stretch off a layaway to reach a good hold on the lip of the roof above. A couple of quick pulls and you are established in the base of a shallow groove. This gives sustained and well protected climbing with one hard move for shorties, that better endowed climbers can 'yawn' past. A few final steep moves lead to ledges and a thorn bush and nut belays.

The final pitch is the obvious short slanting crack sprouting a big fat peg. On closer inspection most of the peg sticks out into space, but good Friend and nut back ups exist. The first move on to the wall is a stinker, a difficult pull on indifferent finger jams to reach better holds. There used to be a creaking jug here that gave the unwary a bit of a shock. It's gone now, doubtless it gave some unsuspecting soul a real fright as it finally parted company with the rock and precipitated them Avonwards. The final wall is steep but the holds are much better than they look and you would have to be really bushed to fail here with success so close. A crumbly last few moves and it's all over, just a short stagger back into the bushes to find a solid tree belay. Although the line of the climb is a little flawed it provides a real insight into the varied nature of climbing on Britains' biggest and best 'City Crag', a great route of subtle contrasts.

THINK PINK: Climbers using the rather serious **KRAPPS LAST TAPE** as an approach to **THINK PINK** which reaches the conspicuous bush by the indefinite flake crack and finishes up the thin slanting crack on the left side of the final wall.
Climbers: Chris Craggs and Colin Binks

FACE ROUTE:
The initial groove of poor (and often damp) rock leads to a black bulge that contains several rotting pegs. It is passed by strenuous undercutting and laybacking. The crux pitch is the second one, crossing a difficult roof, fortunately the protection and rock improve as height is gained.
Climbers: unknown though the leader may be a Berzins.

78: FACE ROUTE

Situation:	Gordale Scar, Yorkshire
Aspect:	South facing
Grade:	E3 (5c, 6a)
Length:	47m (160ft)
Equipment:	A normal rack with a few extra medium and large wires plus extra extenders for the in-situ pegs.
First Ascent:	R.Moseley, J.Mortimer, 1956
First Free Ascent:	P.Livesey, J.Sheard, October 1971
Guidebook:	*Yorkshire Limestone* published by the Yorkshire Mountaineering Club in 1985.

Approaches: Gordale Scar lies just off the minor road that runs eastwards for one kilometre out of Malham village and then turns into a grass track. There is limited parking at the roadside just past a small bridge. A level path leads into the jaws of the gorge, in less than five minutes from the road. FACE ROUTE is the gob-smacking line dead ahead as you round the corner into the ravine.

The Route: A strenuous groove with a number of old pegs leads to a fierce roof. Protection is good but some of the rock is a bit rattly.

Description: Rather illogically FACE ROUTE takes the most obvious groove line on the Left Wing of Gordale Scar. The first pitch follows the groove throughout to a small roof which is passed on the right. Above this steep face climbing leads to a small stance in a mini-cave on the right. The second pitch traverses to the left to below a bulge, this is passed directly or on the right. Continue up into a yew tree. Many parties belay here and then abseil off, but the top is only a short distance above and the descent back through the

gorge is well worthwhile.

FACE ROUTE

FACE ROUTE and the other great line of the gorge, CAVE ROUTE, were put up on the same day in 1956. For many years they were sought out by climbers wishing to sharpen up their aid techniques for use on beetling Dolomite walls, and there is no doubt it was a great way to spend a miserable mid-winter day. An early start was needed to beat any rivals, and a great rucksack of ironmongery was essential. Then a long strenuous day, spent slowly bashing your way upwards, stacked pegs, tied off knifeblades, mouldy old bits of in-situ tat, then usually a finish by torch light before going off to the boozer to relive the day in detail. Altogether more memorable than another session in the gym, but times change.

In those distant days FACE ROUTE was a fairly amenable aid route (graded A2) and a competent party could do it in four to six hours depending largely on the amount of gear that was already in place. Today the route should take an equally competent party an hour or so. The initial groove gives straight forward bridging to a bulge which is passed strenuously to reach more open climbing on large but spaced holds. The climbing is distinctly butch and although there are still plenty of peg runners in place many of them are decidedly grotty, so the odd back up nut is a good idea. A ragged crack line gives more strenuous climbing to a superb semi-hanging stance where there is a dramatic improvement in the quality of the rock. The second usually storms up this pitch and pronounces it mild, as he has not been unduly worried by the possibility of running out of steam on strenuous ground or the state of the fixed gear. As he found it so easy then it is obvious who gets the second pitch!

An easy traverse leads left into another cave-like recess above which glowers the crux bulge, slit centrally by a thin crack. The most obvious way to attack this is to thug your way over the bulge but this involves a vicious lock-off to reach better holds, fortunately with perfect protection. A rather more devious and slightly bolder approach is to lean out rightwards where better holds are hidden, allowing a quick sprint to easier ground. Just above is a gnarled yew tree that has to be fought

through to reach an easy groove leading to the grass slopes at the top of the gorge. Perhaps now is the time for a return to those traditional values we hear so much about these days; whose round is it anyway?

79: NEW DIMENSIONS

Situation:	Castell y Gwynt, Great Orme, Llandudno, North Wales
Aspect:	North facing
Grade:	E3 (5c, 6a, 5a)
Length:	40m (130ft)
Equipment:	A standard rack.
First Ascent:	R.Edwards, T.Jepson (using three points of aid), 11th October 1975. The crux pitch was climbed free a short time later by J.Moran and P.Williams. The route had its first completely free ascent the following year by R.Edwards.
Guidebook:	*North Wales Limestone* by Andy Pollitt, published in 1987 by the Climbers' Club.

Approaches: (Access to the Great Orme is under review due to rock fall, though thus far (1991) Castell y Gwynt has not been affected - check on the latest situation.)

From Llandudno follow the Marine Drive round the headland of the Great Orme for three kilometres to a white lighthouse. Park and cross the wall just before the lighthouse gate. Follow the wall into a steep gully which is descended until the crag appears on the right. Impressive.

NEW DIMENSIONS: The crux consists of "a black groove composed of strange bumpy rock", the bolts and pegs in it are in a very poor state.
Climbers: Colin Binks and Chris Craggs

The Route: An action packed and varied route which feels longer than it is. Much of the fixed gear is in a poor state.

Description: Start in a small cave with thread belays. Climb strenuously out of the roof of the cave then step right, go up and right again to a bulge which is passed

on the right to gain a steep groove. This is followed with increasing difficulty to a small stance on the left. Bolt belays. Gain the groove on the left and climb it past some 'funny farm' bolts and very old pegs until steep moves reach the break. Traverse right to a belay below a steep corner. Up the corner (old peg) to an exit on the left, belay further up the slope.

NEW DIMENSIONS

I remember the occasion well. It was the first Live Aid concert and we were climbing on the Yellow Wall at Pen Trwyn. We had the car stereo cranked up, Quo were bashing out 'Rocking All Over The World', it all felt so apt - then the rain started. So what's new?

We bundled the gear into the car and sat there with long faces, listening to the crowds enjoying the sounds and watching the rain drops running down the windscreen. I suggest to Dave that we go and have a look at Castell y Gwynt instead of sitting and moping. He was not very keen but grudgingly agreed - anything to stop me getting depressed.

By the time we had reached the lighthouse the sky had lightened a few shades though it was still spitting fitfully. I pointed out that we might as well take the sacks down 'just in case' and Dave gave me a funny sideways look. The descent gully was just plain evil; wet, vegetated and slippery. There was a distinct feeling that a misplaced foot would send you shooting down the gully like a manic one man bob sleigh, straight over the cliff edge and out into the sea.

When the crag appeared on the right it proved to be mighty impressive, like "Kilnsey by the seaside". It was extremely steep, capped by a big roof and streaked with long sooty ribbons. Added to this was the gripping drop BELOW the crag; the whole place was distinctly uninviting. Even so, having got this far we (or should that read 'I') decided to at least have a bash.

The rock was remarkably dry because the rain was blowing over the cliff top, so I led off. The start was a bit of a battle, out of the roof of the belay cave to reach more open rock. Above things were rather more straightforward to another bulge from which hung a big peg and a karabiner locked together by flaking red rust. A steep groove gave more strenuous climbing and a difficult exit landed me on a small stance.

The old belay bolts were in a poor state but good threads up and right made things nice and safe (a substantial new bolt has recently been placed on the stance). Dave came up the pitch like a steam train and he was soon tied into the belays, he was beginning to enjoy himself.

Pitch two is a black groove composed of strange bumpy rock. This is very compact and aid bolts were inserted to facilitate the first ascent. Today it is possible to bridge past the bolts (I would not fancy pulling on them anyway) up the ever steepening groove. The last few moves to the break felt pushy, a long stretch found me hanging from wet holds feeling distinctly harassed. A short traverse right reached a small ledge with good belays and a chance to regain my composure. Dave was out of sight but the rope moved in steadily, and then it stopped. I shouted down to see if he was O.K.

"I will be when I get my foot in this bloody sling" came the reply. A few minutes later a red face appeared, uttering just one word, "Desperate".

The grade of the final pitch suggested that it should have been a cruise, but it proved to be steep and strenuous with distinctly unfriendly rock. The exit onto steep wet grass provided a final few anxious moments, certainly no place to take up flying lessons. I put in a double ration of belays and brought up the long suffering Dave.

His raised eyebrows said it all.

"O.K. Tomorrow you choose" I said.

80: LADDER OF DESIRE & THEM

Situation: Unknown Area, Avon Gorge, Bristol
Aspect: West facing
Grade: E3 (5c, 6a)
Length: 60m (200ft)
Equipment: A standard rack is adequate for both routes.
First Ascent: LADDER OF DESIRE R.Harrison,1978 THEM P.Littlejohn, C.King, 1977
Guidebook: *The Avon Gorge* by Steve Monks, published by Dark Peak in 1981. A new guide is due out in late 1991.

Approaches: The first pitch of this combination of routes starts on the piece of rock closest to the A4 (Portway) that links Avonmouth with Bristol city centre. Parking is available on the grass a short way beyond the route or a little further on in a small lay-by.

The Routes: A combination of two routes set one above the other giving superb wall climbing. The lower one is more devious, the upper one more strenuous. Protection is sound but occasionally spaced.

Description: LADDER OF DESIRE starts eight metres in from the stone wall in a small clearing amongst the scrub. A short tricky wall leads to better holds and a flake crack. Above this a short 'blank' wall is climbed to better holds that lead up and left towards the edge of the wall. From here traverse back to the right passing below a concrete handhold to reach a short crack. This is climbed on the right to reach a good pocket which allows a swing back left (old bolts) to good holds and the top. There are a couple of good peg belays cemented down the crack at the back of the ledge, or a substantial 'fence' on the ramp a little higher.

THEM starts from the very tip of the ramp at a pole. Traverse a short distance left then follow cracks steeply rightward passing two peg runners to good nut slots. Step back down and traverse the wall on the left to a shallow groove which is laybacked (peg on the right) to a resting place. Continue up the groove then move left to finish directly up the final steepening via several more peg runners.

LADDER OF DESIRE & THEM

In the mid 1970s Avon County Council decided that the part of The Unknown Area that towered over the road was a danger to the public that scurried past its foot on their way to and from the city centre. Accordingly the road was closed and the contractors moved in. It was a great time to climb in the Gorge, by driving around the barriers it was possible to experience a rare tranquilly unspoilt by the continuous roar of the passing traffic.

The workmen removed plenty of dense ivy, flakes and loose blocks and then decided to really go for it and demolished half the buttress, removing several million tonnes of solid rock. It rather put normal 'creative cleaning' methods adopted by some climbers into perspective. When the dust had settled there was time to take stock. There were sad losses, especially the classic long routes of UNKNOWN GULLY and UNKNOWN BUTTRESS. These were reduced in stature by fifty percent and altered out of all recognition. At the same time there was a definite plus. The lower walls of the buttress had been well cleaned and a whole new area of rock had appeared containing some fine steep crack lines; rare birds indeed at Avon.

LADDER OF DESIRE rapidly achieved classic status and when combined with THEM on the upper tier a memorable outing is guaranteed.

A short tricky wall bars access to the 'ladder' beyond. A layaway high on the left is the key to reaching better holds and then a flake crack allows for rapid progress to the foot of a smooth looking wall. A couple of well hidden finger holds allow you to make a high step up and long reach for good scalloped jugs. A bit of a loop is now necessary out left and back right until below an oblong concrete jug. Purists will sneak below this others will grab it, thank the council, and swing smartly to the right.

Now things begin to rear up and a short flake crack points the way. Large

127

LADDER OF DESIRE & THEM: Starting the fingery and technical crux section with a lot of rope out already. THEM lies just above and provides a logical extension pitch.
Climber: Derek Carter

81: TREVALLEN PILLAR

Situation:	Trevallen Cliff, St Govan's, South Pembroke
Aspect:	South facing
Grade:	E4 (6a, 5c)
Length:	45m (150ft)
Equipment:	A standard rack.
First Ascent:	Jon de Montjoye, I.Parsons, 20th June 1981
Guidebook:	*Pembroke* by Jon de Montjoye and M.Harber published by the Climbers' Club in 1985. A new two-volume guide is due out in 1992.

Approaches: The cliff lies roughly midway between the St Govan's car park and the descent to St Govan's cliff. An abseil descent from any one of a series of spikes above the cliff is the normal approach. The best descent is down a shallow rounded gully (with twin spikes above it) and from the foot of this the route is some distance to the left (facing the sea). The base of the route is inaccessible at high water if there is a swell running.

The Route: Two pitches on immaculate rock, the lower one is delicate and safe the upper one is strenuous and bold. Low in the grade.

Description: Step onto the pillar from a block and climb easily to a horizontal break. A couple of tricky moves gains a small thread and good wires, the crux follows and is climbed leftwards to reach a short groove and then a comfortable stance.

The second pitch climbs the unprotected blunt arête above the belay to a good ledge. The leaning wall above leads into the final groove.

TREVALLEN PILLAR

From above, the delights of Trevallen cliff can only be guessed at. Peering cautiously over the grassy rim, the upper part of the cliff appears as a hotchpotch of poorly

layback holds further out to the right allow a couple of teetery moves to reach small holds and just a little higher a good three finger pocket. A bit of prior planning is worthwhile here to ensure you get the pocket with the right hand, (is the right hand the left hand in this case? There is only one way you will find out!). A quick swing left leads to big jugs and a short steep wall gives out onto the giant ramp system.

THEM starts at the very crest of the slab where a tubular steel spike protrudes from the solid rock. The pitch kicks off with a traverse out left above a big drop, on rather crusty crystaline rock. Steep cracks are then followed to some large well-scarred nut placements. It is worth placing a few runners here to bolster your confidence for the next section which is rather bold. Swing

out on to the wall to reach a poor layaway, then make some committing moves into the groove further to the left. A couple of gripping-feeling layback moves are needed to actually get established in the groove where a peg runner gives you a chance to relax again. The rest of the pitch is still steep but it is more straightforward than the lower section and solid fixed protection arrives with satisfying regularity.

Positive finger holds and small sharp foot holds allow for steady progress up and left to a rather sudden finish. A couple of routes like these make you think; perhaps man-made climbing walls aren't that bad after all.

TREVALLEN PILLAR:
The technical crux of the route is at the top of the thin slanting crack in the lower pillar, while the second pitch offers easier but strenuous and bold climbing. Here both pitches have been run together to cut out the rather uncomfortable stance.
Climber: Colin Binks

cemented horizontal rubble bands and mud, that degenerate even further as the cliff top is approached. From below, the true magnificence of the rock becomes apparent. Large areas of the cliff are severely undercut, but above this major inconvenience are a superb collection of white walls, clean cut corners and striking crack lines. And all this only five minutes from the car!

Walking towards St Govan's from the foot of the abseil the undercut base of the cliff becomes oven more impressive, until it reaches an area of 'futuristic roofs', where superb hand jamming cracks dangle tantalisingly out of reach, not too far from the ground but a long way from the back wall. Just around the corner from these overhangs is one of the most striking features of these cliffs, a magnificent square-cut pillar of superb grey rock. The route is like a magnet drawing you on - it just has to be done.

The undercut lower section of the pillar is avoided by stepping in from a great block, and gives straightforward moves on sharp holes to a knobbly horizontal break. This can be filled with runners, and you may as well get rid of all your large nuts and any Friends you have brought, as you will not be needing them any higher up! An awkward move to stand in the break is followed by a couple of pulls on sharp holds and you can clip an in-situ thread around a fairly insubstantial piece of rock. Fortunately a solid Rock 5 is available just to the right. The crux moves follow and the required technique is obvious - you need to be standing on the good holds by the thread. A step up and frantic search of the rock above reveals the truth; all you require is one good fingerhold, but it does not exist. After considerable groping around you convince yourself of this fact and make the move using a pathetic sloping edge. Once started, the holds improve (though none of them are worth jumping for) and after a short runout you reach an excellent stance on the crest of the pillar. There are good thread belays in the ledge.

The second pitch is a total contrast to the first. Instead of being technical and safe it is butch and bold. A wire can be placed in the groove at head height and though it hardly seems worth the effort, there is nothing else for quite a while. A large flat hold on the right can be reached after a tricky move, and a powerful pull and long reach gains another 'flattie'. From this an

even longer long reach should see you hanging from a pinch grip on the crest of the buttress, in a position of no retreat. A fall from here would probably land you squarely on the second's head unless he has had the sense to crawl into the horizontal break at the back of the ledge to belay. One more pull and the situation eases. A good ledge is reached where you can calm down and get rid of some of the ballast you have carried thus far. The steep wall above has excellent holds and leads into the base of a solid corner that can be bridged easily to the cliff top.

TREVALLEN PILLAR might not be desperate at the grade but it is a superbly varied route on magnificent rock, one of the best around.

Situation:	Kilnsey Crag, Upper Wharfedale, Yorkshire
Aspect:	East facing
Grade:	E4 (6a, 5a)
Length:	50m (165ft)
Equipment:	A standard rack backed up with a few extra mid range wires should be enough.
First Ascent:	J.A.Austin, B.Fuller, 1960? using aid but with some free climbing.
First Free Ascent:	P.Livesey, J.Sheard, 1973
Guidebook:	*Yorkshire Limestone* published by the Yorkshire Mountaineering Club in 1985.

Approaches: Kilnsey Crag is the unmistakable wall of rock looming over Wharfedale almost overhanging the B6160, ten kilometres north of Grassington. Parking is available in a large parking spot, with

refreshments, a few hundred metres north of the cliff.

Permission MUST be sought from the farm (North Cote) at the northern end of the cliff and is not given at weekends due to sightseers blocking the road to essential services. The farmer has requested that no dogs be taken on his land, please respect this.

The Route: A fine wall climb, with a fingery and very safe crux followed by easier but bolder climbing above.

Description: Towards the right side of the long frontage of the cliff is a massive corner, the DIEDRE. To the left of this is a fine sheet of grey rock, which although it is well to the right of the centre of the cliff is called CENTRAL WALL. This area is undercut throughout its length, but a left slanting weakness where the bulges are rather narrower offers a way on to the wall. Climb up and left until a peg on the right can be reached. Swing past this (crux) then head up and left to a resting place. From here climb more or less straight up the wall to three horizontal breaks, the top one of which is traversed to the left to a tree belay. Pitch two follows the rather floral groove behind the tree to the cliff top.

CENTRAL WALL

When Pete Livesey free climbed CENTRAL WALL in 1973 he was already well into his plan of setting the climbing world on its head and making himself famous. This route was an obvious contender for a free ascent, being only partly aided and not too much on the wrong side of vertical. The rock is manifestly magnificent and if the stories are true the route was no match for 'Mr Fingers', despite it being climbed in a thunderstorm.

The start is an awkward (i.e. hard) overhang containing arguably the hardest move on the route, but eminently suitable for bouldering out. You may need a spotter as sheep do-do all over your lycra rather spoils the image. Once over the bulge a few moves diagonally left up a shallow corner, laughingly described as a slab in the guide book, allows you to clip a peg out on the right. Passing this is the crux, but with the peg by your chin, you will not find many safer moves anywhere. A difficult finger change, or a jump for technical dunces, reaches better holds and a rest is available

just a little higher. A semi-detached block complete with threaded slings can be clipped while you get your breathing back to normal.

Thus far the climbing has been ideal for climbers who have spent the winter training on the wall; technical, fingery and safe. The upper part of the pitch is a push-over by comparison but this is where all the 'wobblers' occur. The rest of the climbing is only 5b, but it is steep and sustained, added to which is the fact that the protection is rather spaced. A degree of commitment is needed, as is the ability to climb away from your gear into the unknown.

With perseverance and possibly a bit of a grip, the horizontal breaks are reached and you can scoot along them to a hanging belay from bolts and pegs (in-situ karabiner) beside the horizontal tree. The H.V.S. groove above you is part of the route, though it is usually omitted in favour of a gentle descent to Earth. Over the years vegetation has taken over again and the pitch has become increasingly overgrown. It would only take a quick trip on an abseil rope, from a public spirited soul to return the rock to its former glory, but until that day you can always claim that you left the summit flags in your rucksack at the base of the route.

CENTRAL WALL: Once the crux moves are passed more difficult moves are needed to gain a resting place. A lot of easier but bold climbing still lies above.
Climber: Chris Craggs

83:
STAR WARS

Situation:	East face of Bosherston Head, Castlemartin Range, South Pembroke
Aspect:	South facing
Grade:	E4 (5c)
Length:	40m (130ft)
Equipment:	A standard rack, with a set of R.P.s and a size 3 Friend.
First Ascent:	B.Winteringham, M.Winteringham, C.Heard, 29th June 1980
Guidebook:	*Pembroke* by Jon de Montjoye and Mike Harber, published by the Climbers' Club in 1985. A new two-volume guide is due out in 1992.

Approaches: Park at the large car park for the St Govan's Chapel and cross the stile into the range, (always assuming that the red flags are not flying). Pass the wide inlet of Stennis Ford and a little further the narrower gash of Huntsman's Leap. Turn left, heading for the sea following the edge of the Leap. Just beyond the entrance to the Leap, the top of a white south facing wall can be glimpsed. The foot of this is reached by a 30-metre abseil from anchors in a small outcrop ten metres back from the edge and a short distance seaward.

The Route: A fine open wall climb. Route finding is quite straightforward but the protection is rather spaced.

Description: Climb the steep corner until a line of holds lead out towards the arête. Move up a shallow groove and a short steep wall to reach a good horizontal break (large Friend runner). Now climb into the shallow groove above and trend rightwards until bigger holds lead away to the arête and an easy finish.

STAR WARS

A typical Easter was well under way. The campsite was packed and every evening the pub was bulging at the seams. The weather was unseasonably cold with a raw north-westerly wind whipping up a big swell and as usual the tides were all wrong. Daily we watched the bright yellow helicopter pick up its unfortunate (or incompetent) passengers from St Govan's for a quick flight to the hospital at Haverfordwest as we climbed on some of the more secluded bits of rock on the coast.

STAR WARS was well up the list of things to do but on three occasions we

STAR WARS: The route offers superbly situated wall climbing on good rock although protection is spaced the runners are good where it matters.
Climber: Chris Craggs

peered over the crumbly cliff edge to catch a glimpse of the ledges at the foot of the route disappearing under a column of spray as waves slapped up the rock. We bided our time and sure enough on Tuesday the crowds went home, the wind dropped and the sun even managed to show itself. We abbed to the ledges at the foot of the route towards low water and sorted the ropes out. Close to the sea, below these big cliffs, there is a special indefinable atmosphere that you do not get anywhere else. A sense of tranquillity and timelessness that provides a great contrast to the windswept and desolate Army ranges only a short distance above.

The initial corner that bars access to the wall was steep and awkward but provided good runners. A short distance up this and a set of discontinuous ledges ran out right towards the centre of the wall. I followed these easily at first and then with greater difficulty until a committing swing had to be made into a tiny groove. The expected runners did not appear and a glance back to the left revealed that a fall would have nasty consequences. A couple of awkward steps up led to better holds and good runners below a short steep wall. An undercut pocket allowed a long reach for good jugs and just a little higher a horizontal break that could be laced with protection. I was beginning to warm to the task and loving every minute of it.

The upper section of the wall has a vague shallow groove running up its centre and this was gained by a couple of delicate moves. I placed several small fiddly wires before moving up and right to where a line of better holds appeared to head up towards the arête. A committing cross-hands move and bit of a swing was needed to reach the holds, though they were not quite as good as they appeared from below. There was no going back so I pressed on and the situation gradually eased as I approached the hanging arête. The positions here were great and I lingered a while enjoying the superb situations and the growing inner glow that comes from a totally absorbing route. As I topped out the trials and tribulations of the earlier part of the week were suddenly put well and truly back into perspective.

84: FLAKY WALL

Situation:	High Tor, Matlock, Derbyshire
Aspect:	West facing
Grade:	E4 (6a)
Length:	40m (130ft)
Equipment:	A standard rack with extra mid-sized and large wires, plus extenders for them.
First Ascent:	D.Scott, C.Davies, 1961 (aid)
First Free Ascent:	P.Livesey, J.Sheard, 16th April 1972
Guidebook:	*Peak Limestone, South.* Published by the British Mountaineering Council in 1987.

Approaches: High Tor is the impressive sheet of rock that towers over the river and road as you drive south from Matlock along the A6. A short distance beyond the cliff is a bridge that gives access to the bottom station of the Heights of Abraham cable-car. There is limited free parking near here and the cliff is ten minutes walking distance. Cross the bridge and go round behind the building (paying the entrance fee if necessary) to a flight of steps. At the top of these is a narrow path that heads back towards Matlock and passes under the cliff. The route climbs across the wall to the right of the obvious shallow groove taken by ORIGINAL ROUTE.

The Route: A long sustained pitch with fingery climbing. Protection is good but awkward to arrange.

Description: Scramble up to the tree at the foot of the groove then climb straight up the crack line above to gain the base of the groove. Now follow the curving flake down to the right and cross the wall to the base of a shallow left facing corner. This is climbed to a difficult exit on to the flakes crossing the wall above. Follow these until they end then finish up the steep wall above. Tree belay some distance back.

FLAKY WALL

FLAKY WALL has an interesting and fairly controversial history as it was transformed from a great aid route to an even better free one. It was put up at the start of the 60s, by latter-day Himalayan guru Doug Scott, who spent many of his formative years bashing hell out of the more spectacular rock formations scattered around our islands. This particular piece of limestone gave them a mini epic, hammering steel pegs and wooden wedges down the back of the rather 'flexible' flakes and finishing the route by torch light, in the obligatory snow storm. They sure knew how to enjoy themselves in those days!

At the other end of the decade Ed. Ward-Drummond approached the line with a bit of lateral thinking. Instead of pegging or free climbing the pitch he came up with the novel idea of a subtle combination of the two approaches and free climbed most of the route, using five skyhooks for aid. He also renamed the route Hook-Crook Wall. Not surprisingly this gripping style of ascent did not catch on. Three years later the route finally got its complete free ascent at the hands (fingers?) of Pete Livesey. He renamed it Bull Dog Wall but it soon reverted to its original name. It remains a great route, a long and devious pitch and despite the comments in the guidebook it is no pushover at the grade.

From the tree belay on ORIGINAL ROUTE the groove directly above you marks the start of the pitch. This is technically quite reasonable but there is not much in the way of gear so a rapid approach will soon see you joining ORIGINAL ROUTE again. It is possible to move up and clip an old peg but this needs a long extension and some form of nut back up. When you are happy with the runners it is necessary to descend the curving flake on the right. It is possible to get a Friend #1 under this, but deciding which rope to clip it with is a bit of a poser. It is perhaps best to try and do without it.

From the foot of the flake a difficult move out right is made to reach good holds and a step down leads to a reasonable rest. Above is a shallow groove in the right wall of which are some good thin cracks that will take a selection of wires. Care is needed here because with the direction the rope is running there is a tendency for it to lift out the runners. At the top of the groove is the crux of the route, a layback move on the old

peg pockets and a long reach for the jug formed by the base of the big flake system running up the centre of the wall. A quick pull and a smart mantelshelf and you are back in balance once again. It is possible to turn round here and with your heels stuck in the flake take both hands off, though this is only to be recommended for the reckless or out and out posers. The flake gives steady laybacking with good protection, though it is all a bit strenuous, until a final steep wall is reached. This has reasonable flat holds, though not a lot in the way of gear and if you are still feeling fresh should cause no problems, though it has been the scene of some mighty fliers. A quick trip through the bushes leads to a commendably stout tree belay and a feeling of a job well done. Now it's your second's turn.

FLAKY WALL:
The fingery and committing moves where the security of the shallow groove has to be quitted in an attempt to reach the eponymous flakes.
Climber: William Gregory

85: PAN

Situation: No-Man's Zawn, Lydstep, South Pembroke

Aspect: North facing

Grade: E4 (6a)

Length: 40m (130ft)

Equipment: A standard rack and good route-finding ability.

First Ascent: P.Littlejohn, L.Foulkes, T.Penning, 22nd April 1984

Guidebook: *Pembroke* by Jon de Montjoye and Mike Harber, published by the Climbers' Club in 1985. A new two-volume guide is due out in 1992.

Approaches: No-Man's Zawn is to be found a kilometre or so to the west of the ever popular Mother Carey's Kitchen. From the A4139 turn into Skrinkle, one kilometre west of Lydstep. Follow the road round to the right in front of the houses then bear left. The road heads towards a wire compound on the headland. Before this is reached turn left and drive past the oddly modern-looking building (a new Youth Hostel) to the car park. The Zawn is the narrow rift 100 metres east of the car park. There are stakes above both sides of the Zawn for abseil anchors, check their solidity.

NOTE: The Zawn bed is only uncovered at dead low tide for a couple of hours, check before you abseil in!

The Route: Magnificent wall climbing in a gripping situation. The climbing is strenuous and route-finding is far from easy. Protection is spaced.

Description: Towards the right side of the wall is a discontinuous crack line rising steeply rightwards. Start to the right of the crack and climb the steep wall to a 'lump', there is an in-situ thread two metres further to the right that can be used as a belay if the sea threatens. Pull into the crack and follow it for six metres to a small deep hole before trending left up the wall for eight metres to an inconspicuous flat-topped spike (tape runner). Continue up the left to a resting scoop at some large calcite crystals. Climb up and right to another shallow recess then finish straight up the impending wall. (Can you remember all that?)

PAN

No-Man's Zawn is well named, its base is a place that rarely sees the sun and is underwater for a large percentage of the year. Stood on the shady sandy beach in the bottom of the slit, gazing at the narrow strip of blue sky far above or the sunlit walls of Frontier Zawn across the way, you feel that you are definitely here on borrowed time. This feeling is reinforced when you look at the high tide level far above your head.

This is certainly no place to belay a leader who is a bit on the slow side unless you fancy following the route in wet boots (and that is, if you are lucky). It is possible to take a hanging stance on a lump of rock at eight metres or an in-situ thread a little higher, but this is only possible if the sea is calm and even then the hassle of keeping

PAN: Emerging from the well named No Man's Zawn, the climbing is devious and not over endowed with protection. To cap it all the tide is in and it is raining!
Climber: Graham Parkes

the ropes out of the water is considerable. If you get the time and tide right (and they wait for no man, not even one in No-Man's Zawn) PAN offers a superb piece of wall climbing.

The start is steep but the holds are good, and once you are convinced of the dryness of your feet it is possible to press on rapidly following the line of a thin discontinuous crack. A small round 'pigeon hole' marks the place where the route begins to head away to the left. There is no real line, and the holds are generally unhelpful. None of the moves are desperate but there is an insistent nagging doubt that you might be going the wrong way, heading up a blind alley, and as there is not a great deal of protection retreat would be tricky or spectacular.

An odd flat-topped spike takes a tape runner and gives you the reassurance that you are on the right track. The next section offers more of the same, absorbing wall climbing, steep sustained and bold. Finally you reach an easing in angle and a proper rest amongst an area of huge calcite crystals (incorrectly described as quartz in the guide). From here the rest of the route is much more obvious and with better protection though it is still not easy. A final few steep moves on suspect rock lead back to the grassy cliff top and the belay stakes.

With an accurate description the route still gives an intimidating piece of climbing. First done on sight, it must have given Pat Littlejohn quite an adventure, though it obviously did not tax him too much as later the same day he made the first ascent of 1984 on the same wall - and that's a grade harder!

86: AMANITA MUSCARINA

Situation:	The Unknown Walls, Avon Gorge
Aspect:	West facing
Grade:	E4 (5b, 5c, 5c)
Length:	77m (250ft)
Equipment:	A normal rack should suffice.
First Ascent:	A.Wilmott, D.Hermalin, (aid), 1971
First Free Ascent:	P.Littlejohn, S.Lewis, 1980
Guidebook:	*The Avon Gorge* by Steve Monks, published by Dark Peak, 1981. A new guide is due out in late 1991.

Approaches: The crag is ten metres from the road. Parking is possible but rather risky on the main road, there is a pull-off 200m towards the city and a major parking place a kilometre further on with toilets and tea wagons.

The Route: AMANITA, as it is invariably known, is a three-pitch climb of escalating interest with the crux in a fine position high on an impressive wall.

The climbing is generally of a strenuous nature and protection is best described as adequate. Some of the rock still requires a gentle approach though it is much better than it used to be.

Description: The first pitch starts at the bottom left edge of the wall at a layback flake, which is followed by climbing a shot hole to a spacious ledge. Pitch two climbs directly up the wall to an unstable band of rock, and then enters the constricted groove that forms the right side of the only major feature of the face, a hanging corner system, to reach a constricted stance under the roof. The final and crucial pitch moves right to outflank the bulges before climbing steeply up the wall past bolts to gain a big peg and the final ramp line.

AMANITA MUSCARINA

As you drive into Bristol from the motorway, alongside the greasy trench that holds the River Avon the first rock to appear on the left is a great yellow crumbling wall. "What the hell is that?" is the usual reaction, as necks are craned from the car to get a look at this bizarre vertical desert of folded rock that towers overhead.

The appearance of the wall was enough to put people off and until the late 60s there were only two routes in this whole area. The original line was UNKNOWN GULLY (1954) of which only the lower half now remains, taking the corner to the right of the yellow wall, and up the slope to the left is the retiring and underrated UNKNOWN WALL (1961).

This was the situation until Tony Wilmott appeared on the scene. He was a free thinking product of the psychedelic 60s, a Pink Floyd fan and well into flower power, flared trousers and open minds. When he started to repeat the hard Drummond routes of the previous five years he adopted the novel approach of starting at the top of the graded list and working down "in case I got frightened going up".

This was the kind of mind that was needed to tackle the virgin yellow wall. With a mighty rack of aid gear he bashed and free climbed his way in an epic ascent right up the centre of the wall to produce THE EXPLODING GALAXY. A couple of years later he was back for more, to create the even more demanding AMANITA MUSCARINA, originally graded A5, with stories of pegs being hammered straight into rock which had the consistency of hard cheese. The name of the route is the Latin name for the red and white mushroom much loved by the illustrators of fairy stories, Fly Agaric. The story goes that the Ancient Britons brewed up the fungi into a drink before they went into battle as it used to make them feel invincible. Maybe that explains a lot!

Today things are a little more sane and sensible, the route is still a bit of a serious undertaking but a lot less so than it used to be. The first pitch is a straightforward layback up a rather sandy flake (imagine knocking pegs up the back of it). Above this an old peg and good small nuts protect delicate bridging moves up a cracked bore hole to the first stance. The second pitch starts with fun and games. Out to the right

is a substantial quarryman's spike almost hidden from view. This is lassoed (easy for cowboys) to protect the next section of the route. It was traditional to shout "Banzai" before jumping off and swarming up the rope. In these puritanical days it is necessary to climb straight up the wall with some precariousness before traversing right to gain the spike, the tip of which is polished to a high sheen from surreptitious use. The pockety wall above leads more easily, though with a tricky mantelshelf, to reach the band of sandy cheese that crosses the buttress. A short traverse left gains a truly pathetic thread around a tiny and largely unsupported flowstone pillar which protects (literally if not physically) the moves up the groove above. This leads to an ungainly constricted stance on a loose block with a variety of dubious belays, all crunched up under the roof.

The final pitch starts with a traverse to the right on sloping fingerholds and crusty footholds, before climbing straight up the steep wall past a trio of the original bolts, they are nearly 20 years old now and so need to be treated with a bit of reverence. Above these the rock bulges and pumpy climbing on big but sloping holds leads to a fat peg, a lot of which protrudes from the face. After recovering a little composure the ramp leading leftwards is followed easily though without much protection to the final short shattered wall and the top. Select a stout tree to lash yourself to then allow yourself a few minutes tò sit and ponder - they don't make 'em like that anymore.

AMANITA MUSCARINA: The second pitch offers the hardest single move on the route where a delicate wall has to be climbed after lassoing a quarryman's spike. The final stance is under the prominent roofs.
Climbers: Unknown

137

87:
OLIVER

Situation: The Quarry, Stoney Middleton, Derbyshire
Aspect: South-west facing
Grade: E4 (6a)
Length: 25m (80ft)
Equipment: A standard rack.
First Ascent: G.Birtles, spring 1979
Guidebook: *Peak Limestone Stoney*, published by the British Mountaineering Council in 1987.

Approaches: Follow the A623 westwards through Stoney Middleton Dale and take a minor right turn towards the village of Eyam. After 100 metres there is parking space available on the right in front of the gates of the electricity sub-station. Pass round the side of the fence to gain access to the fine wall to the left of BROWN CORNER.

The Route: A fierce strenuous wall climb, protection is good but rather spaced.

Description: Five metres to the left of the corner and just to the left of the crack which provides the start of MILLIONAIRE TOUCH is a steep groove. Climb this to bulges then swing left and boldly climb the wall to a break. Swing back right and stand up with difficulty, then easier climbing leads slightly leftward up the wall to the top.

OLIVER

I doubt if there are any climbers in the country who would describe Stoney Middleton as their favourite crag. Even so, despite some failings the place retains its popularity. In the summer climbers pop in to do the polished classics on the high and exposed Windy Buttress, or in the tree-shrouded bays. In the winter the local habituées from Sheffield and Manchester can be seen skulking about in the mud in search of a dry patch of rock to do a bit of bouldering on, or top roping WEE DORIS

OLIVER: The crux moves where a sudden transition has to be made from strenuous to delicate climbing, many leaders are caught out.
Climber: Mike Appleton

for the 'n'th time in search of the ultimate pump.

A little further up the dale lurks a rather esoteric looking quarry in the shape of a great open corner, containing an electricity sub-station that buzzes away quietly to itself. There used to be a mighty elm tree growing close to the corner with its uppermost branches brushing against the rock high on the wall. The tree fell victim to Dutch elm disease and so to avoid the possibility of it destroying the sub-station it was removed by an obliging feller (thanks to the guidebook for the joke). With the tree out of the way the wall was revealed in all its glory, quite simply it is the finest vertical piece of rock in the dale.

Geoff Birtles had the central line on the wall eyed up for a time and after top roping it, and doing a bit of constructive

cleaning he led the route and named it after his son. The route was originally graded E3 but in reality it is a pretty tough E4 (not that there's anything wrong with a good honest sandbag). The climbing is bold and strenuous and at the present time has not suffered the death by top rope that has afflicted some of its better known companions further down the valley.

The initial groove is climbed on good though rather spaced holds to reach a bulge, where a variety of runners can be placed. Almost immediately it becomes apparent that the climb is going to be hard work, the holds in the break are rounded and slippery, and the footholds are awkwardly placed. A gentle ache in your forearm indicates that it is time to move on. The wall directly above bulges and so a swing out to the left is required. A pull on a couple of razor edges leads to a large flat hold in the centre of the wall. There is a tiny crack here that is scarred with countless attempts to place small wires, but you are best off saving your energy and pressing on. A long layback move gains better holds in a scalloped break where good runners can be placed. Unfortunately the break is at full stretch and placing good gear is a distinct battle; pull up, peer into the break, select a runner, pull up, poke about in the crack, select another runner, pull up etc., etc. By now the buzzing from the sub-station is being drowned out by a more insistent buzz from your bulging arms.

A swing back to the right gains rock of a marginal easier angle and the crux moves. An initially strenuous and then precarious mantelshelf has to be made to gain a standing position in the break (hint: face right). The move is technically hard, but it comes as a real shock to the system because of the sudden contrast in styles - many attempts flounder here as a spectacular backflip. Once a standing position has been achieved you can shake some of the lactic acid out of your tired limbs and place decent protection without being continually harassed. The rest of the pitch is much easier and can be enjoyed to the full. The wall is steep but the holds are mostly quite generous and protection is adequate. Some of the better holds are protruding lumps of silica (almost a kind of natural glass) and it is not unknown for them to snap off suddenly (speaking as one who knows), but with a little care you should reach the top where a cluster of stout saplings provide a solid belay.

If anyone quizzes you about the climb you could perhaps reply "Oliver? A great route, I got a real buzz out of doing it".

88: MORTLOCK'S ARETE

Situation: Chee Tor, Wye Valley, Derbyshire
Aspect: West facing
Grade: E4 (6b, 6a)
Length: 40m (130ft)
Equipment: A normal rack is adequate, though the faint of heart may want to carry a few extra wires.
First Ascent: C.Mortlock, L.Noble, P.Hutchinson, November 1962 (aid)
First Free Ascent: T.Proctor, G.Birtles, 1976
Guidebook: *Peak Limestone, Chee Dale* published by the British Mountaineering Council in 1987.

Approaches: The shortest and fastest approach to Chee Tor is from Wormhill which is reached via a minor road heading south from Miller's Dale. There is limited parking on the left just before a farm gate. Walk back down the road a few metres and turn right along a small track past a cottage. At an open grassy area a small path drops down to the right and soon reaches the River Wye. The crag is to be found five minutes upstream on the other side of the river, and the route takes the prominent hanging flake towards the left side of the cliff, (not to be confused with the much easier hanging flake of RAVE ON which is still further to the left).

The Route: A well protected and technical lower wall gives access to a strenuous flake. The upper pitch is delicate and bold.

Description: A difficult wall and unobvious traverse guard access to the flake. Once reached it gives sheer hard work until a technical exit reaches ledges. The second pitch takes a shallow groove directly above and is in delicate contrast to the butch goings on in the shady depths now far

below. After a few precarious moves, better holds are reached in a horizontal break and easier climbing leads to the top.

MORTLOCK'S ARETE

Named after the leading member of the first ascent team, (that's one way of making sure your name doesn't get forgotten easily), "MORTLOCK'S" is one of the Peak District's greatest routes. It is on the sports plan of every up and coming 'hot shot' and is a hidden hope in the back of many a 'wrinkley's' mind. And not without reason: the line is a stunner and the climbing an elegant mixture of strenuousness and delicacy.

As an aid route it was pretty *passé* almost as soon as it was put up, with solid flakes and good pockets allowing rapid and safe progress (the fact that as a neophyte, I pulled a peg from under a loose block and took a 40-footer is neither here nor there!). But as a free route MORTLOCK'S ARETE is quite simply outstanding.

The initial wall is tricky, and is taken on small sharp pockets and subtle layaways to reach a big ring peg at ten metres. This lower wall now contains a couple of well jammed and extremely battered wires, and although they are nice to 'go for' they are going to cause problems when the cables eventually break.

From the peg a less than obvious traverse leads down and left to the base of the flake. This pitch was originally graded 5c though the loss of holds (or a reassessment of yet another classic sandbag) means the moves are now graded 6b. Once the base of the flake is reached speed is of the essence, for he who lingers is lost. Laybacking is the easiest form of progress though this approach tires the arms and mind at an alarming rate. With a little luck and not a little stamina, an easing in the angle is reached as the flake fizzles out into blanker rock above. In reality this is no resting place but compared to what has just passed it feels like a slab. Good wires protect the technical and pushy moves needed to reach the sanctuary of ledges above.

The second pitch used to be regarded as 'perfectly protected' when the route was first free climbed in 1976, though nowadays the same pathetic thread and inverted peg do not instil a great deal of confidence. The groove is technical and delicate de-

progress upwards. Fortunately the difficulties are short-lived and good holds and excellent protection are soon reached in a horizontal break. The rest of the pitch is no pushover but the friendlier atmosphere and the knowledge that all the real difficulties are below you allows real enjoyment of this final section. Before long it is all over and you must parachute back to the land of the giant rhubarb, with another quick tick in the book or the fulfilment of a life-long ambition. Either way you will carry a smug smile for the next day or two.

89: WALL OF THE WORLDS

Situation:	Boulder Ruckle Far West, Swanage, Dorset
Aspect:	South facing
Grade:	E4 (6a)
Length:	40m (130ft)
Equipment:	A standard rack with plenty of extenders.
First Ascent:	M.J.Crocker, J.Robertson, 12th June 1983
Guidebook:	*Swanage* by Gordon Jenkin, published by the Climbers' Club in 1986.

Approaches: From the car park at the Durleston Head Country Park (two kilometres due south of Swanage) follow the tarmac road down to the lighthouse and continue along the coastal path for 900 metres to reach a stone wall with a stile, marking the western limit of the Country Park. Directly below this is a shallow gully with twin belay stakes. A 40m abseil from these runs down an overhanging wall to boulders. The route starts ten metres to the right of the foot of the abseil.

MORTLOCK'S ARETE: A good hold is reached after the crux wall. The angle of the rock means that no real rest is possible and there is a lot of difficult and strenuous climbing to come,
Climber: Graham Parkes

spite its steepness, and the holds are rounded dimples in stark contrast to the sharp edged and flaky rock of the lower walls. Precarious bridging and laybacking (of a much subtler nature than that which went before) is required to make teetery

The Route: A fine sustained pitch with good protection up a continuously leaning wall. The finish is rather unstable and folks not at home with normal Swanage exits might benefit from a short fixed rope. As the belay stake is missing at present this will have to be attached to the stile and run across to the top of the route.

Description: To the right of the centre of the wall is a very shallow groove above the conspicuous horizontal break. Climb thin cracks to a small ledge, and continue to the break (spike runner). Pull on to the wall and continue with sustained difficulty to eventually reach a pair of peg runners. Pass these rightwards to ledges and then a thread before exiting slightly to the right.

WALL OF THE WORLDS

There is a lot of steep impressive rock at Swanage. This usually takes the form of vertical walls offset by large horizontal roofs. These structures are a direct result of the interaction of the erosional forces of the sea and the strong horizontal layering of the beds of rock hereabouts. Winter storms batter these cliffs with almost unimaginable power, great rollers bearing down with a momentum picked up over hundreds and even thousands of miles of open ocean. In the last few tens of metres before the cliffs are reached the shallower sea bed lifts the waves higher and higher until they expend their energy in spectacular death throws. The water and enclosed compressed air is forced into every minute crevice in the cliffs and the results can be explosive. The cliff becomes increasingly undercut until gravity lends a hand and another house-sized block heads seaward. The rock here may be fairly hard but the ocean has time on her side, in the geological blinking of an eyelid these cliffs will be reduced to sand.

In Boulder Ruckle Far West the strata is slightly tilted and so instead of the alternating walls and roofs there exists a series of walls that quite simply lean and lean. Apart from the odd aid route these were generally avoided by the Swanage pioneers until quite recently because of the intimidating (and obviously desperate) nature of the climbing, even though the rock was blatantly excellent.

The two most impressive sections of wall were breached by Martin Crocker in one busy weekend in June 1983 and the crag was brought more in line with developments in other parts of the country. The style of climbing on WALL OF THE WORLDS has a very modern feel about it. There are no desperate moves on the pitch but then again there are no easy ones. The holds tend to be adequate rather than generous with good jugs being few and far between. Then, of course, there is the angle - the rock is tilted well the wrong side of vertical and so considerable stamina is required to stand a chance of success.

WALL OF THE WORLDS: This shot shows the intimidating nature of the upward view on this route. The climbing is obviously very strenuous and there are no resting places worthy of the name.
Climber: Graham Parkes

The climb starts kindly enough and good holds lead to a small ledge. Trickier moves are then required to get to a horizontal break where a sling can be draped over a good spike and stock taken. From here the upward view is distinctly intimidating as the rock continues to lean in a most menacing fashion. Difficult laybacking and small fingerholds lead up to a good jug mentioned in the guidebook, but unfortunately it is only big enough for one hand at a time. A bizarre ritual now takes place here as you hang off one hand and rest the other, and then change over until it eventually dawns on you that you are not going to recover on rock of this angle.

Just a little higher a stainless steel peg protrudes rather a long way from a horizontal crack. The move to pass this (a long reach or a short jump) would be no problem if you were close to the ground and fresh, but up here and in your present state it presents a formidable obstacle. If you manage the move better holds begin to arrive and a fairly insubstantial thread can be clipped while you recover. All that remains is one last steep move and a careful exit onto a grass bank where you can lie down at last and rest those burning forearms.

If on the other hand you thought the route a pushover, there is an even more impressive leaning wall a little further to the west with a route called THE LEAN MACHINE on it. This was put up in the same weekend as WALL OF THE WORLDS and is a grade harder. Maybe that will slow you down a bit.

90: ATMOSPHERES

Situation:	Pinfold North, Eglwyseg Valley, Clwyd, North Wales
Aspect:	West facing
Grade:	E5 (6a)
Length:	25m (80ft)
Equipment:	A standard rack of wires is more than adequate.
First Ascent:	(As THE BULGER - A3): unknown, possibly R.Dearman and party in the late 1960's.
First (almost) Free Ascent:	J.Codling, A.Grondowski, 28th July 1984
Guidebook:	The route is mentioned (as the aid route THE BULGER) in the 1983 *Clwyd Limestone* guide by Stuart Cathcart (Cicerone), it is renamed and described as a free route in the 1986 *New Climbs* volume, edited by Gary Gibson and published by the British Mountaineering Council.

Approaches: The cliff lies in the Eglwyseg valley a short distance to the north of Llangollen. If approaching from the A5 cross the river in the centre of Llangollen, then turn right and immediately left by a strange turreted building (the local taxidermist's) into Dinbren Road. Follow the road up over the canal then bear left and continue for three kilometres to a T junction. Turn left, then just before the road drops into a minor valley is a lay-by on the right. Park here and walk down the road a short distance to a gate on the right, signed Bryn Goleu. Pass through the gate and walk up to the cliffs at the head of the valley. A narrow footpath traverses out to the left and eventually passes round a corner to an area of impressive overhangs. Fifteen minutes from the road. ATMOSPHERES breaches the left side of the over-

hangs and then follows the steep rightward trending flake line.

The Route: Powerful climbing with lots of fixed protection and an aid bolt to get started.

Description: Lean out and clip the bolt on the lip of the roof. Using this gain a good hold on the left then swing right to reach the foot of the flake line. This gives strenuous undercutting and laybacking to a rest below the roofs. More hard moves around the corner reach the slightly more amenable groove which is quitted on the left. Easy rock leads to the top and a belay some distance up the bank.

ATMOSPHERES

Despite the public relations job that Stuart Cathcart did in his 1983 *Clwyd Limestone* guide, the Eglwyseg valley remains a real backwater. Spring bank holiday 1990, the weather was great and we spent three days climbing on five different cliffs and did not meet another party, I wonder what it was like at Malham? The rock and the routes are generally excellent with something for everyone, and the nearby flesh pots of Llangollen are only ten minutes away when you fancy a break, or your fingers finally give out.

From the road it is obvious that there is plenty of good rock in the valley, though much of it is not of a great height. When you round the corner and get a first good look at ATMOSPHERES it suddenly appears more than high enough.

An aid bolt on the lip of the roof is clipped and a foot in a short sling lets you reach a good flat hold on the left. Cut loose and a quick swing round the rib on the right reaches a thin thread and an old bolt (nut back-ups are available). The upward view is both impressive and oppressive. A long reach for a hanging rib and you are on your way. Wild undercutting and laybacking, with no prospect of a rest, lead up and right round a veritable bevy of bulges. Eventually a sharp edged crack is reached, a big pull should find you bridged below the roofs. There are two in-situ nuts here tied together with tape, so you can clip in quickly and have a breather.

Another bulge lies between you and success, blind groping round the corner should find jams and a large hidden foothold, from here a swing out left reaches

91: TALES OF THE RIVERBANK

Situation:	Dovedale Church, Dovedale, Staffordshire
Aspect:	South-east facing
Grade:	E5 (6a)
Length:	30m (100ft)
Equipment:	A standard rack.
First Ascent:	Climbed with one point of aid by J.Flemming, C.Calow in 1978, freed by R.Fawcett shortly after.
Guidebook:	*Peak Limestone South,* published by the British Mountaineering Council in 1987.

Approaches: Dovedale Church lies on the west bank (Staffordshire side) of the River Dove, almost opposite Tissington Spires, and so is closest to the southern end of the dale. Parking is available, for a fee, just north of Thorpe which lies a few kilometres from the main Buxton to Ashbourne road (A515). A well-made footpath leads up the right side of the river (looking upstream) and over a hill to reach the open flat area below Tissington Spires. Dovedale Church is on the other side of the river and is reached by wading. A large party may wish to carry one pair of size 11 wellies, so that the whole team can cross dry shod.

The Route: A long groove pitch, well protected but exhausting.

Description: A left arête of the riverside face of the cliff has a fine groove set in it. Reaching this is difficult and staying with it is strenuous. If successful belay on top of the tower on a tree which also provides the anchor for the abseil descent.

TALES OF THE RIVERBANK

Dovedale Church is a most peculiar piece of rock. It is a pair of towers, (or is it two pairs of towers?), with a couple of arches thrown in for good measure and an excellent collection of strong vertical lines. The whole thing is rather like a Victorian folly,

easy ground. Before you top out a quick look down the line of the ropes and then at your forearms should start you wondering, the name of the aided version of the route was remarkably apt.

ATMOSPHERES: An aid bolt is used to pass the initial overhang, above this the route is just plain hard work involving sustained laybacking and undercutting. Fortunately there is a considerable amount of fixed gear from the old aid ascents.
Climbers: Colin Binks and Graham Parkes

TALES OF THE RIVERBANK: A thuggish bulge has to be passed to gain access to the groove above, though this offers little respite for tired arms.
Climber: Chris Craggs

a beauty of a V.S. and if you are into overhanging fist cracks PHIL'S ROUTE should be right up your street, (if you really are into overhanging fist cracks a visit to a 'shrink' might be in order, as soon as you have done the route).

Hiding away in the left arête of the tower, beneath brushing branches is a rather more subtle but still mighty powerful route, a lovely sinuous groove guarded by a shattered wall and nasty bulge. Easy rock leads up and out left to the bulge where an inverted peg and good wires are available to protect strenuous laybacking on slippery finger jams. Once established in the groove the difficulties begin to pile up. The runners are good but awkward to place in the near parallel walls of the crack, and the climbing is very sustained. Footholds are poor and skiddy and the jams in the crack are both insubstantial and painful. An easing in the angle gives a promise of respite so you press on ever hopeful, but things are not what they appear. The crack closes and you are forced out left on sloping holds, just as you are starting to get really pumped - it's a cruel world. Above you another crack rises from the left and it obviously contains some jugs, all that is needed is to crank out a couple of stiff pulls, still on slopers and you have the long awaited good holds.

But wait, something is wrong; sure the holds are large, but now you are laybacking and the damned thing has steepened up again. Now it's a well known fact that placing runners from a laybacking position is nigh on impossible, so it is do or die, push on or fly, (or maybe both), as your last gear is now some way off. One more hard move back into the main crack and you can bridge, get a rest, calm down and lace the crack; and not before time. From here things take on a rosier hue and the rest of the route gives straightforward bridging until you can graze your way up to the meadow in the sky. The situation on this little elevated island is most unusual, a great place for a picnic perhaps, or to laze away a summer's day, if it was not for the self-imposed access restrictions. It is certainly a grand spot to soak up the sun as you tow the ropes in, with only the occasional grunt or swearword carried up on the breeze to let you know your partner is enjoying the route almost as much as you did.

and you get the impression that odd bits have been stuck on willy-nilly to give the present bizarre configuration. The tops are capped with lush meadows and several substantial trees, which provide a means of escape for those who make it to this miniature lost world.

The front face of the eastern tower has a couple of strong lines, SNAKES ALIVE is

92: MINOTAUR

Situation: Huntsman's Leap, Range East, Castlemartin, South Pembroke
Aspect: East facing
Grade: E5 (6a)
Length: 40m (130ft)
Equipment: A standard rack is adequate.
First Ascent: J. de Montjoye, H.Sharpe, 7th January 1984
Guidebook: *Pembroke* by Jon de Montjoye and Mike Harber, published by the Climbers' Club in 1985. A new two-volume guide is due out in 1992.

Approaches: From the car park for St Govan's Chapel cross the stile into the Range and walk past the first impressive inlet (Stennis Ford) to the second more impressive inlet, Huntsman's Leap. Abseil 40m (130ft) from a selection of stakes in the N.E. corner of the Leap to the shingle beach.

The Route: A pitch with a big feel. The lower wall is bold and strenuous, the upper bulge provides a contrast in the form of a short safe crux.

Description: From the tip of the triangular block under the west wall of the Leap, climb cracks for a short distance until they end. Head right across the wall to reach a brown lump and climb onto it. Traverse back into the crack and follow it all the way to the overhangs. Cross these rightwards with great difficulty to a final easy groove.

MINOTAUR

The west wall of Huntsman's Leap is a superb piece of rock; 40 metres high, and over 100 metres wide, and all of it overhanging. At first glance there are no obvious lines, just the odd crack going nowhere, a few hanging flakes and lots of unfriendly looking water-worn rock. A closer inspection reveals at least one line of weakness (although there are actually over twenty routes) on the wall. A thin ragged crack starts from the tip of a big wedge-shaped block and points up into wild country beyond. At high tide the block is partly submerged and resembles a huge

MINOTAUR: The bold lower section of the route leads to better protected face climbing where "long reaches for flat holds and strenuous pulls lead up the wall". Above is a tough but safe crux where the wall starts to bulge.
Climbers: Colin Binks and Graham Parkes

reptile wallowing in the shallows, waiting for unwary prey to be washed in on the swell.

Treading warily on the back of the beast in case you waken it, the climb starts up a convoluted crack containing some bits of 'foreign' rock. This is followed easily but steeply until the crack disappears. A line of holds leads out right to a lump of sandstone 'stuck' on the wall in a most unusual position. There are two ways of looking at the next few moves and the stability of the 'lump'. Firstly; it's been there for thousands of years so it is bound to be OK or alternatively it's going to go one day and today might just be the day. Either way a 'gentle' mantelshelf, if such a thing is possible, is probably the best approach.

From a standing position it is possible to traverse quickly back to the crack line and get a decent runner in (at long last). The 'crack' has in fact turned into a wide, rounded and largely holdless groove, not unlike the inside of a drainpipe, and something of a 'shimmy' is needed to get up it. Above this the climbing becomes a little more obvious though not much easier. Long reaches for flat holds and strenuous pulls lead up the steep wall passing a discreet peg runner, to eventually reach a widening in the crack. Here it is possible to rest using fist jams and a leg lock before embarking on the crux. There are plenty of good runners around including a fiddly but very solid thread that is well worth getting on. Above the rock leans menacingly. With one good hold this section would be butch but brief; sadly the one good hold has been replaced with a finger flake and a small pocket. From these a massive reach is usually not quite enough to gain the jug hidden around the bulge and 'dyno' is required, to make those last few centimetres. The rest is a gentle stroll back to daylight and safety after the rigours of the labyrinth below.

93: AXLE ATTACK

Situation:	Mayfair Wall, Craig Pen Trwyn, the Great Orme, Llandudno, North Wales
Aspect:	East facing
Grade:	E5 (6b) (French 7a+)
Length:	20m (65ft)
Equipment:	Ten quick-draws
First Ascent:	The route was originally an unfinished aid project by C.Lyon and P.Elliot. The bolt ladder was completed and the pitch free climbed by M.Griffiths and L.McGinley in June 1981.
Guidebook:	*North Wales Limestone* by Andy Pollitt, published by the Climbers' Club in 1987.

Approaches: Craig Pen Trwyn is the long line of rock that runs above the Marine Drive on the Great Orme, to the north of Llandudno. The first large wall on the left is the home of AXLE ATTACK, it takes the central bolt ladder starting up a hanging corner.

NOTE: There have been some access problems due to rock falls, please check on the present situation.

The Route: Sustained wall climbing well protected by in-situ bolts and pegs.

Description: Pull into the hanging corner then move right and follow the bolt ladder to a belay, sustained. Lower off.

AXLE ATTACK

In the late 70s and early 80s there was a growing move to place occasional protection bolts on difficult limestone pitches to enable them to be free climbed. Not all climbers were happy with this and in several cases the offending metal was removed and the routes were ignored. There were the usual ambiguities; it was fine to place

bolts for aid, for example, even on routes that were largely free, and some protection bolts were accepted while others were not. It appeared as if it depended on who was putting the bolts in, as much as where they were being used, or how many were placed.

AXLE ATTACK started life as an aid route so bolts were fine, but it was completed as a bolt-protected free route, tut tut. Luckily, at the time, nobody gave a toss about what was happening on some poxy limestone cliff on the North Wales coast, and so the route was not tampered with. Gradually there was a realisation of the potential of the Great Orme, but by the time the balloon went up and the scramble for first ascents was on, the route was already an established classic. Of course if it was OK to use bolts on one route it was OK on others and so the rest of the cliffs in the area were developed very much in the modern idiom.

The route is short and safe, but it is no pushover, offering a sustained and strenuous pitch. The E5 grade in no way relates to the seriousness of the climb (if so it would be E1) but rather to the effort required to do the route in a single push. Only climbers who operate regularly at these grades do the climb in good style. The route has been climbed often enough by people who normally operate at E2/3, but the style of these ascents is often a bit 'tatty' (and that is being kind!).

A fingery pull into a hanging corner at the foot of the face is followed by a difficult swing out right on to the wall. This is climbed to a vague ledge (rest possible by stepping right) below a shallow bulging groove. This provides the crux of the route and is climbed with difficulty using a *'monodoigt'* to jugs just out of sight. Once these are reached the rest of the route is a romp up to the belay bolts, from which you can quickly lower back to the ground, all very French.

AXLE ATTACK is like many of the other harder bolt-protected routes that are appearing up the steepest and blankest sections of our cliffs, ethically rather dubious perhaps but offering superb climbing. Don't knock it until you have tried it.

AXLE ATTACK: A typical example of a 'modern' bolt protected climb; offering a safe but hard piece of exercise. The climber is on the fingery rib that leads to the resting place' with the crux still to come.
Climber: Colin Binks

94:
GET SOME IN

Situation:	St Govan's Cliff, South Pembroke
Aspect:	South facing
Grade:	E5 (6a)
Length:	30m (100ft)
Equipment:	A standard rack of wires.
First Ascent:	B.Berzins, C.Sowden, 22nd August 1981
Guidebook:	*Pembroke* by Jon de Montjoye and Mike Harber, published by the Climbers' Club in 1985. A new two-volume guide is due out in 1992.

Approaches: From the car park at St Govan's follow the coastal path eastwards towards the coastguard lookout. The descent is reached in about five minutes and lies down a polished chimney where a large pinnacle stands a metre away from the cliff. Care is required. From the foot of the descent scramble down boulders and cross to the foot of the largest buttress on this part of the cliff (home of the ARROW). GET SOME IN climbs the steep cracks in the right face of this buttress and starts from a large ledge.

The Route: A very strenuous piece of crack climbing which is fortunately exceptionally well protected.

Description: Climb leftwards up the wall to gain the base of the crack, which is then followed throughout to a small niche below the top of the cliff. Swing right to gain the final corner. Tough stuff.

GET SOME IN

What is in a name? This route was put up in the early 80s when quite a few leading climbers suddenly realised they were being left behind in the new route gold rush occurring on the South Wales coast. The name could well be an evocative reminder of the stampede that went on with over 150 new routes put up in Pembroke in each of

the first three years of the decade.

On the other hand it may refer to the leader's dilemma on this continuously leaning wall. There are no desperately hard moves on the pitch but then again there are no particularly easy ones. To dally is to fail for all but the strongest climbers, so perhaps the leader's philosophy was to 'get some in' and go for it.

Either way the route remains a stern test of stamina. There are plenty of good wires but very little in the way of good holds. A forceful approach is needed as is the ability to conserve energy. The initial wall leads up and left to the foot of the crack where the problems begin. A thin crack wriggles its way up the wall and this is climbed on good finger locks and flat-edged layaways. The footholds are generally poor, doing little to ease the strain on wilting arms. The crack can be filled with wire runners but care is needed to avoid running out of steam and also to avoid blocking all the best finger jams.

Just as you begin to think that the route is in the bag, the crack becomes even more unhelpful and strenuous laybacking on spaced edges is needed to gain a small niche a short distance from the top of the route. An ungainly half rest, or at least a poor shake-out is possible here before launching yourself at the final problem. This presents itself in the form of a small roof protecting entry into the final groove, and passing this is problematical. This is no place to fall from, because although the gear is good, ethics dictate that you should return to the last no-hands rest, and that is precisely where your stalwart partner is patiently stood, right back at base.

Once around the roof good holds come to light at last, and even the tiredest man in the world should be able to drag his weary body up those last few moves. There is a large stake in the grass at the top of the route, and after tying on you can ponder the name again; after an effort like that you deserve a pint - it is time for your mates to get some in.

GET SOME IN: "A thin crack wriggles its way up the wall and this is climbed on good finger locks and flat edged layaways."
Climber: Nick Hallam

95: BASTILLE

Situation:	High Tor, Matlock, Derbyshire
Aspect:	West facing
Grade:	E5 (6b)
Length:	40m (130ft)
Equipment:	A normal rack, with a few extra extenders and a set of R.P. type nuts.
First Ascent:	B.Moore, J.Land, October 1966 (aid)
First Free Ascent:	A.Brown, J.Peel, 1979
Guidebook:	*Peak Limestone South.* Published by the British Mountaineering Council in 1987.

Approaches: The route takes the centre of the large 'blank' wall at the right side of High Tor. Just to the south of the cliff an iron bridge crosses the river to gain access to the lower station of the prominent cable-car. There is limited parking here. Cross the river and pass behind the building to a flight of steps (paying for access if you are challenged). From the top of the steps a path leads back towards the cliff, which is reached in about ten minutes from the road. The foot of the route is reached by scrambling up to the tree at the bottom of the obvious groove of ORIGINAL ROUTE and then traversing carefully to the right to reach a ledge with an old tree stump.

The Route: A long and tough pitch offering very fingery climbing. The lower section is hard and not too well protected, the upper section is just plain hard.

BASTILLE: After the harrowing lower groove the upper wall provides safer, bolt protected climbing. However, the technical difficulties remain of a high order with a selection of poor pockets being used to make progress. *Climber: William Gregory*

Description: Above the stance are two old bolts with a newer one between them. Clipping the top one is desperate unless you use one of the other pair for aid. The proficient or the brave may totally ignore the top one. Climb the wall a little to the right of the bolts to a small overlap which is passed to get into a steep shallow groove. This gives difficult climbing to an exit rightwards past an old peg. From here traverse to the left wrapped around the overhang to reach a good resting place (the stance on the aided version of the route). Sustained pocket pulling leads up and right past several bolts to a poor rest. A difficult series of moves up and left are followed to the easier but bold upper section of FLAKY WALL. Breeze up this to the top.

BASTILLE

After the major lines on the crag had been pegged in the early 60s the technicians looked to the blanker spaces to practise their arts. The big white face to the right of FLAKY WALL was an obvious blank on the map and so BASTILLE came into being. The rock is very compact though it is liberally peppered with solution pockets. At a later date these would provide scarey placements for 'sky hooks' but these were still a few years away so a number of bolts were placed, two on the lower wall and a spattering on the upper section, plus a pair at the belay ledge near the centre of the face.

In the 70s the latest free climbing revolution was under way and in 1976 Pete Livesey, of long neck and steel fingers fame, reduced the aid to a single bolt, (though I have often wonder how he clipped it!). Just a year later, visiting American Mike Graham bypassed this remaining aid point by climbing a line a little further to the right, though he failed to finish the route off, much to the relief of local climbers. British honour was finally restored in 1979 when Andy Brown free climbed the whole pitch. Thirteen years from the hardest aid route on the crag to the hardest free route on the crag - how times change. This is almost the end of the story except that in the late 80s a new bolt was added to the two in the lower wall. This addition is easier to clip and better protection (marginally) for the crux - those old guys must have been good! In 1990 the old bolts on the upper wall were replaced with large new ones. Thankfully the lower groove was not tampered with.

With the two (or three) bolts clipped the route steps to the right and thin reachy moves are made up the wall to a bulge. A long reach over this should find good small fingerholds which allow you to pull in to the base of the shallow groove. This does not prove to be the safe haven it appears from below, and in fact gives steep technical climbing with poor protection from small wires. It is a battle to stay in control and fix solid runners as your legs get pumped, and you realise that a fall may well see you back on the belay ledge again. Once you are happy with the gear more strenuous moves lead up and right to a peg which on closer inspection appears to be pretty pathetic. More fiddling with wired nuts is required to protect the nasty traverse to the left, which is best tackled with your hands above and feet below the bulge. If you get the sequence right a hands-off resting ledge with two good bolts is your reward.

A good long blow can be taken here, safe in the knowledge that the dangerous climbing is below you, though the remainder is no pushover. When you are suitably refreshed, the route follows the line of bolts up the superb pockety wall to a final tricky (or should that read 'hard') sequence of moves out to the left to the sanctuary of the upper section of FLAKEY WALL. This consists of a short flake crack and a steep little wall, the moves being no more than 5b, but they are not well protected and can be quite a strain on tired arms. A small path beaten through the bushes leads to a big solid tree belay. Tie on and take in the ropes, you are entitled to a pat on the back and you probably feel you deserve it.

Situation:	Gordale Scar, Malham, Yorkshire
Aspect:	North facing
Grade:	E6 (6b, 6a) (French 7b+)
Length:	50m (165ft)
Equipment:	A selection of wires to supplement the in-situ gear, and plenty of quick draws.
First Ascent:	J.Sumner, A.B.Knox, 1956
First Free Ascent:	R.Fawcett, 1982
Guidebook:	*Yorkshire Limestone* published by the Yorkshire Mountaineering Club in 1985.

Approaches: Gordale Scar is two kilometres to the east of the village of Malham and is reached by turning right in the village and following a minor road over a hill. At the far side of the hill and just beyond a bridge there is restricted parking, the crag is five minutes walk away across the flat grassy field. Once in the gorge you should not need an M.L.C. to find the route.

The Route: A magnificently sustained route up the finest crack line in Britain - bar none.

Description: Follow the right-hand crack to a niche, the wall above is the technical crux, then sustained work leads to the cave. Pitch two gains the smaller cave and exits to the left.

CAVE ROUTE

Gordale Scar is an oppressive place at the best of times, in poor weather it is a sinister spot indeed. It is best visited for the first time on a winter' eve; you turn the corner into the gorge and the whole place bursts upon your senses. The towering walls, the sighing wind and the crashing water are suddenly revealed in all their grandeur; it all makes you feel rather small.

On a summer's day when the waterfall has dried up and there is no wind, the place feels a little more amenable, though I

CAVE ROUTE: **The climber is just pulling into the resting niche below the crux wall. Above this the crack is followed with sustained strenuosity to the cave. The tourists gaze on in disbelief.**
Climber: Graham Parkes

folks would say it's better than that!), but fortunately it is blatantly desperate.

Put up in 1956 as a major aid route (by the left-hand start) CAVE ROUTE was used as a winter training route to Alpine aid extravaganzas by the proficient, and as a place for a good old fashioned epic by those less well versed in the mysteries of pegging. Bivouacs in the cave were not uncommon, and Yorkshire winter nights can be long and cold!

By the early 70s local guru Pete Livesey was beginning to assess the route as a free project. He had worked out that the upper part of the crack was on, but the lower section of the left-hand crack proved too tough. When he found out that a local lad by the name of Ron Fawcett (Force it?) had been soloing up and down the first ten metres of the right-hand start the dye was cast. The story of that ascent, with three resting points and Livesey jumping for an aid climber's rope on the left-hand crack in sheer desperation is well known. Even with the rest points the route was well ahead of its time but it was largely ignored; perhaps it was just too hard for the competition.

By 1982 Fawcett had improved his stamina enough to climb his way into the history books with the first totally free ascent. The route was renamed TIGER MOUNTAIN but this did not stick. For good measure he did the left-hand crack as well, and that was a full grade harder. CAVE ROUTE RIGHTHAND now gives a superbly sustained pitch with a good rest in a shallow niche at 15 metres. Above this is a short wall, the technical crux, but it is still a long way to the sanctuary of the cave, and the possibility of running out of steam is a very real one. Many people do not bother with the top pitch, dismissing it as an irrelevance. Despite this it has a couple of 6a moves on it and is certainly no pushover. Perhaps folks are worried that they might fail on it after the exertions of the big pitch, and that would be a bit of an embarrassment!

Today CAVE ROUTE stands as a superb testimony to the gigantic leaps that rock climbing has made over the past 20 years. Although there are those who (seriously) consider the route to be rather too straightforward, it is the ultimate objective of many climbers operating at the E5 level. To lesser mortals it is a route to stand under and gaze up in slack-jawed awe.

would never describe it as friendly. Under these more favourable conditions you can consider rock climbing here, given a chance to concentrate on the route without the 'atmosphere' getting to you too much. CAVE ROUTE is the finest line on the cliff and perhaps on British limestone (some

THE PROW:
The steeply leaning
second pitch of the
route is climbed on
good but spaced
layaways to reach
the superbly
situated stance.
The climber is doing
the first two pitches
in one run out;
impressive stuff.
*Climber: Pete (POD)
O'Donovan*

152

97: THE PROW

Situation:	Raven's Tor, Miller's Dale, Derbyshire
Aspect:	South facing
Grade:	E6 (6b, 6b, 6b) (French 7c)
Length:	50m (165ft)
Equipment:	A rack of quick draws.
First Ascent:	R.Dearman, J.Gerrard, July 1963 (aid)
First Free Ascent:	R.Fawcett, G.Fawcett, July 1982, except for the first 12 metres which were free climbed as REVELATIONS by J.Moffatt in August 1984.
Guidebook:	*Peak Limestone, Chee Dale,* published by the British Mountaineering Council in 1987.

Approaches: A three-pitch 'super route' offering a devious traverse, fierce fingery face climbing, and a tough overhang.

Description: The desperate direct start is usually avoided by a traverse in from the left after using the battered tree to get started. Once the main bolt ladder is reached it gives sustained face climbing with only the occasional good hold until the bedding plane is reached. Move right for a belay or press on. The second pitch climbs the leaning wall right then left to reach a hanging groove until it is possible to escape out left to a superbly situated stance. For the final pitch step back right and follow the steepening groove and capping roof to a big tree on top of the Tor.

THE PROW

Throughout the late 60s and most of the 70s THE PROW was the premier aid route of the Peak District, the only other comparable route in terms of popularity being the DIRECTISSIMA over Kilnsey Main Overhang, in West Yorkshire. There were plenty of routes of greater technical difficulty but these two stood out because of their length,

their sustained interest and the impressive ground they both crossed.

Ascents of THE PROW usually began with a Friday night bus ride from Sheffield or Manchester to the Angler's Rest in Miller's Dale. You were accompanied by a rucksack that would not look out of place on a Himalayan expedition containing all your ropes and hardware plus sleeping bag, stove, iron rations and anything else you could cram into it. The licensing laws of the pub were pretty relaxed and so sometime in the small hours you would weave your way down the dale to spend the rest of the night in an alcohol-induced stupor in the shallow cave below the crag. Dawn was usually grey and cold and breakfast was forced down begrudgingly or done without. The start of the route was the technical crux (it still is!) with poor pegs, stacked together and tied off, allowing precarious progress until the start of the bolt ladder was reached and a sense of safety returned. The rest of the pitch was straightforward apart from an ugly restricted groove which invariably wrecked your knees as you thrashed up the back of it. The stance out on the left was (and still is), superbly situated with a row of perfect pegs sprouting from a horizontal crack and a tiny footledge just where it does the most good.

The top pitch was always a bit of a gripper, as some of the pegs were a bit wobbly and the exposure was (and still is!) terrifying as you headed out beyond the second, while he hung securely strapped to his tiny stance muttering words of encouragement. Fat pegs walloped between loose flakes allowed the transition back to the right side of vertical and a massive multiple-trunked tree gave you a chance to get your sanity back.

Today things have changed, steel pegs have been replaced by steel fingers, and a couple of years spent learning the mystical art of aid climbing have been replaced by a couple of years spent losing skin and sweat on a climbing wall.

The start of the route is blatantly "impossible" and so most people avoid it, but of course if you want to free climb the PROW you have to do all of it, and just like the old days, once you have done the start, the rest is a cruise. If you opt for the variation start, the whole climb is a much more even standard, i.e. desperate, with the final roof feeling rather just a little more desper-

ate than the lower pitches. Either way despite its changed status the route remains a mega classic.

98: MALHAM MAIN OVERHANG

Situation:	Malham Cove, Yorkshire
Aspect:	South facing
Grade:	A2 or E6 (6c) (French 7c+) and A2
Length:	36m (120ft)
Equipment:	Depends on the intended style of your ascent, either ten quick draws, or a bunch of karabiners and a couple of knotted slings. (Traditionalists can go up into the attic and dig out their dusty old étriers.)
First Ascent:	J.Sumner, D.Sales, 1964
First Free Ascent:	R.Gawthorpe, 1984 (Pitch 1 only!)
Guidebook:	*Yorkshire Limestone.* Published by the Yorkshire Mountaineering Club, 1985.

Approaches: Park in the village of Malham and follow the well-signed and well-made path to the Cove. The route takes the obvious huge black roof up and right of the centre of the cliff, this being approached along a narrow and exposed path that leads in from the right.

MALHAM MAIN OVERHANG: The lower leaning wall gives "a sustained piece of climbing on the tiniest of holds", whilst the upper pitch remains classic aid territory.
Climber: Mike Owen

The Route: The lower pitch gives desperate but safe wall climbing. The roof remains classic aid territory.

Description: Start directly below the broadest part of the overhang. The first pitch is either E6 (6c) or A1, though many ascents use a strange combination of free and aid styles. The top pitch is all on fixed gear and is a very exposed A2.

MALHAM MAIN OVERHANG

In the olden days when limestone was only any good for bashing pegs in, the bigger and more impressive the bit of rock you were hammering away at the better. At Malham the two most obvious choices were the Central Wall and the Main Overhang. In reality the climbing was straightforward and safe, though putting up the routes must have been mighty laborious, drilling away for hours on end using the most rudimentary harnesses and some pretty primitive rope techniques.

Once the routes were established they became very popular, offering safe all-weather climbing in spectacular situations. With all the gear fixed, ascents were made in very rapid times. In 1972, two of us knocked off the Central Wall and the Main Overhang in a leisurely three hours of climbing. We tied onto a 150-foot rope, 50 feet apart and moved together with about a dozen bolts between us, using the extra 100 feet of rope, tied in a loop, to pass the karabiners, stripped by the second, back up to the leader. Great fun in wild positions.

As free climbing standards rose dramatically in the 80s the bolt ladders were scrutinised closely to see if there was any free climbing potential and the first pitch of the Main Overhang fell to Rob Gawthorpe, a super fit product of rigorous climbing wall training.

The lower section of the wall gives a sustained piece of leaning wall climbing on the tiniest of holds. The exact sequence of moves required to succeed is difficult to work out and all but the most gifted people (or should that be strongest?) have to 'work the route' to guarantee success. The climbing is, of course, perfectly safe (the 20-metre pitch sprouts at least 20 bolts at the time of writing) and some folks might argue that the pitch is really only E1 (6c)!

If you are not up to finger-shredding 6c wall climbing it is still possible to get a lot of pleasure out of the route. Straightforward aid climbing leads to a spectacularly positioned stance under the roof. From here a couple of moves up the leaning wall lead to the ten-metre ceiling which is crossed on a series of large but rusty bolts. This section often has its own personal shower leaking out of the roof. Once on the head wall a couple of pegs lead to a low cave to belay in. There is a massive thread in the cave and it is possible to crawl round this doggie fashion to create a truly 'bomb proof' belay. From here it is possible to escape off left along a narrow and very exposed ledge, though TERRACE WALL, a short but very exposed V.S. is right above you and provides a fitting contrast to the simian antics that went on below.

99:
THE SUPER DIRECTISSIMA
(TOTALLY FREE)

Situation:	Malham Cove, Yorkshire
Aspect:	South facing
Grade:	E7 (6c, 6c, 6c?) (French 8a+)
Length:	75m (250ft)
Equipment:	Twenty-two quick draws if you intend to do the route in one pitch! If you are intending to split it a smaller number will do, 14 for THE GROOVE.
First Ascent:	J.Sumner *et al.* late 1960's though the lower section had been ascended by P.Biven and T.Peck in

1959 on their original ascent of the Central Wall. They then traversed left to the tree on the terrace before bolting the wall behind it.

First Free Ascent:	J.Dunne, autumn 1988
Guidebook:	The mixed version of the route was described in *Yorkshire Limestone*, 1985. The first free ascent was reported in *New Climbs 1988* (BMC).

Approaches: From the village of Malham a well-signed footpath leads to the Cove. From the 'cat walk' above the stream, the route follows a line just right of the obvious shallow weakness (?) up the centre of the leaning wall, and then climbs the fine white face above to a small stance before tackling the capping roof via a leftward slanting line.

The Route: A true 'super route', bang up the centre of the most impressive limestone wall in the country. Originally climbed in one pitch it is now usually done as two separate routes. The short top pitch has been largely ignored to date.

Description: The first long pitch (THE GROOVE, E7, 6c) takes the shallow weakness in the centre of the wall, passing a major bulge with great difficulty to a 'shake out' on a large layaway. Desperate face climbing leads to a semi-hanging stance. The second pitch (FREE AND EASY, E6, 6c) can be gained by a traverse from the right (5c) and then climbs the sustained and fingery wall, easing as height is gained, to a small stance under the capping bulges. The short final pitch, is climbed leftwards. This last pitch has only had one ascent at the time of writing and a consensus on its grade has not been reached.

TOTALLY FREE

When a series of tiny bolt-protected routes were put up above the 'cat walk' at Malham in the mid 1980s a large percentage of the climbing world scoffed. The routes were only ten metres high, at the foot of an 80-metre wall, and they ended up beneath 'impossible' bulges. Undeniably hard, they all appeared rather trivial. At the time the routes were developed not so much to produce French style routes here, but

THE SUPER DIRECTISSIMA (TOTALLY FREE): Alone in the centre of the finest limestone wall in the country, at the 'resting place' on the first pitch.
Climber: Alan Murray

largely because the rock stayed dry through a series of particularly atrocious summers.

As people became stronger and more confident they tackled more and more arduous routes on the steeper sections of this lower wall. With hindsight these short routes can be seen in their true perspective; as stepping-stones to ever longer and harder pitches. The second pitch of John Sumner's bolting tour de force, the SUPER DIRECTISSIMA had already had a free ascent by Ben Moon in 1984 and by the summer of 1988 things had moved on enough for an ascent of the whole route to be a possibility. John Dunne spent a considerable time working on the route and in the autumn of that year he made the ascent in a most impressive style. He climbed the lower groove to a resting place below the upper wall, and then hung there while the ropes and seconds were reorganised so that he could press on to the top without excessive rope drag, effectively doing the route in a single pitch.

Repeat ascents have not used this (rather eccentric?) style. The lower pitch is done as a route in its own right at Hard E7 (isn't that E8?) 6c called THE GROOVE. The second pitch stands at E6 6c and is referred to as FREE AND EASY, and although it is the former, it certainly isn't the latter. The short upper pitch is a bit of an enigma. There have been stories of epoxied jugs and their subsequent removal on the final bulges, as well as rumours of loose rock, though it certainly used to be solid enough when it was aided. Either way it has not seen much traffic to date.

It may be some time before a climber steps on to this wall at the bottom and pulls over the top, having done the route on sight with no falls, but it will happen. As climbing history has always shown, the greatest achievements of one generation are the training routes for the next.

NOTE: In the few short months since I wrote this final paragraph Simon Nadin has flashed the first pitch, on sight. This is a truly awesome feat which is a significant pointer to the future.

100: THE DIRECTISSIMA
(MANDELA)

Situation:	Kilnsey Crag, Wharfedale, Yorkshire
Aspect:	East facing
Grade:	A2, or E3 (5c) and A2, or E8 (5c, 6c, 4c) (French 6b, 8b)
Length:	80m (280ft)
Equipment:	This depends largely on your intended style of ascent. The route is almost fully equipped so a collection of quick draws and a few mid-range wires to back up some of the in-situ rust on pitch one is all that is needed, along with a couple of knotted aid slings or étriers for the top pitch. If you intend to do the whole route free you can leave the étriers at home!
First Ascent:	R.Hields, R.Hirst, 1958 although the first pitch had been climbed by J.Brown in 1953 and the roof had been crossed as the ORIGINAL ROUTE by R.Moseley in 1957.
First Free Ascent:	Pitch 1: R.Fawcett, A.Evans, 1975
	Pitch 2: M.Leach, 1988
Guidebook:	*Yorkshire Limestone* published by the Yorkshire Mountaineering Club in 1985.

Approaches: Kilnsey Crag is to be found in Upper Wharfedale about eight kilometres north of Grassington where the unmistakable cliff almost overhangs the B6160. Parking is available 200 hundred metres beyond the cliff in a large lay-by.

NOTE: Climbing is only to be carried out with permission from the farm (North Cote) opposite the right (northern) end of

the cliff. Permission is not normally given at weekends because of spectators blocking the road to essential services. Dogs are not welcome because of farm animals, so please leave them at home.

The Route: A three-pitch mega-classic up one of the country's most impressive rock formations. The roof is usually aid climbed!

Description: The first pitch follows the slim twisting groove that runs up towards the centre of the massive overhangs. This can be free climbed at E3 (5c) or aided on the in-situ grot. The second pitch climbs the "dry stone wall" up to the roof and then follows the flake out to the lip (a long way away). A small stance is available just around the end of the overhang. It is possible to make a spectacular abseil from this final stance but if you are after the full tick the top pitch gives straightforward climbing with the odd peg runner hidden in the grass.

THE DIRECTISSIMA (MANDELA)

Joe Brown made the first foray up under the 'big umbrella' in 1953 by pegging up the central groove to reach a small stance below the overhangs. He described the upward view as resembling the reflection of the floor, in the mirrors on the ceiling of a ballroom, such is the vastness of the roof. Four years later Ron Moseley finally crossed the overhang by starting up the corner to the right of the overhangs and following the flake that zig-zags its way towards the lip. He lowered off on several occasions, gripped stupid, convinced that he was prising the whole thing away from the roof. Eventually after a mammoth 11-hour session in étriers he made the first ascent. The route was reported in the press. The following year the initial groove was linked to the flake and the DIRECTISSIMA came into being. It quickly became the most sought-after aid route in the country and even appeared on TV in a Grandstand outside broadcast one Saturday afternoon.

With most of the gear in place the route became quite straightforward but no less gripping. The area of rock just above the stance weeps a regular little stream for a large part of the year and the fixed gear in this area rots quickly. A few years ago I remember looking up the bulging wall that leads to the roof and being somewhat startled to see that all the bolts except one had gone the way of all flesh. A piece of grubby white tape hung down, attached to something out of sight above and to a peg on the stance. Small loops were tied into the tape every two feet and it was wrapped around the remains of a bolt in the centre of the bulge. This piece of kit was affectionately known as 'the suicide sling' and all that was required was to aid up it from loop to loop. As you moved the whole thing creaked and dirty water oozed from the tape. Passing the half-way point was especially frightening because as you transferred your weight past the old bracket the tape slid around the back of it in a way guaranteed to fray it, and your nerves at the same time. Thankfully this idiocy is no longer necessary as the bulge now boasts nice new metal men.

In 1975 Ron Fawcett free climbed the bottom pitch at 'H.V.S.' - he was obviously better at climbing routes than grading them! Today it gives a superb pitch at E3 (5c). There is plenty of fixed gear to clip, but the climbing is sustained and deceptively steep, and a bit slippery. An abseil descent from the stance under the roof gives you some idea why the pitch is such hard work.

Of course the roof has now been free climbed by Mark Leach and renamed MANDELA (because they said it would never go free!) but there is still enough fixed gear to allow an aided ascent if you so wish. This is a civilised attitude as it would be a great pity to lose the route to 99.999% of the climbing population. Clipping the new bolts that were fixed to facilitate the free ascent may present you with a bit of an ethical problem, but do it anyway, it will calm your nerves as you swing about like an oversized bat, suspended from the ceiling. The route may one day become 'an easy day for a lady' but in the meantime do it any way you can. A mind expanding experience is guaranteed.

KILNSEY MAIN OVERHANG: The lower pitch offers a great piece of well protected climbing at E3, the upper overhang remains the domain of only the most talented, or alternatively it can still be climbed on aid to give an insight to how good the good guys really are.
Climber: Colin Binks

Kilnsey - at the end of the day.

PRINTED BY THE GOLDEN CUP PRINTING COMPANY LTD.
HONGKONG